Y0-ADB-536

BILLY
THE CLASSIC HITTER

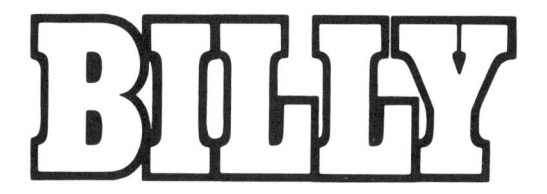

by BILLY WILLIAMS
and Irv Haag

illustrated with photographs

RAND MCNALLY & COMPANY
Chicago • New York • San Francisco

Special Acknowledgments

Many thanks for the splendid cooperation and assistance by Chuck Shriver, Manager, Information and Services, Chicago Cubs, Sports Editor Cooper Rollow of the *Chicago Tribune*, Editor John Kuenster of *Baseball Digest;* our deep gratitude also to Bill Loughman, whose endless supply of background material and statistics made our task so much easier, and to the late A. B. (Bernie) Clapper, peerless audio engineer and president of Universal Recording Studio, for his masterful touch in recording "Hey, Hey! Holy Mackerel!"

Copyright © 1974 by Rand McNally & Company
All rights reserved
Library of Congress Catalog Card Number: 74-8753
Printed in the United States of America
by Rand McNally & Company

ISBN 0-528-81980-1

First printing, 1974

Contents

FOREWORD	5
THE MAN	11
THE INVISIBLE SUPERSTAR	21
THE CLASSIC HITTER	26
EARLY LIFE	40
MINOR LEAGUE BALL	51
FIRST MAJOR LEAGUE START	62
WINTER 1959	66
ANOTHER CHANCE	70
ROOKIE OF THE YEAR	74
BILLY HITS HIS STRIDE	82
THE EARLY DUROCHER ERA	107
1969—THE BIG YEAR	117
THE NL'S NEW "IRON MAN"	131
"MUTINY ON THE WRIGLEY"	143
THE BATTING CHAMP	153
"IT WASN'T DUROCHER, AFTER ALL!"	162
1973—A POSTMORTEM	181
A NEW BROOM, A NEW SEASON	193
BILLY WRAPS IT UP—A POSTSCRIPT	203
BILLY WILLIAMS' LIFETIME RECORD	207

ABBREVIATIONS

G	Games
AB	At-bats
R	Runs
H	Hits
2B	2-base hits
3B	3-base hits
HR	Home runs
RBI	Runs batted in
TB	Total bases
RP	Runs produced (runs + RBIs − HRs = RP)
SO	Strike-outs
BB	Base on balls
IBB	Intentional base on balls
E	Errors
FA	Fielding average
BA	Batting average
SA	Slugging average
ERA	Earned-run average

Foreword

I'm supposed to be a pretty unemotional guy, at least that's what you might think from what you've read or heard, or when you've seen me play baseball. But I got excited when I was asked about doing this book. Believe it or not, I've been excited and emotional other times too. Few people know that I actually cried alone back in the tunnel behind the Cubs dugout one day during my rookie year of 1961. It was the third time they'd brought me up for a chance with the "big club." I was there only because they thought I could hit. It certainly wasn't for my fielding, which was not very hot at the time, and that's putting it mildly. And I wasn't hitting like I had in Triple A. There I was, back on the bench, trying to figure out what happened. It looked like back to the minors again, maybe even out of baseball, and I just broke down.

It was a thrill just to know somebody wanted to do a book about me. I think anybody would feel that way. But I wanted to do it for a lot more important reasons than that.

For the first time, I have a chance to get certain things straight. Fans have a tendency to worship professional athletes—too much sometimes I think. They want to know as much as possible about their favorites. I can't speak for other ballplayers and I like my privacy too, maybe more than most, but I feel fans have a right to know. It's not like we're going out and doing the regular-type job. When we become major league ballplayers, paid the kind of salaries some of us are, the public gets to be part of our lives, and that's how it should be.

But let's face it. Even though writers have been good to me, a lot of stories give the wrong impression. Sometimes I get the idea that if you've read one story about Billy Williams, you've read them all. I come off always the same way . . . quiet, mysterious, in a world all my own, nothing ever bothers me. I'm sure you get what I'm driving at.

Some of the writers spent only a little time with me, some didn't talk to me at all but picked up things from here and there, from interviews with others about me, and so forth. And, to be truthful, maybe I scared some of them off too. When I'm thinking about something else, I guess I can look pretty mean, like a person you don't feel like walking up and talking to at that moment.

I've always thought it's too bad people judge a person by his ways and actions and not by speaking to him or really getting to know him. Over the years, I've found you might meet somebody on a particular day. He has something on his mind, he's thinking about something else. He's angry or he says or does something you don't approve of. Maybe it hits you the wrong way. Like me out at the ballpark. I'm out there strictly to play baseball. Sure I meet people and chat with 'em, but I don't get into my personal life. That's the way I'm built, the way I was brought up.

So for the real story, all of it, and to let people know how I honestly feel not only about baseball but life in general, a book's the best way to do it.

When one man heard about this book, the first thing he said was, "I'll bet Billy doesn't say one thing that's controversial." See the kind of reputation I've got? I've never said things *just* to *be* controversial, and I try not to say something bad about somebody unless I believe it *ought* to be said.

People are always asking, what's been wrong with the Cubs, how did you feel about Leo Durocher, what really happened in that "hassle" [there were *several*], what about this ballplayer or that one, how do you feel about the Cub trades over the winter, the chance of *you* being traded, etc. You'll find the answers to these questions and a lot more, with no beating around the bush.

I've had some big moments in baseball and some big disappointments, done some right things and some wrong things. And after turning the other cheek, trying to give the other guy the benefit of the doubt, there were times I got riled up, spouted off, and was plain boiling mad, just like anybody else.

The time I felt I was done an injustice by the Baseball Writers Association of America—that's one example. When I lost one Most Valuable Player Award I *could* have won and, two years later, was deprived of one I know darn well I *should* have won. One magazine article that really rubbed me the wrong way.

Funny things, dramatic events, little-known facts and statistics, inside stories. Like what happened after Sandy Koufax threw a perfect game against our Cubs. Some very upsetting things about

1973 and some other seasons. There's a lot of that kind of stuff too. Some sides of Billy Williams, my family, personal life, and opinions you haven't seen or heard before, because I've never told anybody before.

Then there are the kids. That's another reason I wanted to do this book. We've tried to make it good for them and all baseball fans, even those who aren't Cub fans. They won't learn any new swear words, but there's a lot of "inside dope" on hitting and the big-league way of thinking. It's not an instructional book, but I think they'll get some good out of it.

Also, I wanted them to know that things don't come easy and no matter how hard you work, you don't do it all by yourself. You have to stop and give thanks to the Master, God, and tell him what you want. I don't mean to be corny, but if a few youngsters are inspired by what other ballplayers and I have been able to do to overcome handicaps and reach the top, I'll be proud and happy.

Getting back to how some write-ups give the wrong idea. One fella said I get bothered because "as usual, nobody recognizes me." I wonder then who that guy is who's had to leave his family so many times when we're all out for a good time, say at a zoo, and go off to sign autographs while they waited, or got tired of waiting so long they went on by themselves. Good thing my wife, Shirley, and my four daughters are so understanding. As she said:

"I've yet to see that place where he won't be recognized. They come up to him when we're out for dinner, they even catch him out in the lobby when we go to the movies. But I've become used to it, because I figure this is a part of his life . . . and the public is his life.

"In Chicago, everybody seemed to know where Billy lived. They'd drive by the house slowly and point it out, and then I'd really get scared. Especially after they announced how much he had signed for. That's the only thing I really hate. I think they should stop announcing salaries. They don't ever really think about the security of a person's family."

And would you believe autographs in church?

Living a Christian way of life is nothing new to me. Back home I went every Sunday, but I'm not a regular church-goer now. The strange thing is that I used to go often in Chicago when I first came up. But people ask you for autographs in church and make a big fuss about it. It's the wrong conception of going to church. I go to worship just like everybody else. You go there to worship God, the Master, not to get autographs, so I just found myself staying away. Out here [in the suburb he recently moved to] it may be the same situation, but I'm going to try though, because I haven't been to church for quite some time.

Then that part about me "craving" recognition. Most of the time it comes out like sour grapes, or that I'm like a spoiled kid who didn't get everything he wanted for Christmas.

I'm like a lot of other superstars. I hope you don't mind me calling myself a superstar. The articles do, and *that* doesn't make me mad! About a lack of recognition . . . the late Roberto Clemente and I had a lot in common. Incidentally, one day Leo got into a hassle with Dock Ellis, and pretty soon all the Cubs and Pirates came off the bench for a big free-for-all. I'm trying to pull somebody off Glenn Beckert. He and this guy are kicking and biting and doing everything down there. Then I feel somebody grab me around the waist. I turn around quick, ready to let go with something, and I see it's Clemente. He was tryin' to do the same thing I was, be the peacemaker. It always seems the peacemaker gets "scarred upon." I got some pretty good knocks and bumps on my legs. The one I felt sorry for was Danny Murtaugh, he was almost having a heart attack. And over on the sidelines, there's Durocher and Ellis . . . *watching!* But see, not too many understood Clemente. For most of his career, he never really got recognized for what a great ballplayer he was. Then after he died, they hurry up and get him into the Hall of Fame right away. It doesn't seem right that those who deserve recognition don't get it until too late and others, maybe a little "flashier," get more than they've earned.

Or take Henry Aaron who I got to know when I was about 14 or 15 'cause he lived around Mobile too. He helped me no end, just by talking baseball with me, telling me about hitting, what to look for and expect, things he'd been through when he was comin' up, and ideas that rubbed off on me—like learning to play the game relaxed and figure what's going to happen will happen. A lot of people said Aaron was lazy. A lot of writers said this. But that's just the way he did his job. Then a few years later, all of a sudden, they notice him. "Hey! This guy's close to Babe Ruth's record, let's start writing good things about him, get on his wagon." Shoot, he's been doing it about the same ever since 1954.

When I go out on the field, I think about getting the job done. Other guys get the job done different ways. Like Jose Cardenal. I call him "Hot Dog." He calls me "Hot Dog." In fact, I'm the one who started that bit about him. You call it to a guy who kind of acts it out a little bit on the field like he's going for an Emmy award or something. At first, you think Jose's "hot-doggin'" it, but after you get to know his personality, you find out he's having fun playing the game. That's his way of getting the job done. Over the past few years, ball clubs have taken him wrong. We've talked about it. He got the reputation of being temperamental, a troublemaker. He is temperamental, but you keep a fella like Jose happy and he'll really perform for you. He loves playing at Wrigley Field, and he's a fine clutch player, a real good ballplayer all around.

There's no way Billy Williams can ever be a Jose. Or vice versa. People don't always understand the so-called superstar. It's not that you'd *like* to be first, it's that you *have* to be first, or at least keep trying to be. That's what makes a guy a superstar. Pride, determination, the love of competition, working hard at his job the way he's cut out to do it. Look at somebody like Tom Seaver. He's pitched his heart out every time for a team that doesn't score many runs, to the point where now he might have to save that fastball for when he really needs it, instead of challenging nearly every batter with it, pace himself more. He's pitched an awful lot of innings and look how few runs he's allowed, his low ERA, year after year.

Or Pete Rose, a guy who never runs out of ways to try to beat you. Willie Stargell. You've got to wonder what big Willie has to do to win a Most Valuable Player Award. He's the leader of the Pirates, has had some great years, broken up all kinds of ballgames, but all he's done has come close when they get down to voting.

Not just because he's my friend, but I think like me Ferguson Jenkins was also misunderstood a lot, especially the last couple of seasons. People got the idea he was getting a swelled head, being a prima donna, and all that. There's your case of a man saying something in the heat of the moment, maybe not thinking it all through, and just letting off steam. Some guys have to do that. Santo, Fergie, Pepitone, Durocher, you know who I mean.

When it comes out in the papers, you see the part where Fergie doesn't feel like coming out to the ballpark anymore. You don't get, or you miss, the part that the reason is he's down on himself, disappointed he's not doing better for the team, trying to give all he's got, and nothing seems to work. Or the time he was kidding about being sent to Detroit because it's so close to his home in Canada. What a big fuss they made about that. And when he said he wanted to be considered "Like Nobody Else." He meant he wanted to be judged on his own record and value, and not on those of the other top pitchers. It's quickly forgotten that for a lot of years in a row, where would the Cubs have finished without Fergie? After all, he was the first to win 20 or more games in the National League for six straight seasons since Warren Spahn and something only one other pitcher did in Cub history.

It's hard to explain this desire for recognition without appearing to be blowing your own horn. It's like a man in any field who spends many years on the same job. He proves himself, doesn't need to be pushed, gets to be a professional, and performs day in, day out without making a big deal about it. He figures he doesn't have to polish any apples, the boss knows he's working. He becomes one of the best in his business. But when it comes to the point where he figures he's next in line for the top position and everything that goes with it, the boss brings in his son you didn't even know he had, instead. I believe you shouldn't have to change the way you work, talk, or think to get what you've earned. You shouldn't have to change your personality, beat drums, or get into some kind of personality contest. Your record should be enough. Maybe nice guys don't finish last, but I guess a lot of times they also don't finish first. When you've got to the top, you don't want to come in second or third just because you're not—what's the word—flamboyant?

Now I'll make a confession. Much of this book at first came as a surprise to me, and here's why. We wondered whether it ought to be in the first person or third person, but we soon found out I'm not the type of man who brings things up on his own, especially when it's me playing the "hero." And we didn't want it to be "just another baseball book." So Irv Haag spent hours and hours with me ("psychoanalyzing me," I called it), using a tape recorder, throwing all kinds of questions at me. He also spent days and days talking to my teammates and to superstars like Hank Aaron, Johnny Bench, Tom Seaver, Lou Brock, Pete Rose, Willie Stargell, Joe Torre, and others for their comments on me (without me knowing what they said). He talked to Shirley, broadcasters, writers, coaches, did all sorts of research in newspapers, magazines, and books, then got my reactions, and put the whole jigsaw together.

So the story's in third person but the quotes in italics are all by me. That's also why it has a lot more in it than if only "the quiet man" told it. I remember saying when we started on this project, after the '73 season was over, that I might learn a lot more about *myself*, and I have. That means *you* ought to find out plenty you never knew about me before too.

Billy Williams

The Man

"He Was Not Easy to Reach"

—Jack Brickhouse, Vice-President
in charge of sports, WGN, Chicago

"I remember when this boy first came up as rookie of the year. I saw this shy, withdrawn, frightened, modest, suspicious—not necessarily happy—young black man come into a white man's world. Or what, in his opinion, was a white man's world.

"He was not easy to reach. He was in a shell. He had a sweet swing and all that, but he still was not quite the affable fella you'd like a fella to be. He wasn't uncooperative, but he answered in monosyllables, and he was a 'Yep' and 'Nope' guy."

Billy Williams chuckled when he read those remarks by Jack Brickhouse, for many years the homey, glib, ever-optimistic voice of WGN Radio and TV sports. Brick's elated "Hey! Hey!" and deflated "Oh-h brother!" have become as familiar to Chicagoans and other midwesterners as "State Street, that great street."

Even today, a lot of people get the feeling I go around with a chip on my shoulder mad at the world, from my facial expression. As a young kid, I didn't go around smiling all the time. In school, I didn't laugh at any little joke I'd hear. I didn't say that much, and I had a habit of staring at people. When Shirley was in the eighth grade, and I was in the eleventh grade I think, her friend used to see me around. I'd stare at her and say two or three words maybe, but the smile wasn't there. All of a sudden, just by looking at my facial expression, she decided I was the meanest man in the world. She even told Shirley that, but I guess Shirley didn't go along with it. Later on, when Shirley and I got more acquainted, her friend was over at Shirley's house a lot, so we got a chance to talk to each other, and she found out I wasn't as mean as she thought I was.

One person who may have helped to bring Billy out of his shell in those early days with the Cubs was "Mr. Perpetual Sunshine" himself.

I was fortunate to be around a fella like Ernie Banks, who took a lot of time with young ballplayers. Ernie and I roomed together my first couple of years, until one time down in Houston. He woke up at about six o'clock one morning, pulled the curtain back and said, "A beautiful day for a doubleheader!" Billy laughed. *And I had just started thinking about playing* one *ballgame! So, I went to the traveling secretary and said, "I like to play with Ernie on the field, but I can't room with him."* Another big grin. *This guy wakes up E-A-R-L-Y in the morning!*

Believe it or not, while you're sitting around in the room, Ernie's the same way you see him on the field. He's a guy who never likes to go to sleep. He likes to stay up most of the night talkin' baseball. A lot of times, he'd be talkin' and look over and I'd be asleep. He'd just wind up turnin' the light off and tell me the next morning I went to sleep on him. That's why he's had so many good years in baseball —he's a typical ballplayer that ate and slept the game. A lot of people think this is a big put-on about him, but he carries on everywhere the same way he does around the field.

Then Billy added, and you knew he meant it as a compliment to Ernie . . . "He's strictly a politician!" Williams revealed he saw Ernie get mad on the ballfield only once—when he figured Jack Sanford of the Giants was brushing him off and knocking him down at the plate too often. (And it may come as good news to duffers everywhere who've always wanted to fling a putter into a pond that Ernie too gets mad when he makes a bad shot on the golf course!)

The trim, neat, slender veteran of 13 full seasons with the Chicago Cubs has an interesting manner of speaking. Sometimes as he's talking, he seems to feel he's using "I" too much, and you realize he's still somewhat shy, still modest, and is measuring his words carefully. Then he switches to "you" and the listener finds himself almost in Billy's own shoes, thinking his thoughts, feeling his feelings.

You find yourself listening intently, first because he speaks softly, though at times quite excitedly and enthusiastically. And secondly, just when you think he's stopped talking, he's suddenly apt to drop in, or end up with, something that comes from a lot of deep thought, revealing his philosophy, or his quick wit, or his warmth. For instance, in telling about a boyhood pal, Eurial Jordan, with whom he had a little bike shop over 25 years ago back in Whistler, Alabama:

We never cut off our friendship after he left town to go into the service and I left to go play baseball. We continued our friendship. . . . And y'know, this is the way it's supposed to be.

"Today, when you talk to Billy Williams," said Brickhouse, "you'll find a proud, highly talented, articulate, intelligent, inspirational type of man. Here's a fella who's good for the other guys on the ball club. He's a fella who speaks a lot of sense."

I like to analyze things before I make any motion. I have a tendency to think about whether what I say is the right thing so that after a while, if you think about it, you know the things you said were true, and the things you said you meant.

The genial WGN sportscaster also had some comments on Billy's often-overlooked value to the ball club. "His words have weight. I have a feeling that at some of those club meetings, the younger boys will listen to Billy, more so than they will other people who are perhaps using up more words in public print."

You certainly won't get any argument about that from Lou Brock, who supplied the missing spark to the Cardinals' offense and was the key man in their drive to the pennant in 1964, the same year he was traded from the Cubs.

"Billy taught me more about hitting than anybody else in baseball," said Larcenous Lou, a fast friend of Williams since the two were learning the ropes in the big leagues under the Cubs' rotating-coach experiment that had begun in 1961. "He made me aware of things to look for, especially in pitchers, little things but important things you might never learn under ordinary circumstances."

Another Cub "graduate" who's gone on to stardom, Bill North of the Oakland A's, is lavish with praise about the Cub leftfielder who outsiders often accuse, wrongfully, of going his own way, in his own world, oblivious of his teammates.

"Billy Williams is the man who's been more help to me than anybody," said North. "I don't know if he's aware of that, but it's true. Williams taught me how to play baseball. As you know, he's the best hitter there is. More important, he's a great human being. Pro isn't the word. He's a man—at his job and living.

"I learned a lot just sitting there and watching him play, although he gave me plenty of hitting pointers too. Mainly, Billy taught me how important it is to relax. Now I know what I have to do is play as hard as I can and not cheat myself. If I don't produce one day, I will the next. Even though I didn't know any of the pitchers over here, getting a chance to play relaxed, the way Billy Williams does, made all the difference," said the speedy A's outfielder who rapped out 158 hits in 1973. An injury kept him out of the World Series.

Billy's not one to force his suggestions on another player—he has

13

to be asked. He's willing to work with anybody, especially if they show the desire and determination he feels separate the "utility" ballplayer from the star. He has little patience with those who have the ability but fail to work at developing it.

In a column he used to do for the *Chicago Tribune*, "The Wonderful World of Ernie Banks," Ernie had this to say:

"Billy, in his own quiet way, makes it a point to encourage youngsters who have just reported to the club. I remember when Danny Murphy, the bonus high school boy from Massachusetts, joined us. He was going to be with the Cubs for a week before joining a minor league team.

"Billy introduced himself to Danny, who answered, 'If you see me doing anything wrong at the plate, will you let me know?'

"Danny returned to the Cubs late that season and Billy watched him taking batting practice. He noticed the boy had a hitch in his swing and suggested he pull more with his swing to quicken it. You know what? In his first game he hit two homers off Larry Jackson, or maybe it was Ernie Broglio. But either way, they were off 20-game winners. Everyone was disappointed when Danny didn't make it in the majors.

"When Billy gives out with a tip, the player takes it seriously. He knows that coming from Billy, who doesn't waste words, it must have merit."

Bill Gleason, brilliant columnist of the *Chicago Sun-Times* and hilarious master of ceremonies, has long recognized how Billy contributes more than his uncanny consistent batting, clutch hitting, long-ball power, and fine fielding. Wrote Gleason in August, 1970: "The leader of the Cubs is, of all people, the quiet man of the clubhouse, Billy Williams. Billy Williams, who seldom speaks in a voice that can be heard beyond his own cubicle, who wouldn't say 'Rah! Rah!' if Phil Wrigley promised him a $10,000 bonus for each 'Rah', is the man to whom the Cubs look for leadership. Although Billy still has the body and the face of a kid, the young players and the veterans who have come to Chicago from other clubs see in him the great player he has become.

"He combines the dignity of Ernie Banks, the determination of Santo, and the competitive fires of Hundley, and he plays every day, every night."

"He's an individual who can change the complexion of a ballgame with two or three words," according to Ferguson Jenkins, for many years the dean of the Cubs' pitching staff and Billy's fishing and hunting buddy and probably his closest friend. "He can say something that's offbeat and bring a smile to your face, break the tension. Plenty of times, he's helped calm me down in a tough ballgame by saying something like 'C'mon, let's get these next guys out fast, the fish are bitin' on the lake'."

Ron Santo, as talkative as Billy is taciturn, reveals how "Whistler," as he often calls him, is a soft-spoken pillar of strength in other areas too. "In the days when you had writers coming in right after you, you didn't have much time to relax. And, of course, at the time I'd speak what I felt. But every once in a while, he'd grab me and I'd realize 'Wait a minute, I'd better keep my mouth shut'." The ex-Cub captain, who is now performing his heroics with the cross-town Chicago White Sox after invoking what some wag referred to as the "Santo-Clause" in the new regulations by refusing to be traded out of the Windy City, continued, "When we'd lose, Billy knew he'd have to kind of get my chin off the ground. I'm a tough loser as well as a happy winner, I guess."

The colorful third baseman loves to tell about Billy's habit of imitating him. "We'd been together so long, he could almost tell what I was going to say the first thing if we won or if we lost. Usually, when I walked on the bus, I'd say to the guy who won the game with a clutch hit or the pitcher who pitched a great game, something like 'Gee, you were fantastic! You were just great!' Billy would impersonate me before I'd get the words out!"

One interviewer, Ron Berler, writing a feature on Billy for the *Chicago Tribune* magazine, said, "Some baseball players are gabby, some are flamboyant. And then there's Cub star Billy Williams who, for his own good reasons, would rather not talk about it." One thing Billy won't talk about freely is his golf score. That alone tells you he's not a machine. Golf, by the way, is the only other thing he does from the left side. He's a natural righthander. Even though he bats lefthanded, he throws righthanded. He also bowls righthanded. Come to think of it, he won't reveal his bowling score either!

But Billy is still baffling to many. When one of Chicago's veteran baseball writers heard we were writing this book, he shrugged his shoulders and said, simply, "A difficult man." Some say it's virtually impossible to get inside the man whose cold, stony glare at the plate can unnerve the toughest pitchers. A man who can be driven into the dirt on a "warning" pitch, then, without a show of emotion, calmly get up, dust himself off, and dig his spikes even deeper into the dirt, an even icier glint in his eye as he dares the pitcher to try and get one by him. Certainly not a man you'd expect to find singing in the outfield.

Y'know, when you're playing the outfield, the traffic's kind of slow. You want to get involved in the game, but still you don't want to get too excited.

In Wrigley Field, you have the people very close to you. But in the bigger ballparks, you're out there by yourself, and you're trying to do something to keep you relaxed. And this is how I try to play the game, relaxed. So, I just start singing. It might be a good tune I heard on the radio that particular day.

Did a ball ever hit you right between the ... choruses?
Billy laughed.

No, this is between pitches. You can't afford to do this when the pitcher's releasing the ball—you've got to think about other things. But I just do it to try to keep in a relaxed mood and give myself company out there. Maybe I start humming a song in the clubhouse or on the bench, and it carries on when I get out in the outfield.

One of his big assets, the reason for his consistency, said broadcaster Lou Boudreau, is his ability to rid himself of worries when he's between those white lines. "If he's worried, he never shows it. It helps him mentally at the plate. I don't think he allows outside matters to affect him once that game gets underway."

Billy's outer calm and inner confidence weren't always there, not by a long shot. They came only after Billy faced and learned to handle such extreme nervous tension that, early in his career, a doctor advised him to give up baseball. He still keeps many things inside. Said former teammate Glenn Beckert, "There are times I think he's aching to explode." But Billy has disciplined himself to cope with tension and turn his nervous energy into the extra adrenaline that makes the great competitor perform so well under pressure.

"He leads his club with his bat and just the way he plays," said Joe Torre of the St. Louis Cardinals. "I think he knows if he blows his stack, it might affect a lot of the young kids, and Billy feels that kind of responsibility to his teammates, and it carries over.

"When he first came up, he was having a rough time in the outfield. But he knew his shortcomings. Instead of goin' out there and working on his hitting which he knew he could do, he went out there and worked on defense which he didn't have to do. But he wanted to be a complete ballplayer, which only goes to show what kind of pride the guy has."

Billy doesn't put much stock in statements that say a player gives 110 percent or 120 percent. He believes all you can give is everything you *have* to give. And he gives everything each time out.

At the end of the Cubs' frustrating 1973 season, Chicago was losing to the Mets at Wrigley Field, 9 to 2. Billy made a desperate try at nabbing a foul ball on a soggy, rain-puddled field.

After the game, relief pitcher Bob Locker told Williams, "Billy, you're a great ballplayer. There's no way we could have won at that stage of the game, but you still gave it everything you had."

He doesn't know any other way to play. If a ball's playable, he thinks it must be caught, regardless of the score.

That's one side of Billy Williams. Another is the Billy who will eagerly take the time and has the patience to show a fellow fisherman the *right* way to put a plastic worm on a hook. He keeps a fishing kit in his locker at Wrigley Field, just in case he decides to stop on the way home to see if the perch are biting.

It's not that he forgets or doesn't care if the club lost that day. He just won't let it tear him apart. Like the evening the Cubs dropped their 11th straight game in '73. As he walked into a restaurant for dinner, he was stopped by a bus driver, a really rabid Cub fan who recognized him. The man talked on and on about the faults of the club, and Billy was patience personified. Finally, the master diplomat, he gave the fan probably the thrill of his life.

"You really know baseball!" Billy said admiringly.

Once inside the restaurant, when the waiter arrived to take his order, Billy, chin in hand, looked up and said, "How about 12 straight wins on rye?"

Nobody took that losing streak harder inside than he did. He just didn't show it. He's determined not to let yesterday ruin today—in a game or in life.

Those who confuse Billy's "cool" with complacency are making a big mistake. Maybe Torre put it best: "The thing I admire about Billy, he's the same person whether he's 0-for-4 or 4-for-4. Anybody can take a 4-for-4 day."

Sometimes you see things happen at the ballpark. Maybe we should have won a game and didn't, things that happen that shouldn't happen. I think about 'em and ask myself, "Is there anything I can do about it now?" If not, I say, "There's no use worryin' about it because nothing's going to change."

But then again, if you feel you can do something about it, that you might help the cause, that's when I get mad or upset.

There's a practical side of Billy too. He's never been thrown out of a ballgame. In his analytical way, he knows it's not going to do his ball club any good if he's ejected from a game. Like any ballplayer, he often disagrees with an umpire's call. A lot of fans don't realize it, but he lets the boys in blue know. Quietly. As he walks by, on his way back to the dugout, and in such a manner that on the next close call he might get the benefit of any doubt.

Things bother me, sure. But I try not to let them get the best of me. If something happens I don't like, I'll voice my opinion about it. I won't accept it with a smile. When it gets to the point where I have to turn beyond the second cheek, that's when you hear about it. With me, it's a matter of trying to give the other guy the benefit of the doubt. But when you get beyond that, when somebody's trying to take advantage of you, that's the time when you have to tell a guy to get off your back.

There have been times I've felt I was too nice. Sometimes I've thought if I were meaner, I'd be a better ballplayer. But I've found out I was wrong. For example, one time at San Diego that fella Eduardo Acosta was throwing at me. He threw a pitch right behind my head. We were leading by 8 runs. It made me mad, and I thought, "I'm gonna show this guy." I squeezed the sawdust out of the bat and gritted my teeth. I wanted to hit one out just to show him. But you just hurt yourself. He got me out with no trouble at all.

Then that time in St. Louis when Rick Wise was throwing at me. I knew it, everybody knew it. The day before, I went 3-for-4, but I didn't do anything the rest of the series. I was too mad.

Some use the word "professional" about Williams as if only ice water flows through his veins. It is true that he's entirely different after a ballgame than before. In the clubhouse, he leaves no doubt that his business is baseball, and he's all business—not just when he arrives at the ballpark, but almost from the moment he gets up before a game. The first thing he does is look at the paper to see who's pitching, and starts thinking ahead, as all those born under the sign of Gemini supposedly do.

He's not the chilly, unapproachable person he occasionally appears to be. Chances are he's deep in concentration most of these times.

I'm usually thinking about different things. And maybe people see me at a moment when I'm thinking about something else. Peo-

ple judge people without getting involved with them. A person doesn't have to smile. It's what comes out of the heart that means something.

Although Billy loves to talk hitting in general, they'll be exporting green cheese from the moon the day he volunteers to tell about some of the batting feats of his that have left others gaping. That's the single most important reason why this book is written in the third person. Where others leap into the limelight by tugging at a writer's sleeve, ready with "hot copy," you almost have to drag inside dope about his personal exploits out of Billy.

Take Ted Williams to whom he's often compared, at least hitting wise. When Ted came up as a rookie, a teammate said to him, "Wait till you see that Jimmy Foxx hit!" The cocky kid popped right back with, "Oh yeah?! Wait till Foxx sees *me* hit!" Nor was the Boston Red Sox rookie bashful about announcing his goal. "When I'm real old and walking down the street someday, I want people to poke each other and say, 'There's the best damn hitter who ever lived'."

But that's not Billy. He'd probably be the same no matter what his profession—let's say a brain surgeon, for instance. Praised for saving a patient's life with a perilous operation, Billy would probably wonder what the fuss was all about. "Wasn't that what I was supposed to do? That's my job."

Stories that he can keep his press clippings in a fishing hat are slightly exaggerated. But when asked if he had any for background material, he allowed there might be a few around . . . someplace, but couldn't quite remember where. When he finally found them, where were they? In beautiful, handsomely bound scrapbooks? Nope. Stashed and stuffed into an old, small, beat-up vinyl case he once used to carry his basketball gear when he appeared in games, mostly charity exhibitions, with some fellow Cubs during the off-season.

Downstairs in the cozy recreation room of his spacious but unostentatious home in a fine Chicago suburb, there's his beloved stereo music ever in the background, a console TV, comfortable furniture, small bar, and, of course, a goodly array of plaques, trophies, and specially marked baseballs and bats. If you'd like to take a closer look at them, you're welcome. He'll answer questions but won't take you on a "Here's the year I did this, and here's the year I did that" tour.

On the other hand, there's undisguised pride in his voice when he says he was National League Rookie of the Year in 1961. There's also a special reverence whenever he uses the term major league ballplayer. He won't tell you of his heroics in that rookie year. And don't expect him to tell you about the mischief he played the same year with Warren Spahn, the winningest—363 games—lefthanded pitcher in history. Lefties are usually poison to lefthanded batters. But Billy, typically, passes off his "luck against lefties" to the fact that he got a chance to see a lot of southpaw slants in Triple-A ball.

You don't get to know Billy, really know him, the first time you meet him or the second or third time. And unless he gets used to you and/or respects you, it's doubtful you'll ever get inside the armor.

He's candid, sincere, has his own brand of humor—more a dry wit than a guffaw—smiles and laughs easily, and takes a ribbing good-naturedly. He also has a way of "counter-ribbing" a ribber, by acting as if it's all going past him, until you see the laughing glint in his eye. You soon learn that nothing you say gets by Billy—if anything, he's way ahead of you. Nor does he find it necessary to use profanity to get his point across.

There's one more especially refreshing quality about him. In a world filled with so many people eager to tell you what they're *against*, Billy generally tells you what he's *for*.

He wanted this to be more than "just another baseball book," and he has worked hard at trying to make it interesting and meaningful.

In fact, before starting his story, I asked him kiddingly, "What if I dig up some *bad* stuff about you?"

Without hesitating, without trying to be humorous, Billy replied:

If you do, print *it.*

The Invisible Superstar

"What If a Kid Reads That?"
—Billy Williams

Billy Williams came to the Cubs with very little going for him—except his ability with a bat. A press agent's dream he wasn't.

He wasn't cut out to write anonymous letters to sportswriters like Grantland Rice, alerting Rice to keep an eye on a fantastic rookie from Georgia—as Ty Cobb did.

Billy wasn't built to stage the headline-making spring holdouts of a Joe DiMaggio, or, as the "Yankee Clipper" did, to fire back contracts without even opening the envelope.

Unlike Dizzy Dean, once a Cub himself, helping pitch the 1938 Bruins to the pennant with his "nothing ball," he couldn't give out two different stories about where he was born to two different reporters.

He didn't inspire the kind of stories told about another ex-Cub, the legendary, stubby, stocky slugger Hack Wilson. After one of his habitual and rougher nights on the town, Wilson was trying to catch forty winks while tending centerfield. He didn't notice that the Cub pitcher was being lifted. Enraged at himself, the hurler whirled and fired the ball off the fence right near where Hack was snoozing. Waking up with a jolt, Wilson played the ball perfectly and whipped it into second base. A moment later, Cub manager Joe McCarthy removed *him!*

Even having such a simple name was against Billy. If it had been say Ossee Schreckengost, who caught for the Philadelphia Athletics, or Carl Yastrzemski of the Boston Red Sox—what writer could ever forget him after hunt-and-pecking a name like those a few times?

And whether Babe Ruth *really* "called" his home-run shot, Leo Durocher said "Nice guys finish last," and Yogi Berra said all those funny things doesn't matter. Most people *think* they did, hence the stories have become a part of their image. Then, now, and forever.

In building up Durocher's image, sportswriters might tell how Leo kicked dirt on umpire Jocko Conlan's freshly shined shoes. And they could always find a new "Berra-ism." For example, Joe Garagiola once mentioned that Berra's always late, then went on to tell about the time Yogi was only 15 minutes tardy. "Gee!" said Yogi, "this is the earliest I've ever been late."

Billy's image? Quiet, shy, modest, colorless, uncomplaining, unemotional. For all but the last couple of years, you could also add unnoticed and unrecognized. Kind of a hardworking, dedicated real square, who knows nothing but trying to do the best job day in and day out, out-of-step in a world that's seeing more goof-offs, oddballs doing their thing, and people looking for a paycheck and a pension and little else.

Of course, those who play against him—pitchers for example—use other words to describe him (many unprintable in a family-type publication like this). Billy has flattened baseballs with such clocklike precision and relentless regularity that one hurler groused, "The only way to pitch to Billy Williams is in a night game at Wrigley Field."

Even after his consecutive-game streak was into the high hundreds, there weren't the usual, natural hot-story ingredients of whether he'd be able to continue or not. And meanwhile, Billy simply went about it day after day.

Milo Hamilton, former Chicago White Sox broadcaster and for the last eight years the "Voice of the Atlanta Braves," commented on some of the reasons for the Cub star's lack of publicity.

"You talk about being unnoticed, unheralded, whatever," said Hamilton, "you've got to remember that Billy came to this town when Ernie Banks was already Mr. Cub . . . then Santo emerged as another star. No matter how you look at it, when the publicity got out, he was always third, whatever he did. I think he was a victim of circumstances. And his endurance record was a big thing too," Hamilton went on, "but even that was overlooked until he did it. Then they started talking about it."

Lou Brock came up with one of the neatest descriptions of Williams. "Some players are the backbone of a ball club, but they always seem to go unnoticed. Billy's been like the third man in a two-man act."

Write-ups over the years have harped on the same things so often you'd almost expect a halo to sparkle over his head when Billy doffs his cap. "He has a perfect disposition," said Durocher. "Nothing bothers him," noted Santo. "Billy's expected to bat third, play left, make all the catches," chortled Banks in his sing-song manner. "He does it. He's a guy who knows what he has to do and he does it. He's a real pro. I've never heard him complain once."

It figures then that Billy caused a wave of national excitement matched only by the thrill of watching paint dry. If you're familiar with the Boy Scouts of America, you'll understand. Billy spent many rewarding days as a Scout, also becoming an Explorer, and thinks highly of the organization. One of his proudest awards is a citation for helping to recruit a large number of boys for membership.

In fact, everything a Scout pledges on joining is a completely accurate description of the soft-spoken Sweet Swinger, from the Scout Motto, "Be Prepared," the Oath to keep himself "physically strong, mentally awake, and morally straight," and the Scout Law that requires members to be: trustworthy, loyal, helpful, friendly, courteous, kind, obedient, cheerful, thrifty, brave, clean, and reverent. Every word fits the steel-tough, durable professional who's been the Cub mainstay the last seven or eight years.

So you can't put all the blame on the writers. After all, people don't buy newspapers to read that "Today, Billy Williams did not throw his batting helmet into the stands after taking a questionable called third strike. He also did not go for a homer in the third inning, but deliberately hit to the right side to advance the runner into scoring position. Nor did he start a row in the clubhouse, call the manager a bubblehead, or challenge him to a fight under the stands. After his hitless day, he went home. And that night he ran off films of himself at the plate, trying to find out what he was doing wrong. Next morning, heading for the clubhouse, he didn't sneer at the gleeful youngsters tugging at his sleeve for autographs or threaten them with a baseball bat. Billy also didn't tell the reporters he'd start hitting again as soon as the bee sting on his elbow cleared up and he got rid of the corn on his big toe."

As a result, he became sort of baseball's "unknown soldier." Only other baseball people and rabid "baseball nuts" who ravenously devour statistics and records were aware of the slender swat-smith. Few fans knew, for example, that Billy's total of 137 runs scored in 1970 was never attained by Stan Musial, Hank Aaron, Willie Mays, Roberto Clemente, Ernie Banks, Eddie Mathews, Roger Maris, or Carl Yastrzemski. As a headline over a newspaper story about Williams once put it beautifully: "Billy Does It All—Except Attract Attention."

A good indication of the average fan's unawareness of Billy's performance is in the voting for the National League All-Star teams. When Billy was playing his first full season in 1961, and through 1969, managers, coaches, and players made the selections. Williams was selected in '62, '64, '65, and '68. But in 1970, when Commissioner

Bowie Kuhn restored the voting to the fans, Billy wasn't named to the All-Star squad, even though he had had the second greatest season of his career. He was ignored again in 1971. And in 1972, his finest season, when his batting average was tops in *both* leagues, he still didn't make it on the fans' vote but was named by Pirate Manager Danny Murtaugh.

The fans did vote for him, finally, in 1973. And those who saw Billy introduced on TV with the other players on the 1973 National League All-Star team witnessed something few rival pitchers ever see—the warm, spontaneous, beaming smile that couldn't hide his genuinely boyish enthusiasm and his delight in having received such an honor.

Meanwhile, the sportswriters, aware of Billy's incredibly consistent, efficient performance in pain or not, game after game after game, without fanfare for over eight seasons, began using phrases like "the quiet gentleman" and "the silent superstar" when referring to him. Later, of course, after he had played in so many consecutive games that he became as much a part of the leftfield scenery in Wrigley Field as the ivy growing on the brick walls, he was "the iron man." Then they began to call him "the machine." Arnold Hano wrote in the magazine *Sport:* "The 'quiet machine' of the Cubs goes about his remarkable way without fuss, with only one thought in mind: to 'keep trying to be the best'."

Hano then went on to quote Lippy Leo. "Billy Williams never gets excited. Never gets mad. Never throws a bat. You write his name down in the same spot in the line-up every day and you forget it. He'll play left; he'll bat third. Billy Williams is a baseball machine." Billy's read this type of thing about himself for a long time now. And he's taken it pretty much in stride.

But one day, Billy picked up a Jim Brosnan article in a national magazine, entitled "THE BILLY WILLIAMS DOLL: WIND IT UP AND IT HITS LINE DRIVES." Leo was wrong. This made Billy so mad he slammed the story into the nearest wastebasket. When other writers picked up the analogy, adding such comments as, "You don't have to wind it up—it's self-winding," it really got under his skin. "Oh, Billy has his moments," Shirley said. "If you rub him the wrong way, he might give you a lecture."

You could tell he had done a lot of deep thinking about it when he told why this type of reference irks him so. And his reason shows a side of him, a depth, a dimension few people know.

What if a kid reads that? Suppose he just reads the top of the story and not the rest. He's apt to get the idea that all they do is put me up at the plate, I just swing the bat and get base hits. Easy. Nothin' to it.

But he doesn't see the part where Billy wasn't hitting and went out to the ballpark early for some extra practice. He doesn't see that on the bench, all the time, Billy's thinking what this pitcher threw him today, what he threw him last, what he threw him with men on base.

It doesn't give credit for me being a good hitter by thinking hitting all the time. Today you find that so many kids, not just kids but people in general, depend on other people to do things for them.

Take your utility ballplayer. He's content to be in the major leagues, but he doesn't have the desire and determination to be a good major league player, the best.

It's pride that keeps you going. A player paid the salary I am, with 40,000 people in the stands and everybody focused on you, has to feel he can't let up at any time. Sure, God may have given me the ability to play ball, but he left it up to me whether I'd use that ability and develop it. To never be satisfied. If you get four hits, you want that fifth one. If your salary's not enough, work at bein' better to earn more. I just think kids ought to know that.

In many ways, you could compare his underrated role to that of Lou Gehrig's, not just because they both played iron men. Most everybody remembers that during the 1932 World Series between the Yankees and the Cubs Babe Ruth pointed to the centerfield bleachers in Wrigley Field, then boomed a homer into almost that exact spot.

But how many remember that Gehrig homered right after the Babe and had a pair of homers in that same game—or that Larrupin' Lou put on one of the greatest hitting displays in Series history, batting .529, with 3 homers and 8 RBIs, in the four-game set. Still fewer recall that in 1927 when Ruth hit his 60 round-trippers, Gehrig was voted the Most Valuable Player in the American League.

For many years, the spotlight just seemed to be pointed in the other direction as far as Billy was concerned. Like the time he homered in the 1964 All-Star Game and the network had cut away for a commercial. Or the time he was asked to send the scorecard from his 1,000th consecutive game to the Hall of Fame at Cooperstown, New York—then spent hours looking for it on a visit there, without ever finding it. As Billy puts it:

When you come up to the major leagues, they put a tag on you and it seems no matter what you do after that, the tag remains.

The Classic Hitter

"His Swing Is Poetry in Motion"
—Willie Stargell, Pittsburgh Pirates

The tiny girl in pigtails races to the living room. She squirms inside the draperies up tight to the picture window. Her daddy's on his way to the garage. Nose pressed to the glass, she watches as he backs out the car with the license plate "BW 26." He stops, looks up, sees her, and waves. She beams, calling "Hit me a homer!" Then she flashes a peace sign. He beams back and returns the sign. It's their own special tradition every morning Daddy goes to work at Wrigley Field.

The Classic Hitter has been punching his time card at the same old place since 1961, the year he won the National League Rookie of the Year Award. One of the finest defensive leftfielders in the game, in 13 full seasons he averaged nearly 30 homers, 100 RBIs, 97 runs, 185 hits, 315 total bases, and 65 extra-base hits per year and batted .300. He topped both leagues in total bases in 1970, with 373, and in 1972, with 348. Three times he belted more than 200 hits.

Getting more than 200 hits a season three times is a lot more significant when you realize that such legendary stars of the past as Ted Williams never attained it. Joe DiMaggio had over 200 hits twice in his brilliant career; famed for hits, Nellie Fox, Chicago White Sox great and 1959 American League Most Valuable Player, achieved it only once. Ex-Cub MVPs, Hank Sauer in 1952 and Phil Cavarretta in 1945, never had that many hits, nor has Al Kaline.

And as he starts the 1974 season, he ranks second in homers among all-time Cubs, with 376, second in extra-base hits (843), and third in RBIs (1,286), hits (2,397), total bases (4,079), and runs scored (1,251). Yet the Sweet Swinger played in fewer games than the Cubs he trails—for example, 432 fewer games than Banks, 180 fewer than Cap Anson.

Over a seven-year period, 1967 through 1973, astonishingly, he *produced more runs than anybody in baseball*, drove in an average of 101 runs a season, slammed out more doubles, triples, and total bases than any hitter in either league, and ranked among the top in virtually every other offensive category.

It's well known that baseball statistics probably have started, rekindled, and prolonged more fights and arguments than anything else, except possibly marriage. Furthermore, neither party is ever fully convinced he's wrong. This is especially true when the discussions involve batting records. The so-called batting championship is based on the batting average only. The Triple Crown winner must have the most RBIs and home runs and the highest batting average. But the Triple Crown winner might not lead in runs scored or in total bases. With so many different kinds of statistics to consider, what formula can be used to determine the most productive hitter in a season?

The "runs-produced" or, as it is sometimes called, the "runs-responsible-for" method of evaluating a player's offensive worth is becoming increasingly popular. It ignores the batting average but takes into account the runs scored and runs driven in. Here's the runs-produced system as described by John Kuenster, editor of *Baseball Digest,* in a recent issue.

"There are all sorts of criteria to measure a player's offensive capabilities in baseball, but through the years, the most generally accepted standards include runs batted in and runs scored. When you tote up a batter's RBIs and the runs he has scored, you've made a start on judging much of his effectiveness at the plate.

"These two figures, however, should be refined further if you are to get a more accurate assessment of a batter's value to his club. Since a home run counts as both an RBI and a run scored, it is logical to deduct it from one column or the other. Once this is done, then you have the net total of runs produced by a batter."

To figure the number of runs produced, add the number of runs scored to the number of RBIs and from that total subtract the number of home runs. Using the runs-produced method, let's compare the records of two great hitters: Frank Robinson's when he won the Triple Crown and the American League's Most Valuable Player Award in 1966 and that of Billy Williams in one of his greatest years, 1970, when he seriously challenged Bench for the National League's MVP trophy.

	RUNS SCORED	PLUS RBI	TOTAL	MINUS HR	RUNS PRODUCED
Robinson	122	122	244	49	195
Williams	137	129	266	42	224

Obviously, such a comparison doesn't take many things into account, such as the number of *opportunities* each man had—or didn't have—to drive in runs or how many times he "gave himself up" by advancing runners, which count as official times at bat without credit for a sacrifice. But by adding other pertinent statistics, we can arrive at a fairly valid, if not infallible, comparison.

	AB	R	H	2B	3B	HR	RBI	BA	TB	RP
Robinson	576	122	182	34	2	49	122	.316	367	195
Williams	636	137	205	34	4	42	129	.322	373	224

Another little-known feat shows why so many fellow National Leaguers, managers, and players alike, call Billy one of the most valuable players *never* to win a Most Valuable Player Award.

Under the Cubs' Offensive Rating system that ranks all players in both leagues, batting .315 and up rates a "one"; .300 to .314 rates a "two," and so on; 31 homers and up rates a "one"; and 90 or more RBIs rates a "one." Over a three-year span—1970, 1971, and 1972—Billy was the only major leaguer to rate a "one" in all three categories. He averaged 115 RBIs, 36 homers, and .319 per season.

Without a doubt, the first Cub player in history to crack the $100,000-and-up salary bracket was baseball's most productive batsman, inspiring such remarks as "Billy's a ballplayer I'd pay to see play," made by the Cubs' vice-president, John Holland.

Though not considered primarily a home-run clouter, Billy's total of 376 through 1973 puts him high on the list of all-time sluggers. He's moved ahead of such former greats as Johnny Mize, Joe DiMaggio, Yogi Berra, Hank Greenberg, Ralph Kiner, Gil Hodges, and Rocky Colavito. Billy is second only to Banks among Cub homer hitters down through history, including Chuck Klein (300), Gabby Hartnett (236), and Hack Wilson, who still holds the NL record for most homers in a season (56) and whose career total was 244.

There's never much talk about "tape-measure" jobs when Billy hits them. Because the ball literally explodes off his bat as a whistling line drive, it's usually just gaining altitude as it slams into a seat or clears the wall. Many hit the wall with such velocity he's often held to a single instead of a double, a double instead of a triple. There's little time for "leg" hits.

Were he not primarily a team player, he might have set even more glittering individual records. As Ernie Banks said, "I can always remember when he was in that consecutive-game streak, and we would be driving out to the ballpark. His main thought was to play the game so he could contribute something to the success of the team. That to me is the true sign of a *professional* athlete who feels he has to prove to the fans and himself each day he goes out there that he *is* a professional—to make a great play, get a clutch home run, or throw somebody out at the plate. Billy is conscious of this all the time."

Much has been made of Billy's "natural swing," one Santo called "probably one of the shortest swings in baseball, and one of the prettiest." Like so many other professionals, he makes meeting the ball look deceptively easy—smooth as butter, seemingly effortless. But on impact, the ball leaps off his bat with such velocity that it's often past a fielder before he can even go down for the grab or it hits the wall and is already rebounding back toward the infield as Billy, no turtle on the base paths, is just rounding first, heading for second.

"We were rookies the same year," said Joe Torre. "He won the 'Rookie of the Year' and I finished second. That's the way I would have voted too. Billy Williams is such a natural hitter, even when he's in a slump he looks good. A quick stroke, real fast wrists, and he just seems to stay over the ball an awful lot, which I think only another ballplayer can appreciate. He scares the hell outa you!"

I don't really know whether my swing is natural or not. It's God-gifted so to speak, but I know I had to work extra hard to keep it natural. When the late Rogers Hornsby was batting coach and I'm still down in the minors, he really took me under his wing. Hornsby was the type of guy who didn't like many people. He had ways of his own. But he was a go-getter and he loved to talk baseball. He had ideas of who was capable of playing major league baseball. And if he wanted you to know something, he wouldn't beat around the bush, he'd tell you point-blank. I think if a person develops this attitude, not only in baseball but in life, you respect him.

He saw that I was so eager to hit, so eager to do good, I was going after bad pitches, and I wanted everything to come at once. He detected that in spring training and this was the thing we worked on most. Sometimes you get into the habit of going after bad pitches because you're looking for the ball in a certain place. So you really have to do more concentrating up there.

Hornsby didn't mess with my basic style, my stance, or the bat I used. He didn't mess with the way I held my arms. He stressed the strike zone, 17 inches wide from your armpits to your knees, said that the only way you can be a good batter is to get a good ball to hit. And make the ball be over the plate.

You get an average of only one good ball to hit each time at the plate. The thing is, when you get it, you're not supposed to miss it. That's the difference between .300 hitters and ordinary hitters. You always have to be ready for that good pitch and connect when you get it.

A squib in *Baseball Digest* verifies that Hornsby did indeed have his own ways. When he saw Williams at San Antonio in 1959 during a tour of the Cubs' farm teams, he wired Chicago: "SUGGEST YOU BRING UP WILLIAMS. BEST HITTER ON TEAM." One of the club officials called Hornsby and said, "He's better than anyone else down there, huh?"

Hornsby shot back, "He's better than anyone up there!"

The "Rajah," who won seven batting championships and hit over .400 three times, posted the highest one-season average—.424—in modern baseball history and led the 1929 Cubs of Manager Joe McCarthy to the NL pennant. Ted Williams also credits Hornsby for his hitting philosophy. In his book, *The Science of Hitting,* Ted wrote, "All they ever write about the good hitter is what great reflexes they have, what great style, what strength, what quickness, but never how smart the guy is at the plate, and that's 50 percent of it."

Chatting about Billy with gritty ex-Cub catcher, Randy Hundley, we asked the "Rebel" if there's too much being said about batters hitting "pitchers' mistakes," rather than giving batters more credit. Randy drawled, "I'd say 80 percent of home runs are hit on mistakes... the pitcher didn't get the ball where he wanted, not in enough or away enough. Other times, a pitcher makes a good pitch where he and the catcher wanted it, but maybe the hitter's looking for it.

"Sometimes the hitters *don't* get enough credit. The percentage is with the pitcher. If he throws right down the middle, six out of ten times a batter will pop up or ground out. But Billy's one of those hitters that a pitcher can make a super pitch on, and he can still hit it—especially if he's looking for it. If he's looking for a pitch low and away and gets it, Billy's gonna hit it hard. A lot of guys can *look* for it, but it's something else to hit it and hit it hard. He has tremendous strength in his hands and his forearms. He's not that big of a guy, but he really hits the ball with a lot of authority.

"Billy's probably one of the best hitters I've ever watched. The thing about it, he studies hitting, he studies pitchers, he concentrates. He sits on the bench and you'll hear him talk about how 'He's gonna throw a fastball here' or 'He's gonna throw a change-up', and you know he's thinking about what a pitcher throws. He might be guessing a lot, but he's sure guessed *right* a lot."

Billy admits to "guessing" at the plate, but he uses the term to mean "calculated anticipation"... what he's noted about the pitcher and recalling how and what he threw to him in certain situations before. In describing the homer he hit off Al Hrabosky that won the game against the Cardinals on September 9, 1973, Billy said:

> *I was guessing. He got me on a fastball yesterday, and started me out the same way this time. I knew he wasn't about to give me anything good to hit if he could help it. He had one strike on me and I was sort of looking for something on the outside of the plate. That's where he put it. I wanted to make sure it was a strike so I waited a little longer than usual before swinging. When I left the ball, all I was trying to do was get on base. Luckily, I got enough wood on it to put it over the wall in left. When I say "leave the ball," I mean I'm now looking and swinging at where I think the ball will be. You hear a lot about following the ball all the way from the pitcher's hand to your bat. Basically, this is what I do. But I've never seen the bat hit the ball—they said Ted Williams could. That's one thing I'd like to do before I hang 'em up—see the bat hit the ball. And actually, this is what batting practice is really for. To help you get your timing. If there's anything I'd like to see to make batting practice better, it's more guys who can get some good velocity on the ball. Lots of times, coaches and other people, not primarily pitchers, throw batting practice. Most of 'em don't or can't throw hard enough.*
>
> *Another thing. I've seen young kids come up and ask the guy to throw fastballs. That's mostly what you get in the minors. They want to hit the ball out of the park. I figure if you know you can hit a fastball, it'd make more sense to work on curves and other pitches you can't hit in order to become a real good hitter. It doesn't pay to let the word get around that they can get you out on a curve, change-up, slider, or something like that.*

Ted Williams was another student in the school of "guessing." Sam Rice, the great Senator outfielder of the '20s and '30s with a lifetime batting average of .322, asked Ted if he ever guessed at the plate. Ted readily admitted he did. "I knew it!" exclaimed Rice, according to Ted's *The Science of Hitting*. "I go around asking these young hitters today if they guess at the plate, and they say 'No' because somewhere along the line somebody has told them 'Don't guess'. And the funny thing is, they're all hitting .230."

But even the Classic Hitter can't win them all. Sometimes the best way to foul up a hitter is for a catcher to tell him what's coming. Wondering if he's getting the straight dope or not, he'll be confused or he'll be thrown off completely. And as Hundley said, given a fat pitch right over the heart of the plate, the best of them are apt to hit a pop-up or a dribble.

Against San Diego in one series, Billy had committed mayhem two straight days on Padre pitching. The next day, San Diego's manager, ex-Cub Don Zimmer, went out to talk to pitcher Eduardo Acosta on the mound. Soon they were both laughing, and Zimmer was chuckling on his way back to the bench. As Billy tells it:

Acosta winds up and just lobs me the ball. I see that blooper coming up there and I take a big cut—miss it by a foot. He keeps throwing me six more pitches the same way. I'm sure one of 'em will be a fastball that he'll try to get past me. You guessed it. I struck out—on one of his bloopers. You should have seen the guys on the bench, they were really breaking up. That's one day I might have slammed my batting helmet down just a little bit harder.

Jim West, TV sidekick of WGN's Brickhouse, who considers the Cub veteran one of his favorite people, likes to tell one of Billy's favorite jokes on himself.

"Billy, some days you hit just like Ted Williams," says West.

"Yeah, and some days, I hit just like Esther!" Billy retorts.

Said Don Kessinger, Billy's long-time teammate and one of baseball's outstanding shortstops, "Not only is he the greatest hitter I've seen in baseball in my time up here, he's the hardest worker at it. He watches films more than any man I've seen. He picks up little flaws that might be giving him trouble. And when he goes into a slump, he studies, studies, studies. You really have to admire a man like that."

I have a movie projector at home, and I keep one reel of film handy all the time. It's one that shows when I'm hittin' good. Barney Sterling of the Cubs films us every day. When I feel I'm doin' something wrong, I watch the first reel, then play the other, and compare 'em, and keep doin' it until I spot the problem.

I'd rather do it that way than maybe go out and start changing my stance or stride, picking out another weight bat, or make some other adjustment that could really throw me off.

Sometimes, I find I've been swinging too hard and that makes my head turn. Or maybe I see I've slipped into my old bad habit of going after balls outside the strike zone. If I think I've figured out what's wrong, I take extra batting practice and work at concentrating on doing what I know is the right way for me.

Billy's fortunate. He has an extra pair of eyes—Shirley—at home helping him spot what may be causing a slump. "When Billy's stance or timing is off, he'll ask me if I notice anything different. Sometimes I can, and I tell him. A lot of times I'd tell him when he came home —I'm always watching on TV—'Billy, you're lunging at the ball' or 'you're swinging too quick'. No, he doesn't get mad. He'll say, 'Well, I noticed that too'.

"When I'd see him just kind of punch at the ball now and then, I'd get so mad, I'd take off my house slippers and throw 'em at the TV set. Other times, I could see the pitchers would think they're outsmarting him. I'd just know they'd come back with a certain pitch, and there I am, warning him, trying to get him to hear me over the TV set," she said, laughingly.

How about when you see him brushed back, or he has to hit the dirt. Do you get scared, Shirley?

"No! I just get mad. I can see it all on TV and he's just watching the ball and I find myself yelling, 'Look out!'"

Of course, in trying to shake a slump, the Classic Hitter is never at a loss for "assistance"—from waiters, bus drivers, bellhops, and fan mail, not to mention some of his fellow players. Thinking about some of the tips he gets, he chuckled.

You can talk to five different guys and get five entirely different opinions. One thing you've got to avoid, and that's doing too much thinking up there. Many times, you'll see me step out of the batter's box. That's because I'm concentrating so hard or ideas are flashing through my mind so fast, everything's like a blur. Then I've just got to clear my mind.

Slumps are mostly a mental thing, I'd say. And it always seems that when you're not goin' good, that's the day you're facing a Gibson or a Seaver and you go up with that in your mind. You can lose your confidence and determination, and maybe most important, discipline—forcing yourself to lay off pitches out of the strike zone or ones you know you can't hit, and to hold back on going for the homer, unless that's what you must have to win.

Billy Williams talks freely about his batting slumps, but for what makes the Sweet Swinger's swing sweet and pitchers religious ("I pray every time he comes to the plate") we must rely on others.

"Well, I think I signed the wrong brother." That was the mournful confession by Buddy Hancken, scout for the Pirates in 1956 and later with the Houston Astros. Hancken was quoted in Joe Heilings' column in the *Houston Post*. "Franklin was a year older than Billy, and I signed him because he could do everything you looked for in a ballplayer," Hancken revealed. "And he could do them better than his younger brother Billy. There was only one problem. Billy stepped into a pitch, really attacked the ball. I would have signed Billy too, but I moved out of that area the next year—the year Billy became eligible to sign." Billy had just annihilated the Astros for the season, with a .446 average—26 hits in 57 at-bats—9 homers, and 18 RBIs.

You can take it from the Mets' superstar pitcher Tom Seaver that what the scout saw in Billy hasn't changed. Seaver, who'll no doubt still look like a freshly scrubbed, clean cut, college kid until the day he collects his baseball pension, was in a jovial mood when cornered in the clubhouse at Wrigley Field at the end of the 1973 season. Little wonder. All the Mets had to do was win one of four upcoming games from the Cubs to make Tug McGraw's battle cry "Ya Gotta Believe!" come true. But he turned serious when talking about Williams. "Billy's probably the most aggressive hitter I've ever faced. Never takes that half cut, he's always looking to drive that ball hard. I think that aggressiveness, always ready to hit the ball hard, and his consistency are his best qualities."

Billy's name first blazed into national prominence, briefly, in 1964. Willie Mays was coasting along with the best average in the league. Suddenly, out of nowhere, there was Billy on top of the list, hitting about .420, some 40 points ahead of the "Say-Hey Kid." He was still batting over .360 late in June when Mickey Herskowitz made some observations in the *Houston Post* about the former star of the Houston Buffs.

"There is sort of an Indian cast to Williams' face with his high cheekbones and dark, wide-set eyes. He is a serious, unemotional fellow who rarely opens a conversation. But he watches when a Mays or an Aaron or a Boyer steps into the batting cage, and *they* watch when Billy Williams takes his turn." He then quoted Dave Roberts of Houston who had played against Billy in his rookie days.

"The rightfield fence in Dallas is 340 feet away, and the wind blows in. The ball doesn't carry. It's a bad park for a lefthanded hitter. One night Williams just flicked his bat and hit a scream-a-reeno over the fence. That's when I decided he has power." Ernie Banks, who was also on the scene, put it in a nutshell. "He stands up there like he isn't going to swing at all, and then at the last instant, he snaps those wrists."

Joe Amalfitano summed up Billy's cool, quiet confidence in the clutch. "Once we're tied in the seventh inning, and I'm walking up and down the bench saying, 'We need a homer to win this one'. Billy looked up and said, 'I'll get it'. And the next time up, he did. Mays does that. He'll call his shot once in a while. A lot of guys say it, but they're usually kidding. Billy wasn't."

But humorous he can be. "Are you a hot-weather hitter, Billy?" he was asked. Wiping his brow in the broiling Texas heat, Billy shot back, "I hope so. It's the only kind of weather I got right now."

Lou Boudreau, who played against Ted Williams, invoked the famous Boudreau shift against him, and later managed the mighty Red Sox slugger, rates Ted and Billy almost on a par.

"The forearm is the key to the late swing and making contact. I'd say that Billy's forearm is just as strong as Ted's. His swing is just as smooth, and his wrists are just as quick.

"Ted might have had more consistent power, but the power's there in Billy too. Both, I think, were underrated defensively. The only edge Ted may have had was in his throwing. Ted probably had the stronger throwing arm."

When Ted Williams heard the comment by the Yankees' catching great, Bill Dickey, that he, Ted, "hit the ball right out of my glove," the "Splendid Splinter" was delighted. That's the way it is with great hitters.

If you really want the scoop on the trouble a batter like Billy causes at the plate, what better man to ask than the guy whose job it is to tell his pitcher what to throw?

(A catcher ran into a dilemma with a fearsome slugger up and Lefty Gomez pitching. He gave Lefty sign after sign, but Gomez shook off every one. Finally, the frustrated backstop went out to the mound. "Well, what do *you* wanta throw?" "Nothing," replied Gomez. "Let's wait a while. Maybe he'll get a phone call.")

And what better catcher to ask than Johnny Bench of the Cincinnati Reds, the game's greatest and possibly the best catcher in baseball history? The sturdily built superstar from Oklahoma City, veteran at only 26 of six full major league seasons and the youngest player—at 22—ever to win the Most Valuable Player Award, in 1970, had a dismal 1971 and took a severe roasting from the Reds' fans. But he came back with a brilliant 1972 season and his second MVP trophy, then rebounded valiantly after serious lung surgery in December of '72 with another outstanding performance to help lead the Reds to the Western Division title in 1973. Baseball's most eligible bachelor, graciously stopping to chat in front of his locker which, appropriately, was equipped with a bottle of S-E-X cologne, put it quite candidly.

"You may keep the ball a long way from Williams, but he can hit to leftfield. And he can hit it out of the ballpark, especially here at Wrigley Field. He can go out and pull the ball to right. Inside, he's got such quick hands that he can get around on any pitch.

"There's really no way to success. All you can do is hope he's having an off day, that the percentages are in your favor, and that he's going to make those seven outs out of ten when your club's around."

Told that Billy was getting static in 1973 from some of the press and fans because, for Billy, it was a below-par season, Bench commented about his own problems in '71.

"We were four games under .500 for the year. It seemed like everything went wrong, and, of course, the blame went to me for the same thing Billy's going through. We're both supposedly leaders, batting in the middle of the line-up, supposedly should drive in runs and hit a lot of home runs. When you don't come through, you're the target. There are a lot of ups and downs, and you just have to learn to accept them—the important thing is that you don't get down on yourself."

Big, awesome, free-swinging Willie Stargell of the Pittsburgh Pirates looked at Billy being under fire in a different light.

"Well, I'll tell you—Billy spoils the fans. It's like Oscar Robertson when he was with Cincinnati. He'd go out and score 30 points every night. People just took it for granted that 30 points by Robertson was an ordinary thing. But the average basketball player will tell you, to score 30 points every night takes some doin'. And performing the way he does is just something Williams has done year after year. The moment he doesn't do as he's always done, people feel it's so easy for him to do it they can't figure out why he's not doin' it.

"His swing is just poetry in motion, really. And he's so consistent. Driving in as many runs as he does is an amazement in itself. Even from the outfield, I can see his immense concentration. He's seldom at the plate without an idea. If a guy's pitchin' him one way, he's thinking of the adjustment he has to make. And I don't think there's anybody who can make the adjustment he can. Billy's the type of hitter who rarely strikes out, but almost always makes contact. He's always the ballplayers' ballplayer, always playing the part to help his team win. Like when there's nobody out and he's hitting with a man on second. Then he's concentrating on pulling the ball so his guy can get to third, and give the man hitting behind him the opportunity to drive the runner in. If he gets a hit, good. If he doesn't, he's still got the man in scoring position. If you get Billy out four times, he just takes his hat and gently throws it aside, and goes out to the outfield to play defense. Even if he went 0-for-20 and his team was winning, I'm sure his attitude would be the same—as long as we're winning, that's fine."

I wonder if Willie'd like to trade years. The great year he had in '73 wouldn't be hard to take. He's right about me trying to concentrate. Usually, I'm able to wipe everything out of my mind. But the fans get involved. Out at Wrigley Field, you're so close to the fans, I hear 'em in the background when I'm walking up to the plate. You know—"Hit the ball outa the ballpark."

If you're not careful, you can get yourself really involved too. Every now and then, if I don't catch myself, I find myself swinging, trying to hit it out, 'cause you'd really like to do it for the fans. Maybe you end up hitting it on the end of the bat, poppin' up or something. So you have to restrain your thinking. Unless it's a situation where you must have a home run to win a ballgame, you have to go up there with only the thought of getting that pitch for a base hit.

Where Williams is practically motionless awaiting the pitch at the plate, Stargell is like a Mr. Coffee Nerves up there, waving his war club, possibly hoping to unnerve the pitcher, causing Billy to comment:

If you notice him out at the ballpark, he uses such a long bat [36 to 38 ounces] that when he goes into his airplane-propeller type motion, sometimes you see the bat actually kicking up dust on the ground. He does it about seven or eight times. And you can notice it seems to get faster just before the pitcher starts to release the ball. His bat's never still, it's always moving. When the pitcher moves the ball in, lots of times it really continues moving! Willie's hit a lot of homers. Some big ones.[Sigh] Some real big ones against the Cubs.

Speaking of homers, does a batter purposely "go" for them, or do they come as sort of a happy surprise when the ball's timed and met just right? Phenomenal hitters like Stan Musial and Rogers Hornsby have claimed there won't be any more .400 hitters because "everybody's swinging for the fences." Hornsby swore he never tried for an out-of-the-park job in his life, yet hit 302 of them. Billy estimates that when he's *thought* homer, he's *hit* a homer only once in about every 50 times.

On the other hand, somebody once asked Babe Ruth if he could have hit .400 if he hadn't been swinging from the heels. ".400? Hell, kid, I'd have hit .500!" bellowed the Babe.

In Mickey Mantle's *The Education of a Baseball Player*, the Mick mentioned he led the league in strike-outs in 1952 and 1954 "because I was almost always going for the seats and was not pushing or poking the ball to pile up singles. When you let fly at a ball with all your strength, you increase your chances of missing it." Mantle exploded 536 round-trippers into the seats.

Musial, who clouted 475 home runs, put it another way in *Stan the Man Musial*. "When I started, I used to slap at the ball or cut for the line drives. Then I got tempted. It's a vicious circle. You hit well when you have your groove. Then you go for distance and lose your groove. Then you've got to go looking for the groove again, with singles."

If anybody's an authority on the long-ball craze that's fascinated the fans ever since Ruth blasted 59 in 1921, it's the man who hit more career homers than anyone in baseball history, Hank Aaron. So, we asked him.

"Hank, Billy says he seldom goes for a home run. Is that pretty much your philosophy too?"

"I think he's right," answered Aaron. "I go up there with the idea of just trying to hit the ball hard someplace. I'm not too concerned about hitting the ball out of the park. If it goes, fine. If it doesn't, well, nothing I can do about it. I think Billy swings the same way I do. He's not looking for a home run. But, if it's a situation that *calls* for a home run ... for example, you go up in the ninth inning and your team is one run behind, well, naturally, he feels it's his job, he's paid to do it, to go up there and look for a homer. I've done this on several occasions but mainly, most of my home runs come just thinking that I'm going to go out and meet the ball, hit it hard."

As the old cliché used to go, "Home-run hitters drive Cadillacs, singles hitters drive Chevies," but there's always the question of which of the two types of batters *really* is most valuable. Though not an answer, it's interesting to note that in 1927, when Ruth hit his 60 homers, the Most Valuable Player Award went to Lou Gehrig, who topped the "Bambino" in nearly every offensive department, especially in such important categories as RBIs, total bases, hits, and batting average.

Then there was the time Leo Durocher asked Willie Mays to stop trying for homers. As he revealed in *Willie Mays, My Life In and Out of Baseball,* the superstar of the Giants had 36 homers before the end of July in 1954. If he'd continued at that pace, Mays, not Roger Maris, might have been first to hit 61—*and* in a 154-game season. But Durocher told Willie he was hitting .316 instead of .340 because those balls that didn't leave the park when Willie was swinging for the seats were being caught, and Leo also changed the batting order so Willie would bat third. This assures at least two innings in which the third man doesn't lead off and brings him to bat a lot more often during the season.

"And Leo was right," Willie confessed. "My batting average did go up." Quite an understatement. True, the "Say-Hey Kid" hit only five more homers, but he wound up batting champ with a .345 average, second in total bases, third in runs, hits, and homers, tops in triples and slugging, and helped pace the Giants to the pennant. He also won his first Most Valuable Player Award.

It's obvious "which" Willie Mays meant the most to his team in that 1954 season. Likewise, the immense value of the Classic Hitter to the Cubs becomes strikingly apparent in comparing Billy's overall performances in 1965, 1970, and 1972 with Willie's two Most Valuable Player years, 1954 and 1965.

		R	RBI	HR	RP	H	2B	3B	BA	TB
Mays	'54	119	110	41	188	195	33	13*	.345†	377
Williams	'65	115	108	34	189	203	39	6	.315	356
Mays	'65	118	112	52†	178	177	21	3	.317	360†
Williams	'70	137†	129	42	224†	205**	34	4	.322	373†
Williams	'72	95	122	37	180	191	34	6	.333†	348†

* Tops in league   † Tops in majors   ** Tied for lead in majors

Both in '65 and '70, Billy produced more runs than anybody in either league in '73. As the record books continually reveal, it seems Billy simply has picked the "wrong" years to have his best seasons!

Early Life

It might make a good story to say Billy Williams always dreamed of becoming a big leaguer. But it wouldn't be true. There were no such dreams for a black boy back in the '30s and '40s.

However, farsighted realists had long recognized that some of America's finest baseball players were black, their talents wasted in the Negro leagues. Branch Rickey, one baseball official determined to do something about it, was biding his time to keep a vow he first made in 1904.

When he was 22, Rickey was a player-coach at Ohio Wesleyan University. His team included the first black athlete in the school's history, Charlie ("Tommy") Thomas. On a trip to South Bend, Indiana, the team put up at a hotel, but the manager told Rickey that Thomas couldn't stay there. The young coach finally persuaded him to allow the black to share Rickey's room. Rickey never forgot the incident.

Rickey went on to become an executive with the St. Louis Cardinals. He started moving closer to his goal in 1943, when he left the Cardinals to join the Brooklyn Dodger organization. He'd fathered the highly successful St. Louis farm system, the first in baseball, and aimed to do the same for the talent-poor Dodgers, but in this case, he would also tap the rich Negro ranks.

Rickey came up with the ingenious idea of sponsoring the "Brown Dodgers" to play in Ebbets Field while the regular Dodgers were away and to compete against other Negro leagues in a new United States League. This would give him the opportunity to send scouts all over the nation to seek out top Negro prospects.

Ironically, in April, 1945, when Rickey held a press conference to announce the United States League, the late, black Chicago sports columnist, Wendell Smith, was present. Smith had just come from Boston where the Red Sox had given a trio of black players a tryout. The players? Sam Jethroe, Marvin Williams, and Jackie Robinson.

Nothing came of that tryout. However, Rickey got Smith's ear, and asked if he knew of any black players with major league ability. The man Smith recommended, of course, was Robinson.

In October, 1945, Rickey signed Jackie to play with the Montreal Royals, the Dodgers' Triple-A farm club in the International League. The color bar had been broken; Rickey had kept his vow. The Royals won the IL championship in 1946, sparked by Robinson's batting—his average, .349, was highest in the league.

Jackie moved up to the Dodgers in 1947—the first black to enter the white man's world of major league baseball. In only his third full year in the majors, he won the National League's Most Valuable Player Award.

Not so well known, however, is that the National League could have seen a minor flood of star black ballplayers in 1944, had a plan by Bill Veeck materialized. Veeck hoped to buy the floundering Philadelphia Phils and stock the perennial loser with the elite of Negro baseball.

Unfortunately for "Sport Shirt" Bill, word of his intentions may have leaked out. Whatever the reason, his offer was refused, even though the Phils were later sold for less than Veeck was willing to put up.

But none of this was known as yet in quiet little Whistler, a town with a population of about 500, near Mobile, Alabama. Here, on June 15, 1938, Billy Leo Williams was born. It didn't take long for little Billy to become aware of how the "White" and "Colored" signs separated things in the world.

The problems his father, grandfather, and uncle had in making a living for their families also showed Billy the cruelty and injustice that could come just from being the wrong color. His grandfather, Louis Williams, was born with an exceptionally light skin color. In fact, he could and did pass for white. He worked himself up to foreman at the wharf and supervised both whites and blacks at unloading fruit boats. Billy's dad and uncle also had jobs there as stevedores. But his grandfather always had to caution them, "Never call me 'father' down here." He feared that if the whites ever found out he was a Negro, they wouldn't work for him. Worse yet, all three of them might lose their jobs.

Billy's dad, Frank, had been a well-known first baseman with the Whistler Stars and had played with Satchel Paige, a native of nearby Mobile. "Ol Satch" told Billy he used to call his dad "Susie" because he was as graceful as a girl. He also felt Frank was probably good enough for the majors, but never, of course, had a chance because the big leagues were then far from ready to welcome blacks. Paige himself didn't make it until 1948, when he was more than 40 years old.

Small as it was, Whistler was strictly segregated. The whites lived in the middle of town, between Fourth and Eighth Streets. Baptist Town and Methodist Town were the two all-black communities—so named because they centered around the Baptist and the Methodist churches—at either end of town. Billy, his three older brothers, Franklin, Clyde, and Adolph, and his sister, Vera, went to all-black schools, and either made their own fun or settled for amusements that called for little or no money.

For many years, Billy's mother, Jessie Mary, did daywork for white families and took Billy along—something he really enjoyed. She often sent him out to feed her chickens and pet ducks in a little pond behind their first home, a four-room house with a hall down the middle.

His parents rented that house in Baptist Town, though they were Methodists. It wasn't the finest house in town by far, but it had a comfortable porch and a chinaberry shade tree to take some of the sting out of the searing Alabama sun.

Billy won't ever forget that house. That's where he learned things he's carried with him all his life. Like not complaining when the going gets tough, but trying instead to find the brighter side of things.

When he was little more than a toddler, he'd have to scurry around to help his brothers put buckets on the floor to catch water that streamed through the roof every time it rained. He'd watch till they got full, and his brothers would empty them. *As the raindrops would hit, each bucket would play an exciting little tune,* Billy recalled. *I guess that's when I started to love music so much.*

There were plenty of lean times. Then one day they couldn't meet the rent payment, and the landlord put them out. The Williams family had to move in with relatives. In about a year Frank had managed to scrape up enough money to buy a small lot at the other end of Whistler—in Methodist Town. *We all had to help build the house to earn our keep,* Billy said.

His dad worked all kinds of hours, sometimes leaving in the middle of the night, depending on when he got a call that a boat was docking. The kids loved to wait up for him because he'd always bring home something good to eat—a load of bananas or other fruit or a special treat from the store. They'd all sit around on the porch, enjoy the food, and chat for a while. Often their dad would ask,

"Who needs school money?" Then he'd flip each of them a bright new silver dollar. That's how he was paid in those days.

Billy's parents were very religious. They had grown up in the Methodist Church and made sure their youngsters did too. They all had to attend services every Sunday and would sit right in the first row. Most of the day—from 9:30 in the morning until about 10:00 at night—was spent in Sunday School and church or in church activities. In between services, they might visit relatives or have group picnics. Nearly everybody liked to sing, so an entire family would put on a recital or entertain another family; the Williams family would sing for the Mosely family, for instance. Said Billy: *I always liked to sing. I used to sing in the choir. Later, I even sang in the outfield sometimes.*

Since Billy's father worked such erratic hours, his mother spent a lot of time with the youngsters.

Mom took us almost everywhere. Most of the time we'd walk. We could go straight up the tracks to the movie or straight down the tracks to Eight Mile Creek. On Saturday nights, we'd head for a place called Hunter's Hall. They used to show silent movies. And sometimes, kids would put on boxing matches with those big gloves. We had some great Saturday night fish fries too. They don't have those much anymore, at least not the way we used to have 'em.

Our biggest thrill for a while was to go over and watch the airplanes take off. You know, those little Beechcraft planes. This was something really exciting to us. We'd seen 'em fly by, but never had seen 'em taking off.

Even though Mrs. Williams enjoyed doing things with them, she was no soft touch. She laid down the law—and was quick to enforce it. She didn't waste her breath scolding or threatening. When one of them sassed back or disobeyed, she delivered a good, sound whipping right then and there.

Billy got his share of hide-warmings. His mother had placed Eight Mile Creek strictly off-limits, but he still liked to sneak off and go swimming in the ice-cold water. One day he and his brother Franklin took off for the creek. They were thrashing around in the water and having the time of their lives when they spotted their mother and father coming up, only a short distance away. They tried to run, but their dad caught up with them, took out his belt, and gave them a healthy walloping on their bare bottoms.

When the family went to Chickasaw Bow, a nearby beach, a week later, the boys decided to show their mother they could swim. Fortunately, she was convinced, and the ban on Eight Mile Creek was lifted. From then on, that's where Billy spent many of his happiest, most carefree hours.

Not all of Billy's lessons were learned in church or at the end of a belt, however. His fun-loving grandfather played a big part in helping to shape Billy's outlook on life. Always young at heart, he got a big kick out of doing things with his grandsons.

His favorite pastime was fishing, and he'd often take Billy with him. That's why today when he isn't holding a baseball bat Billy would just as soon be holding a fishing pole. But something that happened after one of their fishing jaunts many years ago still sticks in his mind.

You could compare the color of my grandfather's skin to any white man's. Well, this one day coming back from fishing, he had me wait outside while he went into a restaurant to get us something to eat. They had the usual signs, "White" and "Colored." Of course, the best food was near the "White" sign. That's where grandpa went. When he came out with some sandwiches, he was sort of laughing to himself.

"What's so funny, Grandpa?" I asked.

"People, Billy, people! When I went inside, they didn't know whether I was white or black. It's the outside of a man they care about. But, the inside is what's important. Never judge a person by the color of his skin."

I still think about that lots of times.

People judge people without getting involved with them. Like two guys leave their town in the South. One's white, one's colored. They don't know each other. They go into service. Okay, they're in the barracks together. They get a chance to talk to each other, live with each other, and discuss each other's problems. And I imagine when they leave the service, they come back to their hometown, and can't wait to get back there to do things together, to get involved with each other. That's all it amounts to.

When Billy was barely big enough to hold a baseball, his dad used to throw the ball to him. If Billy would catch one, he'd say, "That a boy, Billy, you're gonna be a ballplayer someday."

His older brothers used to swipe his bike and go off to play ball all the time. It wasn't long before Billy joined them.

When I first played baseball, I had a three-fingered glove. And I remember the first time I wore baseball shoes. I was about eight. My brother Adolph had bought a new pair. But when he saw how big my eyes got when he showed 'em to me, he hid 'em in his room. The first time he went out without 'em, I looked and looked till I found 'em, then sneaked out of the house with the shoes under my shirt. I put 'em on and spent the whole afternoon at the park practicing slides on the grass. I got some raspberries on my behind for doin' it, but it was worth it.

After the family moved to Methodist Town, Billy and a couple of new friends would round up some of the other kids from the neighborhood, meet in a vacant lot, choose up sides, and play baseball. Some of the kids were white. Billy and the other kids didn't look at it as blacks and whites—but just a bunch of boys having fun together playing baseball. Before long though, the parents saw what was going on, and the white kids didn't show up anymore. *Maybe if they'd have let us alone, we might have shown those grown-ups something about getting along,* Billy said.

Billy got into his first important game when he was 13 by a fluke. By this time, all three of his brothers were members of the Mobile Black Bears, a semi-pro team that had uniforms and even went on road trips. If the game was close by, Billy would go along just to watch.

One day his brother Clyde, who was slated to pitch, took sick on the bus. Someone suggested that one of the fellows who played third could pitch, but that still left the manager with no third baseman. Franklin piped up that maybe Billy could fill in.

"Billy? He doesn't look big enough to hold a bat."

The youngest brother wasn't short, but he sure didn't pack much meat on his bones.

"He's good!" Franklin kept repeating.

With no other choice, the manager told Billy to put on Clyde's uniform and shoes and take over third.

Billy managed to hang in there, but certainly didn't rip the cover off the ball. In fact, batting both righthanded and lefthanded, he didn't even get a hit, but he did meet the ball better from the left side. And he played well enough to earn a compliment—and a valuable tip—from the Bears' manager afterward.

"Nice game. When you're a little older and heavier, come back. Maybe we can play you at third some more."

Then, almost as an afterthought, he told the string-bean kid that he'd probably be better off hitting lefthanded all the time, because that seemed to be his best side.

Williams has batted lefthanded ever since.

It's easy to see why Billy never had a weight problem. When he wasn't playing baseball, he was pedaling his bike, swimming, or pushing a lawn mower for two or three hours to earn a dollar or so for spending money. Even today, he's only about 20 pounds over what he weighed in high school.

And when he transferred from Whistler Elementary School to Mobile County Training School, the high school for blacks, it was a four-mile hike.

Those were really exciting days. I got to see and use things I never knew existed—you know, things like volleyballs, tennis racquets, horseshoes. And I liked doing things with my hands, so I took a lot of shop courses.

Meanwhile, he kept building up his athletic skills and developing his body until it looked like a coiled spring covered with rawhide. He ran the 440 on the school track team and played junior varsity basketball.

He had joined the Boy Scout Troop from his church when he was younger. He became a Den Chief and joined an Explorer Troop in his teens. The boys frequently lugged their packs ten or fifteen miles for midnight or weekend camp-outs.

Camping out, living outdoors, spending time away from home for the first time—that was a big thrill for a kid like me. I had plenty of happy times, and I really learned a lot from Scouting. It's a great organization.

But baseball was becoming more and more a part of Billy's life. When school was out, he organized his own team, and it competed in the summer league of the Mobile City Recreation Department. The boys practiced three days, and played three league games a week.

We'd start up at about nine in the morning, meet on Fifth Street— that wasn't a baseball park, it was a vacant lot—and we'd play until about eleven. By that time, it was getting plenty hot, so we'd head for Eight Mile Creek, have sack lunches or maybe pick up a water-

melon, and do some swimmin'. Then, we'd go back and play baseball till it got dark.

We had a pretty good little team—one year we won the league championship. And believe it or not, the name of our team was The Cubs!

His high school didn't have a baseball team. Its big sport was football. Billy wanted to go out for football right away, but his mother put thumbs down on that. So did Franklin, who was on the team. They were afraid that he'd get hurt because he was so slight. Later on, when he was a senior, they changed their minds, and Billy became good enough as a 155-pound defensive end to get a crack at a scholarship from Grambling, maker of pro-football players.

His first high school football game was against Moss Point, Mississippi. After the game, a girl walked into his life—literally. They were both strolling toward the bus that went to Whistler. Billy had often noticed her in school assemblies because she was so pretty. He also figured she was shy, so he broke the ice.

"Hi."

"Hi."

"Goin' home on the bus?"

"Yes."

"Me too. Like to ride with me?"

"Okay."

On the way home, chatting about this and that, they became a little more at ease with each other. He found out she *was* shy, that her name was Shirley. (They should have suspected they were "meant for each other"—her last name was Williams also.)

Finally, he worked up the courage to ask her to go out with him the next night. To his happy surprise, she agreed. Soon, she began waiting to walk home with him after football practice and became his regular girl, his date for movies and parties.

When the future Chicago Cub was 16, he became the regular third baseman on the Mobile Black Bears. He might have won the job earlier, but his mother refused to relax her ruling: he had to wait until he entered 11th grade. Even then, Billy had to be home by no later than 11 at night, which meant he could go on no road trips and so missed about half the games. It was tougher to take too, because his brothers on the Bears—Clyde a pitcher and Franklin and Adolph outfielders—went out of town, while Billy had to stay home. At most, each game netted him about four dollars.

Meanwhile, the color line had been broken. Franklin signed with the Pirate organization and began to play minor league ball. Some of Franklin's friends and professional players like Willie McCovey and Henry Aaron used to come over to their house and talk baseball. Billy, listening in, began to have faint flickers of hope that he might find a career in baseball.

When Aaron started playing, even the remotest thought that he—or anyone else for that matter—would someday break Babe Ruth's home-run record of 714 was ridiculous. One of eight children, he had starred in football and softball at Central High in Mobile. But, like Billy, he was skinny—only 160 pounds as a baseball rookie—and began as an infielder.

Aaron had also played some games with the Mobile Black Bears. When he was 17, he caught on with a well-known Negro professional club, the Indianapolis Clowns. He was hitting over .450 when a Giant scout got on his trail and offered him $250 a month and the chance to play Class-A baseball.

However, a scout from the Boston Braves, Dewey Griggs, also showed up and countered with a promise of $350 a month and a start in Class-C ball where Hank would be under less pressure. It's been told how Griggs didn't get to see Aaron field but was so impressed with his swing (he was then holding the bat cross-handed) that he told the front office he'd pay the money out of his own pocket rather than pass up such a tremendous prospect. At any rate, the Braves bought Aaron's contract from the Clowns for $10,000 and dispatched Hank to play shortstop for the Eau Claire team in the Class-C Northern League in 1952. After hitting .336 with Eau Claire in 87 games, Aaron tore apart the Class-A Sally (South Atlantic) League in 1953 with the Jacksonville team. The front office didn't have to see any more—when Williams first met him, Hank was already with the Braves, who had moved to Milwaukee in 1953.

I don't really think I patterned myself after any ballplayer. But the one I admired the most was Aaron.

Billy could readily see how an Aaron could be "discovered" in such a way that it smacked of a plot for a "B" movie, but he never imagined it could happen to him. Not even when he was entering the gate for a Sunday game and the guard happened to mention that there was a scout in the stands to take a look at Hank's brother, Tommy. He told the guard he hoped Tommy would be signed.

That day, Billy banged out a homer and a double and made

several fine plays at third. He had forgotten about the scout—he had more on his mind. He was about to graduate and had to study for his final exams.

A couple of nights later, he had his books spread out, studying, when his dad answered a knock at the door.

"Billy, there's a man here who wants to see you."

It was Ivy Griffin, a baseball scout. Griffin's hometown was in Thomasville, Alabama, so he spent a lot of time looking over the talent around the Mobile area, which has produced a good number of players, including Tommie Agee, Amos Otis, Milt and Frank Bolling, Tommy Aaron, and Cleon Jones.

In three years with the Philadelphia Athletics, Griffin had seen action in only 185 games. Like Billy, he batted left and threw right.

After they'd talked a little baseball, Griffin asked what Billy planned for the future. Billy replied that he was considering going into carpentry or, as so many of his friends were doing, into the military, maybe even make it a career if he liked it.

"If you had a chance to play baseball, would you be interested?"

"I sure would." Then Billy told him how he had always hoped he might follow in Franklin's footsteps. Griffin mentioned there was a possibility of getting him started in Class-D baseball. Although eager to jump at the opportunity, Billy asked if he could think about it for a few days.

"Sure," replied the scout. "It's against the rules to sign you until after graduation anyway. When do you graduate?"

"Friday."

"Good. We can get together over the weekend," he said as he was leaving.

Billy and his dad were wide-eyed in disbelief. Then they started to laugh. Both of them suddenly realized they hadn't even found out what team he represented.

Several days later, Billy was also contacted by a scout from the Pirates. He didn't make any specific offer but on learning about Griffin's interest, he asked to be given a last chance before Billy signed anything.

When Griffin phoned Sunday, he told Billy he was with the Chicago Cubs, and revealed that he'd followed Billy for quite some time, including games he'd played in Birmingham, Alabama, and Hattiesburg, Mississippi.

Then Billy called Franklin. His brother was all for him going with the Cubs but pointed out that a lot of ball clubs were giving bonuses, just for signing. Remembering how he himself had missed out, he said to make sure they held out for some cash. They promised they would.

When they met with Griffin, his dad fully intended to bring up the bonus. But as the discussion went on, he became so excited he forgot all about asking for one. So did Billy. He smiles about it now.

Whatdya mean I didn't get a bonus? I got a bus ticket to Ponca City, Oklahoma, and he gave Dad a cigar!

Later on, Billy also discovered that the same Pirate scout who signed Franklin had obtained an okay from his club to pay Billy $10,000 for signing.

Franklin was so disgusted, for a while he wouldn't even talk to us. I wanted to go off and play baseball so much I guess that somewhere along the line, the bonus just slipped my mind. From that point on, I took the attitude that everything's done for the best. For one thing, they didn't have very much invested in me. Maybe I got more of a chance than somebody else might have got. And they say opportunity knocks only once. Maybe I was afraid I wouldn't get another chance.

On June 21, 1956, Griffin sent in his report to the Cub front office. Griffin didn't go overboard on rating Billy's arm, fielding, or running—he gave him a 2, for "good." But in hitting, he indicated a 3 plus, for "above average." Under salary, he penciled in $200 a month. And in the space calling for him to recommend Billy's highest eventual capability, Griffin wrote M.L., for "major league."

On the back, under other comments, he added:

"Billy Williams runs good, throws good, hits good, and fields good in outfield. Have not seen him play third base, but saw him take workout there. Handled ground balls well and looked good. He was 18 last week. Tall, rangy boy. Loose, and should go all the way if he develops normally. Comes from good, honest colored family, and has had proper training at home. Has brother playing at Clinton, Iowa, in Midwest League."

Future reports would not always be as favorable or as optimistic. But Billy wasn't worried about that . . . he didn't even think about it. All he knew was that God had given him an opportunity. It was a start. That's all that really mattered to him.

Minor League Ball

In late June of 1956, Billy was jouncing along on a bus, heading for the Class-D club at Ponca City, Oklahoma, to start earning his $200-a-month salary. The trip took almost three days. It seemed like forever to the kid who looked skinnier than ever now that he'd shot up to six foot one—and had never been away from home for more than a day or two.

At the same time, the Chicago Cubs were heading nowhere, slipping and sliding into an eventual eighth-place finish and one of the Bruins' worst won-lost records in history. It was the third and last season as manager for Stan Hack, once the tremendously popular star third baseman who had played on all of the last four Cub championship teams.

The Cubs of 1956 included a slender young home-run-slugging shortstop, Ernie Banks, other infielders Dee Fondy, Gene Baker, and Don Hoak, outfielders Walt ("Moose") Moryn, Monte Irvin, and Pete Whisenant, catcher Hobie Landrith, and utility man Eddie Miksis. Among the pitchers were Bob Rush, who, with only 13 wins, topped the staff, "Toothpick Sam" Jones, Turk Lown, and Jim Brosnan, a fading hurler who was gathering material for a book he'd write, *The Long Season*.

Back in Ponca City, Billy's bus finally pulled into the terminal. He got off, frightened, bewildered, unsure of what to do next. Then came the first of two shocks.

"Billy Williams?"

"Yes."

A middle-aged Negro stuck out his hand. He said he worked at the hotel where the white ballplayers stayed and had been told to pick up Billy and take him over to his house.

He was Mr. Reed. He knew I was a homesick kid and that this was my first time away from home. I imagine he could see it written all over my face. I found out that every black ballplayer that came into town stayed with his wife and him. They had about five black ballplayers living there at that time.

I was really surprised. Being from around Mobile, you'd figure that Oklahoma would be integrated, that you could go practically anyplace you wanted. I never thought I'd have to stay in a private home. I thought I'd move into a hotel where the other players were living, and keep in contact with the ball club.

Everything turned out fine, however. The Reeds made him feel at home. But, even though he was dead-tired from the long trip, he was so concerned about his next step, to prove he could play ball, that he had trouble sleeping.

The next day he got his second shock. When he reported to Don Biebel, the manager, he was told he'd probably do only pinch-hitting the rest of the season. Billy's chin also dropped when he learned that Class-D clubs were always short on money and couldn't afford to take everybody on road trips. Since the line-up was pretty much set—Ponca City had a good chance to make the Sooner State League playoffs that year—Williams would stay home until the team got back.

Hardly a glamorous or encouraging introduction to organized baseball. He appeared in only 13 games, went to bat 17 times, banged out 4 singles, drove in 4 runs, and scored 4.

I played in only 13 games that first season and hit .235. That wasn't a very impressive record, but it didn't bother me. I was only 18 and having a lot of fun with my friends in town. I guess the manager wasn't very excited about me. He left me home on road trips. I'd fool around every day and wait for the team to come back home.

Billy also had his first adventure—or misadventure—in the outfield. Playing under lights was brand new to him. As Biebel told it: "I remember the first ball he tried to catch. He wound up flat on his stomach." Billy also slashed his wrist on that fielding attempt and still has the scar to remember it by. His first manager also went on record to add:

"I get as ecstatic about his swing as I used to about the picture swing of Ted Williams."

However, in the report Biebel sent to the Cub home office, he included such remarks as: "Looked good at first with the bat, but of late hasn't done too much," and "Biggest weakness is in his fielding, and has to play to work at it." Otherwise, he rated him as average in running, throwing, and hitting, and recommended another season of Class-D ball.

After spending the winter in Whistler, talking baseball with Aaron and Franklin, dating Shirley, and generally taking it easy, he received some thrilling news. He was to report to Mesa, Arizona—his first spring training program with the "Big Club."

Thrilling news but nerve-racking too. He had to show enough improvement to earn the chance to play regularly at Ponca City. The first days at the Cubs' camp did little to take off any pressure—nobody paid much attention to him even though he went all out.

But near the end of the week, when Billy was in the batter's box, whipping those wrists and savagely lacing into fastballs from the pitching machine, a gruff old-timer wandered over to the batting cage to watch. It was Rogers Hornsby, his attention caught by the crisp, clean, solid smack that only a really well-met baseball can make as it flies off the bat.

Billy's time was up, and he started to step out of the cage, but Hornsby waved him back in, telling him to take some more cuts. Every time he'd make solid contact, Hornsby would say, "Nice cut, Williams."

About ten minutes later, without a smile, Hornsby told Billy to call it quits and added, just as unemotionally, "You've got a good swing."

Billy didn't know what to think. Did he like him or didn't he? A reporter told the rookie he'd made a valuable ally, that every player Hornsby liked eventually found himself at Wrigley Field.

This was perhaps the most important single break Williams received in his career. From then on, Hornsby took him under his wing.

It might be said that if a rattlesnake ever bit Hornsby, the snake would die. He was blunt, hard-boiled, stubborn, tactless, opinionated. He never "yessed" anybody, never took back anything he said. As a hitter, few righthanders were good enough to carry his spikes. As a manager, he spent more time in hot water than all the lobsters in Maine: he was *fired* from more jobs than many baseball men ever *had*.

Hornsby even got himself fired after he played with and managed the 1926 St. Louis Cardinals to the first pennant and World Series triumph in their history for his refusal to accept only a one-year contract.

He's the only manager to get bounced by a father and son, both times—twenty years apart—for the same reason: he wouldn't tolerate front-office interference. Bill Veeck, Sr., gave him the ax when he was president and general manager of the Cubs in 1932. And Bill Veeck, Jr., of whom Hornsby said, "He oughta run a circus," bounced him as manager of the St. Louis Browns in 1952, while the "Rajah" was still in the first year of a three-year contract.

But when Hornsby talked hitting, smart men listened. Just a glance at his record was enough to have them hanging on every word.

In his last full year as a player, he helped power the 1929 Cubs to the pennant with 40 homers, 149 RBIs, 156 runs scored, 229 hits (including 47 doubles and 7 triples), and a batting average of .380. Twice voted Most Valuable Player and twice winner of the Triple Crown, the latter in 1922 and 1925, Hornsby still holds the National League records for most total bases in a season, 450, the highest lifetime slugging percentage, .577, and the best slugging mark for a season, .756. And he had a lifetime batting average of .358.

The last man to hit .400, Ted Williams, credits Hornsby for impressing him with the most basic rule of batting: *get a good ball to hit.*

Even though the best righthanded hitter of all time maintained that great hitters aren't born, that they're made by practice, fault correction, and confidence, Hornsby made an exception in the case of Billy Williams. He didn't alter Billy's swing, stance, or style in the slightest.

But he did pound away on knowing the strike zone. "Seventeen inches wide from your armpits to your knees" he'd repeat again and again. And he'd keep mixing in the secrets he'd accumulated in 2,259 major league games.

"You don't have to swing hard to hit a home run. I never tried to hit one, I never *knew* when I'd hit one."

"Just try to meet the ball. Don't try to get fancy. Try to hit the ball in the largest safe area, straight up the middle of the diamond."

"Timing is 50 percent of hitting."

"Try to let the bad balls go by."

"Many major-leaguers ruin themselves by swinging at about everything pitched to them."

"There won't be any more .400 hitters—too many guys are swinging for the fences."

And back to the strike zone. "Most of the time, you're not going to get anything by hitting pitches outside. If a ball's in the strike zone, you can hit one pitch as well as another. Doesn't make any difference if it's a fastball, change-up, curve, or slider. Just swing level and stride into the pitch. Try to hit the ball through the middle... if you do it right, the home runs will take care of themselves."

As valuable as were all these batting tips to the raw rookie who'd seen less than 15 games in organized ball, more important to him was Hornsby's attitude toward baseball in general. Hornsby's philosophy really rubbed off on Billy. The following briefs, which were expressed by the "Rajah" in *My War With Baseball*, typified his attitude toward the game:

"They claim I was stuck up as a player. Like hell I was. I wanted to be a success at playing ball. If anybody wanted to talk about the pitcher we were facing, or offer some suggestions, I was tickled to death to talk. But no bull."

"No player ever owed me anything as a manager. He owed it first to the fans and second to himself to give a 100 percent effort."

"When we made a mistake that cost us a game, or we were in a slump, we'd sit around the clubhouse for half an hour or so and discuss ways to improve ourselves. Players don't do too much of that today, because they have other interests. Baseball was all we knew."

"There are only two kinds of players as far as I'm concerned—the guys who put out and the guys who don't."

"God gave everybody just so much ability, and if he gave you the ability to hit .210 and you hustled and hit .220, you've done a lot better than the most talented guy in the world who hits .260. You don't have to be ashamed of anything. I've found out that it's a good thing not to have to hang your head."

Billy could thank his lucky stars Hornsby was in his corner for that brief spring tryout. Player reports on him in April and May of 1957 were extremely pessimistic, and some all but ruled out any chances that he'd ever make it to the big leagues.

Comments included "just average power"; "I do not think he is a prospect"; "average arm and fielder and a slow runner"; and "Rate him Class A tops and Class D for this year."

Thanks to Hornsby, he headed back for his first full season with the Ponca City ball club with greater confidence and almost fanatical dedication and determination.

When he arrived, however, he quickly discovered he had more to conquer than getting the jump on a flyball or gloving windblown pop-ups or skittering grounders. This year, he was the only black on the roster.

He had many occasions to recall what his grandfather had said about the "inside" of a man being most important, but it couldn't stop the hurt, even when his "outside" won him respect on the field as the team's leading hitter. Off the field, the players steered clear of him.

When the team played at home, it wasn't so bad. He was still staying with the Reeds and was able to make friends in town to keep from being lonely. But on the road, even though this was Oklahoma and the signs "White" and "Colored" weren't there, they might just as well have been. Blacks weren't welcome in restaurants. The team traveled in station wagons and when they stopped for meals, Billy had to remain in the car. He ate only if and when one of the players remembered to bring him a sandwich.

He managed to smother his disillusionment and frustration—all but once. He was playing poker in the clubhouse one day, and a white teammate from Georgia was dealing.

"How many cards, Smoky?"

"My name's Bill."

"I said how many do you want, *Smoky* . . . can't y'hear?"

"Yeah, I can hear . . . and I can do more than that," retorted Billy, rising. The big Georgian glared at him, and a moment later they were trading punches. A coach broke it up. As he had many times before—and has since—Billy decided to turn the other cheek by staying clear of the instigators.

A few days later, however, the kid from Georgia was released, and the club president, Dave Sutton, made it clear that there would be no more poker playing in the clubhouse and no more reference to color.

By August, with 126 more games behind him, Billy's performance changed his player reports from "good" or "all right" to "excellent." From "just average power," it became "above average power," and any doubts that he was a bona-fide big league "prospect" had vanished.

Biebel wrote in September, 1957: "This kid looks like a better hitter every time you look at him. He hits the ball right on the nose and hits it with power to all fields. Waits till the last second and then whips the bat. He keeps improving at every phase of the game. He has an excellent chance, and every manager in this league likes him a lot."

Under player weaknesses, he noted: "Needs an awful lot of work on both flyballs and ground balls. Doesn't have the real good arm, but throws well enough and it seems to be improving."

Still and all, Billy had earned himself a pleasant winter. He had rapped out 140 hits, of which 60 were for extra bases, and his 40 doubles were tops in the league. He also belted 17 homers and 3 triples, collected 95 RBIs, and hit .310. Unfortunately, his 25 errors were also tops in the league.

At the end of the 1957 season, beer flowed like champagne in Milwaukee, with the baseball-mad fans toasting their first pennant since the Braves moved from Boston. Then the town rocked deliriously for days after the Braves became World Champions, outlasting the Yankees in a seven-game World Series.

The 1957 Cubs had little to celebrate. Under Bob Scheffing, who'd replaced Hack as manager, the team barely avoided ending up in the cellar, finishing in a tie for seventh. But Wrigley Field attendance dropped to its lowest since 1945, a total of just 670,629. The continued slugging of Banks and the performances of a pair of right-handed rookie pitchers were all that the fans had to cheer about.

Ernie blasted 43 homers, second only to 44 by Aaron, while Dick Drott won 15 games and Moe Drabowsky 13.

No other Cub pitcher that year, not even veteran Bob Rush, could win more than six games. The new players on the roster included catcher Cal Neeman, infielder Jerry Kindall, centerfielder Chuck Tanner, now White Sox manager, reliever Don Elston, and second baseman Bob Morgan.

In 1958, instead of sending Billy to a Class-C or B club, the Cubs elevated him to the Class-A club at Pueblo, Colorado, in the Western League. But with the season barely underway, he began getting stomach pains. The trainer thought it might be something minor and temporary and advised Billy to wait a day or two and see if the pains went away. They didn't. He was in for the shock of his young life.

When I was at Pueblo, I didn't feel right all year. I started getting pains and was in and out of the doctor's office. Then he took a lot of tests and wound up saying that my best bet was to forget about baseball and do something else. He never did tell me what was wrong. But he did call John Holland in Chicago, that same day I think, and it's a good thing. Mr. Holland suggested I come to Chicago for a real thorough examination.

The Cub vice-president wasn't giving up on his promising rookie that easily. He sent Billy to Wesley Memorial Hospital in Chicago for all sorts of tests. After about five days—frustrating news. They couldn't find anything wrong with him. Holland let him work out at Wrigley Field for a few days, then sent him to Burlington, Iowa, a club in the Three-I League. It was Class-B ball, but it would give him some of the playing time he'd missed. At Pueblo he'd appeared in only 21 games, hit .250, with 2 homers, 2 doubles, and a triple, 11 RBIs, and 2 errors.

The Cub executive also gave him some other cheering news. Just a few days earlier, with his characteristic candor, Hornsby had told Holland that after looking at all the Cub minor league prospects, he should keep only Williams and a kid named Ron Santo and get rid of all the rest.

"So we're not about to lose you to a stomach-ache!" smiled Holland, to Billy's relief.

He finished the 1958 season under manager Walt Dixon at Burlington. In 61 games, he hit .304, with 10 homers, 7 doubles, and 38 RBIs, while holding his errors to 4.

Dixon, who considered him definitely a top major league prospect, also commented that while Billy was with his club, "Girls were throwing themselves at him. But Billy wasn't interested. As he put it: 'They're not going to help me get to the big leagues'."

In his final season report, Dixon pointed out that Billy had good power to all fields, was a hustler who really wants to play, doesn't swing at many bad balls, and hangs in well against lefthanded pitchers. On the other hand, he was critical of Billy's fielding and base-running. In fact, he suggested Billy might be better off playing somewhere besides the outfield, possibly at first base.

Regardless, Billy moved up again—this time to Double-A ball with Grady Hatton's San Antonio team in the Texas League. Here he met and became a friend of "that kid Santo," who'd also made such a good impression on Hornsby. And, as Dixon had suggested, he got some work at first base as well as in the outfield.

Ron Santo recalled that 1959 season, when he and Billy were both rookies in San Antonio. "Billy was actually not a good fielder. In fact, he played first base, and I remember he couldn't even catch pop-ups. They moved him to the outfield and he had trouble adjusting, and even when he got to the major leagues the first few years, he had problems."

Williams jumped off to a red-hot start at the plate and was soon sharing the team batting lead with his roommate, J.C. Hartman. But his stomach had started to kick up again. Then one night, he gave his brother Franklin a call back home in Whistler. He was having a great time fishing and hunting, Franklin told him. After they finished talking, Billy came down with another ailment—homesickness.

I just felt like going home. I was happy there at San Antonio, but I could have been happier at home doing things with guys I'd grown up with. My stomach was hurting, like it was all tied in knots. I felt something was wrong, but didn't know what.

The murderous Texas heat didn't help much either. They were driving back to San Antonio from Victoria, Texas, and the jabbing, throbbing pains were like a bellyful of toothaches. He began to think about leaving the team and going home. Thoughts of swimming in that ice-cold water in Eight Mile Creek and catching those big croakers and striped bass made it all the more tempting.

By now, he was feeling so miserable he was hardly able to think straight. They pulled into San Antonio at about three o'clock in the morning. Billy had made up his mind. He told Hartman he was going home and asked if he'd drive him to the depot.

Hartman tried every argument to talk him out of it. But Billy was in no mood to listen, and finally told him he'd call a cab.

Seeing that nothing would change his mind, Hartman drove him to the train depot, and seven or eight hours later Billy arrived in Mobile.

I might have missed everything if it hadn't been for my father, Buck O'Neil, the black coach who helped a lot of black ballplayers get adjusted to the big leagues, and Mr. Holland. When I got to Whistler, I just left my gear at home and went out fishing. Dad was waiting for me and started lecturing me for jumpin' the team—telling me I could get fined or suspended. I went fishing again the next two days. But by about this time, I started to have second thoughts and started worrying about what might happen.

I didn't know my dad had called Mr. Holland and told him where I was. All of a sudden, O'Neil shows up. Mr. Holland had sent him to take me back to San Antonio. Buck and I talked for a while, then he asked why I'd come home. I told him it was my stomach again and I couldn't play. He said, "Fine, let's have a doctor look at you when you get back!" I was still stubborn and told him we'd gone through all that before and nothing happened. "Okay," he said, "let's see a doctor here then." That was fair enough.

59

We saw the doctor. The next day, he told me I had an ulcer, but that it wasn't serious. He gave me some medicine and I started to feel better almost right away. Buck convinced me to go back to the team. I felt pretty sheepish, facing my teammates. It wasn't as bad as it might have been, though—Buck told me the San Antonio club didn't plan to fine me or give me a suspension, if I'd promise not to do it again. Since then I've often wondered what might have happened to my career if the Cubs had just said, "Forget him, get somebody else."

Knowing he was lucky to be back in a San Antonio uniform—and that he'd better produce or else—Billy tackled every game with more fervor and gritty determination than ever. He was still hounded by the same old bugaboo, subpar fielding and throwing—with 21 boots. But as usual he was a terror at the plate. He wound up the season pounding the ball for a .318 average in 94 games, with 118 hits, 79 RBIs, 22 doubles, 7 triples, and 10 homers.

His batting record won him a promotion to Fort Worth, a Triple-A club whose season was still in progress. He was supposed to finish up there, but after only five games and ripping the ball at .476, Billy got a long-distance phone call.

"You've had quite a year, Billy." It was Holland calling from Wrigley Field in Chicago. "How'd you like to finish up here? We'd like to see how you do against big league pitching." Billy was stunned.

He's not sure Holland heard his mumbled answer. He vaguely remembers packing and hurrying to catch a plane and was still in a delightful daze a few hours later when he checked into the Sheridan Plaza Hotel.

The first thing he did was call his dad in Whistler to blurt out the exciting news. *They'd brought him up...he was in the majors!* After Billy said goodbye to his dad, he tried to collect his thoughts and calm down a little.

What a difference from that first bus ride to Ponca City. Hornsby had been right. If you want to play professional baseball, there's only one place to be—in the big leagues. To hell with things that won't help you get there. Your life has to be baseball, baseball, baseball. It's worth every ounce of effort you can give it.

This time though, he was like everybody else. Not shuttled off someplace where the black ballplayers have to stay, away from the rest of the team, but in his own, big, comfortable room at a fine hotel.

Not at all like things were in the Texas he left a few hours ago, either. Billy thought of how the white ballplayers just went down to the restaurant at mealtime, while he had to order something and eat in his room. Or if he wanted to get out of the room, they'd make him sit in the kitchen near a hot stove.

Billy arrived in Chicago on Wednesday, August 5. In Thursday morning's *Chicago Tribune*, Richard Dozer wrote about the game Wednesday afternoon at Wrigley Field. The Cubs had gone down to their seventh straight defeat, losing to the Phillies, 6 to 4. At the tail end of his column, Dozer wrote:

"The Cubs Wednesday purchased the contract of outfielder Billy Williams, 21, from their San Antonio farm club. Williams batted .318 in 94 games with San Antonio. He hit 10 homers and batted in 79 runs. He is expected to join the Cubs Thursday. Pitcher Elmer Singleton was sent to Fort Worth to make room on the roster for Williams."

His first major league "story." Billy was about to see Wrigley Field again—but this time as a Cub. What would they write when he got into his first game?

First Major League Start

Good thing Billy had his ulcer under control when he reported to the Cubs that first morning, Thursday, August 6, 1959.

When I walked into that clubhouse, I felt strange. Y'know, first I'm black, and I came from a small southern town into a real big city. Then I see big league ballplayers I'd read about, guys with pictures and records on trading cards and things. All of a sudden, I'm in their environment, in the same clubhouse with them. I didn't want to say anything, I guess I was afraid I'd say something wrong. Yosh Kawano got me a locker and a uniform, and I started putting it on, but I kept looking over from my locker to see how these major league ballplayers carried themselves.

This was in the old clubhouse upstairs over the parking lot, and the manager, Bob Scheffing, had his office away from the players. Next thing I know, he comes walking over and says, "Williams." Here I am still trying to figure out how to put on a major league uniform and he tells me I'm in the line-up that day. We were playing Philadelphia.

After a while, all the veteran ballplayers came up and said "Glad you're here," "Welcome to the Cubs," and things like that. It's normal for 'em to try to make a new guy feel welcome. Even the fellas who played my position. Maybe they didn't really mean it, 'cause there weren't that many jobs those days with only eight teams in the league. When a rookie would come up, it might mean somebody could be out of a job. One thing helped a lot, though. When I went to spring training with the big club, I got a chance to know some of the fellas—like Ernie and Tony Taylor. We went out to dinner a couple of times. No, my uniform didn't fit just right, but I was so excited to be there, I was glad just to have that major league uniform on. The number they gave me at the time was "4" I think. The wind currents out in leftfield? Nobody said anything

to me about that. I guess they wanted me to find out for myself.
  I really can't remember much about taking fielding or batting practice or anything. I'm sure I must have, but I was nervous. Nervous but psyched up too. And, of course, when I saw the fellas on the other team, players with good records in the major leagues, all I could think was, "Now I've gotta face 'em." By that time, there wasn't much I could do except try to relax, do the best I could, and hope for the best.

  Just being told he was starting, batting third, and playing leftfield was enough to give any rookie the jitters. The atmosphere of Wrigley Field got to Billy too. When he trotted out to his position, he was about in front of where Gabby Hartnett's home-run blast sailed through the dusk and crashed over the wall, to break the hearts of the Pirates in '38. Over in centerfield, maybe in line with the spot where Babe Ruth hit his "called shot" homer in the 1932 World Series, was Bobby Thomson, who had hit one of the most famous homers of all time with two on in the last of the ninth to win the pennant for Durocher's 1951 Giants.

  (Later, Billy heard how Thomson was approached by a "fan" who offered to sell him *"the"* ball he'd hit into the stands. As you might not expect from a gent born in Glasgow, Scotland, Bobby quickly bought it. When he got to the Giant clubhouse and showed the ball to his teammates, they roared with laughter. About a dozen other "fans" had already been there, offering to sell *them* "the" ball!)

  Another hero of that same Giant-Dodger 1951 playoff game was now a Cub too. Al Dark, who singled to start the four-run rally and scored on Carroll ("Whitey") Lockman's double, usually played third base, but today he was on the bench, getting a day of rest.

  At shortstop was Banks, who had been voted the National League's Most Valuable Player in 1958. And, even though the Cubs were in the second division again, Ernie's great record gave him a good chance to repeat in '59.

  The rest of the line-up included Art Schult in rightfield, Jim Marshall at first base, Tony Taylor at second, Earl Averill at third, Sammy Taylor catching, and lefty Art Ceccarelli pitching.

  The Phils failed to score in the first inning. Tony Taylor opened the Cub half with a single off Phillie starter, Jim Owens. Marshall followed with another single, the fleet Taylor scooting to third. Here was Billy's initial chance to be a "hero" or a "bum."

  The one thing he didn't want to do was strike out—that could set up a possible double-play and let Owens off the hook. Billy knew that if nothing else, he had to make contact, hit the ball someplace. He slapped out an infield grounder and was thrown out at first, but Taylor sped in to score.

Up in the WGN Radio broadcast booth, the late Jack Quinlan, the very popular, always exuberant, play-by-play man, happily told his listeners: "Williams, the kid just up from Fort Worth, has driven in a run the first time he batted in the majors." His sidekick, Lou Boudreau, smiled his approval too.

The Cubs broke a tie in the bottom of the eighth and won, 4 to 2, to snap their seven-game losing streak.

Billy was hitless in three other trips to the plate. In fact, he was the only Cub starter who failed to get at least one hit. The next day against the Pirates he again went hitless. On Saturday he drove in another run—also with an infield out. But on Sunday, August 9, he rapped out his first and second major league hits in a losing cause as Pittsburgh won, 5 to 3.

The rest of the season, Billy appeared mostly as a pinch-hitter, starting no more Chicago fires. In 18 games and 33 at-bats, he managed only five hits, one of them a triple, and two RBIs, for a batting average of just .152. One bright spot, he handled 18 outfield chances without an error.

Planes from Texas to Chicago also flew the other way. As Billy cleared out his locker at the end of the 1959 season, he took an extra-long look at the clubhouse before he stepped outside.... He was pretty sure which way he'd be going for the 1960 season.

In '59, the Chicago White Sox stole much, but not all, of the city's baseball thunder. They delighted Chicago's No. 1 Sox fan, Mayor Richard J. Daley, and all the other pennant-starved South-Siders with their first flag in 40 years. This made Al Lopez the only manager to prevent the Yankees from winning 16 straight American League championships. His 1954 Indians and 1959 White Sox were the only other AL teams to win pennants between 1949 and 1964.

Even though the Cubs didn't have the zany, exploding scoreboard—boisterous brainchild of impish Bill Veeck—that erupted after every Sox homer at Comiskey Park, they did have the booming bat of Banks.

Ernie again dominated the league so thoroughly both in hitting and fielding, he was voted the National League's Most Valuable Player, the first in the NL to win it in two successive years. It was one of the few times the MVP award went to a player who was not on a pennant-winning team, and rarer still, a player from a second-division ball club.

This was also the only time both Chicago baseball teams had an MVP. Little Nellie Fox, who Lopez said, "hustled his way to stardom," won it in the American League. The glue-fingered second baseman led the majors in singles seven straight years, went 98 games without striking out and 12 years with the fewest strike-outs, and five times topped the AL in double-plays for a second baseman.

Ernie hit 45 homers, drove in 143 runs, had 351 total bases, and set two new major league records for a shortstop—highest fielding average, .985, and fewest errors, only 12 in 155 games. Banks also had more assists in a single season, 519, than fabled Honus Wagner.

The Go-Go White Sox, whose typical rally was a walk, a steal of second, an advance to third on an infield out, and a score on a sacrifice fly, lost the World Series to the Dodgers in six games.

For the second straight year, the Cubs wound up tied for fifth place. Back home in Whistler, Billy spent an eventful winter, to say the least.

Winter 1959

It was not a happy homecoming for the slender 21-year-old slugger. His unimpressive "cup of coffee" (brief trial) with the Cubs was disappointing enough. But over the summer, he had also broken up with Shirley.

She wrote me sort of a "Dear John" letter, I guess it was mostly my fault. I was back and forth out of town a lot, and I never did like to write. And at that time, I was trying to save money, so I didn't call her much. Times went by when she didn't get a letter or a call, so I guess she figured we didn't care very much about each other and maybe we ought to forget the whole thing. I accepted the letter but, of course, I was really thinking about it a lot because we'd put in a lot of time together.

The other "love" in Billy's life wasn't going well, either. He was still kicking himself for failing to do better in his first real chance in the big leagues. On the other hand, he felt he hadn't had enough opportunities to prove anything, sitting on the bench so much while being used only as a pinch-hitter. Then there was a problem about salary. He thought he'd earned a raise by his good showing in the minors. But farm-club officials didn't agree. In fact, they gave his ego another smack by indicating they felt his top potential was only Class-A baseball. By now, his state of mind wasn't good, and it was getting worse.

I was upset and down on myself. I was trying to prepare for my future, and it didn't look like baseball was going to be it.

Then Billy thought about the last time he had acted in haste, and how he might have ended his career when he jumped the team in San Antonio. This simmered him down, and he decided to have a talk with Aaron as he had in other off-seasons. If anybody understood, it would be Henry. He'd been through a lot of the same things as Billy and had given him many tips about swinging the bat and what to expect in professional baseball.

(Hank had come a long way in just six full major league seasons. He won the 1956 NL batting title, with a .328 average, and led the league in hits, with 200, including 34 doubles, also tops. In 1957, his 44 homers, 132 RBIs, and 118 runs scored were highest in the league, and he was named Most Valuable Player. He appeared in two World Series. He hit .393, smashed three homers, and drove in seven runs in the 1957 Series, helping the Milwaukee Braves beat the Yankees in seven games. Hammerin' Hank also played in six All-Star Games.)

When the Braves were at Wrigley Field in August, 1973, Aaron graciously took time out from his pursuit of Babe Ruth's home-run record—and the relentless pursuit of *him* by press, radio, and TV—to talk about his conversation with Billy that winter of '59.

Even as he was giving the exclusive interview, the batboy was handing him all sorts of things to sign, and Hank patiently obliged.

"Well, I don't know whether I was the main reason for Billy staying in baseball," said Aaron in his soft voice. "Billy's always been a very mature person and had his own mind as to which direction to go. But Billy had several good years in the minor leagues and thought he should have been in the big leagues."

The batboy was back. Henry looked at him, shook his head, smiled, and signed. "I just told him that with all the talent Chicago had at the time, they were probably just waiting for the right time to bring him up, and that they were going to make sure that he'd be able to play regularly."

As he had hoped, talking with Aaron helped Billy sort out his thinking about his baseball career. And he arrived at a decision: He'd seen enough of the big leagues to realize that was the only place to be, but he had changed his mind about one thing.

After being up with the big club, and not doing too well up there, I wanted to go to the minors in '60, play Triple-A ball if I could. They wanted to keep me with the Cubs, but I said I'd prefer going some place where I'd be playing instead of sitting on the bench. I thought I might better myself and be ready the next time I got a chance. It was good I had that chance to chat with Hank. He didn't have it easy when he started, either. But you could tell he felt it had all been worth it. That got me encouraged again too.

As the months went by, other things began to fall into place for him. If, as so many have said, Billy was "born to bat," it now began to appear that another part of his life was also charted for him. As Billy tells it:

One night, a friend of mine, Elliott Turner, and I decided to drive over to Mobile for a dance at the Alabama Branch of the State College.

Shirley was going to school there, but I had no idea I'd see her. Then all of a sudden, you can guess who's about the first person I run into. We said hello and talked for a while—we were both sort of embarrassed, y'know. Anyway, a little later, we took off. On the way home, Elliott told me that someday Shirley was going to be my wife. "Yeah, sure," I said. "Some chance of that!" He said he was willing to put five bucks on it. I gave him a look, then I told him, "Okay, you've got a bet."

Now that I was back in town, everything seemed to get normal again after we met that night. We gradually got back to seeing each other and got more involved.

It turned out too that Billy was given a major league contract at the minimum salary then in effect, $6,500, and he also got his wish to return to the minors. He was assigned to Houston of the American Association, a Triple-A ball club.

On February 25, 1960, Billy dug into his pocket for a five-dollar bill to pay off his bet with Elliott. Then he married Shirley.

Billy chuckled a little when he told it.

I married her, but I didn't change her name. Her last name was already Williams!

A few days later, Billy was on his way to spring training, Shirley remaining at home with her folks.

It was a different Williams who reported to the ball club that year. A lot of the boy was gone. He always had intense desire and determination, but now he began to realize it may have done him more harm than good, that he had been brooding too much.

I do know I had the kind of temperament to keep everything inside me. Maybe this could have been a problem.

Billy was referring to the possible reason for the doctor in Pueblo suggesting he give up baseball.

Nervous tension. It must *have been nervous tension. And I don't know why it waited until a couple of years after I'd started playing professional baseball. I kept complaints and things that happened inside. A lot of times I'd go to the ballpark, play the game, and then go back where I was staying and just keep to myself. No, I didn't necessarily replay the game over and over in my mind, but I wanted to be a good ballplayer so badly, I suppose I did give a lot of thought to that.*

Somewhere between his return to San Antonio after skipping out for a "homesick holiday" and the time he was back in uniform at Houston in '60, Billy had begun to develop the mental discipline that was the key to his becoming not just a major league ballplayer, but a great one, a professional in every sense of the word. Here's how he put it:

In San Antonio, I asked myself, "What are you worried about?" This is the thing I guess that helped me start to take life in stride. I took the attitude that what's going to happen is going to happen, and everything's done for the best. I think if you can sit down and deal with the problem in this respect, you'll feel better.

And he did more than just talk about it. When he'd go 0-for-4 or boot one in the field, he began to force himself to shove it out of his mind, stop brooding about it, leave it at the ballpark in past history where it belonged—then tackle the next day, the next game with a fresh determination to go 4-for-4 and to grab anything they hit his way. He'd learned that no matter what obstacles or bad breaks came his way about the only time he could be licked was when he got down on himself. That's something no really professional athlete can afford to do.

Billy's stomach-churning zeal was rapidly being replaced by an inner calm and quiet confidence. And with the added responsibility of a wife and a family soon to come, he set his sights on earning that next chance with the big club. Billy didn't know when it would come, but he knew it *would* come . . . and he'd be ready.

Another Chance

Finishing in a tie for fifth in '59 didn't cause any run on champagne by Cub fans, but not many ended their disappointment by going over Niagara Falls in a barrel, either. This time, they could utter "Wait till next year" with a little hope. In his third year as manager, Bob Scheffing had brought the Bruins to their best record (74–80, .481) since 1952. Not too bad for a team whose highest finish in 13 years was third way back in 1946.

But shortly after the season ended, owner Phil Wrigley let loose with a thunderbolt. Fans and sportswriters alike were dumbfounded to learn that Charlie Grimm would come back to replace Scheffing as manager for 1960. Wrigley released the story in a press conference with a comment that "Every time we call on Grimm, the Cubs win a pennant." He was referring to the '32, '35, and '45 seasons. He also remarked that he had always thought baseball ought to have relief managers as well as relief pitchers.

Charlie had spent almost five years managing the Braves. He brought that club from seventh place in 1952 to second in 1953, third in 1954, and second again in 1955, but left when Fred Haney took over during the 1956 season. He'd been a coach with the Cubs since 1957.

Grimm went back on his vow to himself never again to hop into the managerial pressure cooker. He accepted the job as Cub manager more out of loyalty than anything else.

It was not a triumphant return for "Jolly Cholly." The Cubs lost 11 of their first 17 games. Charlie was suffering painful heel spurs and no doubt would soon become the target of the slings and arrows that start perpetual Ping-Pong games in the stomachs of most losing managers. But Wrigley came to his rescue, with one of the weirdest swaps ever made in baseball.

This one traded Grimm from the dugout for Lou Boudreau in the

WGN Radio broadcasting booth. To say the announcement was shocking would be to put it mildly.

Unlike Charlie, Boudreau welcomed the challenge, tackling the job with gusto. He donned a Cub uniform with the number "5" he'd made immortal as player-manager with the Cleveland Indians.

Boudreau was 25 in 1942 when he took over as the Indians' manager, the youngest in baseball history. The great shortstop batted, fielded, and led Cleveland to a tie for the pennant in 1948, hit two homers and two singles to lead the Indians to an 8 to 3 victory over Joe McCarthy's Boston Red Sox in the only American League playoff game ever played, and to the World Championship over the Boston Braves of Billy Southworth. That year, Lou was the overwhelming choice as Most Valuable Player, hitting .355, driving in 106 runs, scoring 116 runs, and collecting 34 doubles and 18 home runs. Trivia bugs probably know it was Lou who made the final fielding play to end Joe DiMaggio's 56-game hitting streak in 1941.

But even with Lou at the helm, there was no stopping the Cubs' skid. A headline on one of the sports pages in July, 1960, gives an inkling of how things were going.

SOX GAIN ON YANKS, CUBS ON OBLIVION

By July 30, after a rash of trades, only two of the original Cubs remained—Banks and pitcher Glen Hobbie.

Meanwhile, at Houston, Williams was proving that playing regularly was the tonic he needed. Billy not only stung the ball for .323, the highest average in his brief career, but he also began to unleash his latent power. In 126 games, he lashed 26 homers, 28 doubles, and 3 triples and sent 80 runs across the plate.

Just as important—or maybe more so—he sliced his error total from 21 in San Antonio the previous year to only seven in 1960. But his feverish desire to improve in the field boomeranged.

This happened in Louisville, Kentucky. Somebody hit a "dying seagull" into leftfield. I made a run at it, then dove at it. Well, it had been raining and my right shoulder stuck in the mud. When I got up and tried to make a throw, the pain ran from the top of my head all the way down to my back. I found out it was a shoulder separation, and they sent me home for three weeks.

That was about a month before the end of the minor league season. The team had gotten into the playoffs, and when I came back, Marty Marion [the former "Mr. Shortstop" of the Cardinals] worked real hard with me for a few days, throwing me batting practice, and so forth. At least I got a chance to get into the playoffs against Denver. But we got knocked out. So they sent me back to the Cubs, to finish the season with them.

This time up, Billy—now wearing number "26"—gave them a real eyeful. In 12 games, his batting average was .277, and his 13 hits included a pair of triples and two mighty home-run wallops.

The first was a tremendous belt, soaring far over the rightfield wall in the Coliseum, and it came off another Williams, Stan, to beat the Dodgers. Not too bad for a rookie—that year, the Dodger fast-baller was among the leaders in strike-outs, fewest hits per nine innings, and earned-run average.

About the only other things the steadily dwindling Wrigley Field crowds had to cheer about were a no-hit, no-run game by Don Cardwell in his first game as a Cub; a new major league record by Banks for most career homers by a shortstop, 269; and the exhilarating performance by rookie Ron Santo who had less than two seasons of organized baseball. The peppery third-sacker from Seattle had come up late in June. He got into the line-up right away and did so well, he was chosen Chicago Rookie of the Year by the Windy City's baseball writers. Playing in all but one of the remaining games, Santo had 24 doubles, 2 triples, 9 homers, and 44 RBIs and hit .251.

The Cubs staggered into seventh place to equal the worst record in Bruin history since 1901—only 60 wins and 94 losses and 35 games behind the NL champion Pirates. Despite this, Boudreau never lost his enthusiasm or his popularity with the fans.

Lou was aching to start off fresh and hammer home fundamentals with the Cubs in spring training in 1961, confident he could turn things around.

But Phil Wrigley issued a statement that seemed to suggest the Cub owner had something else in mind.

"Just this morning, I met with John Holland and asked him to give me his file on the Pirates. It showed they have 17 players who came up from their farm system. Other winners in recent years—the Yankees, Braves, Dodgers—have the same history of developing their own."

Wrigley, however, went on to say that he'd make no decision until after he met with Boudreau. Meanwhile, Lou told the press that he planned to ask for a three-year contract and, among other things, would recommend moving Banks from short to first base to prolong his career. Boudreau also predicted that Billy could become another Ted Williams.

True to his word, Lou told Wrigley he wanted a long-term pact. Lou was turned down, and he returned to the radio booth.

Nobody else became manager either. Wrigley again bewildered everyone. He sprang his revolutionary rotating-coach system, in which various coaches would make the rounds in the minors while a few others would stay with the "Big Club" and take turns serving as "head coach." The primary purpose behind all this, said Wrigley, was to insure better and faster development of talent in the Cub system.

Rookie of the Year

With his fabulous spring training performance in 1961, it looked as if Billy might tear the National League apart in the regular season. He led the club in RBIs with 25 in 23 games, and writers began pinning labels on him like "the terror of the exhibition season." Meanwhile, he spent hour after hour sharpening his fielding and throwing. When he left camp, he was still far from a polished outfielder, but did show improvement.

He was still swinging a hot bat when the White Sox and the Cubs met in an exhibition game three days before the regular season opener. The Cubs beat the Sox, 4 to 1, with Billy driving in two runs with a double and single.

The Bruins were now playing under the rotating-coach system—the so-called College of Coaches. At various times during the '61 season, the head coaches were El Tappe, Vedie Himsl, Harry Craft, and Lou Klein.

Billy had won a starting position—but was in rightfield, not left. In the season opener at Cincinnati, he was a complete bust. He hit into a double-play in the first inning and failed to get a ball out of the infield all day. In the next game, he managed to get into the hit column, but Jerry Lynch—who holds the major league record for pinch home runs, 18—came off the bench and boomed a three-run blast to down the Cubs, 5 to 2.

The Cubs electrified 11,299 half-frozen fans with an exciting finish when Billy appeared in his first opening-day game at Wrigley Field against the Braves. He put the Cubs ahead, 1 to 0, in the third, rifling a liner into center, one of two hits he had for the day. Cub starter Bob Anderson yielded only three hits, but two of them were homers, and the Braves led, 2 to 1, as the Cubs came up for their last chance to bail it out.

What a script. Last of the ninth, two out, one on base, and a 3-and-2 count on the batter—catcher Sammy Taylor. Bob Buhl came in with the pitch, and Taylor drilled it over the wall in left center, nearly 400 feet away. It was 3 to 2 Cubs and happy hysteria at Wrigley Field.

There wasn't much celebrating in the next seven games for the freshman rightfielder, however. It was downhill all the way. He got a few hits here and there and came up with a sparkling outfield play. After the first game of a doubleheader which the Cubs lost to the Phils, he was taken out of the line-up. The next day Ed Prell wrote in the *Tribune:*

"Billy Williams, touted during the exhibition season as a possible winner of the National League's Rookie of the Year Award, was benched in the second game. He had gone hitless 13 successive times, and his average dwindled to .143. Williams played every inning of the 10 previous games."

Back in the line-up April 29 against the Dodgers, he had a double and single and another pair of hits in the following game. It looked as if he had really hit his stride when the San Francisco Giants came to town May 2. He went 4-for-4, smacked the first grand-slam homer of his career, and added a fifth RBI to rout the league-leading Giants, 9 to 4. (The day before, incidentally, the Giants' centerfielder, Willie Mays, had become only the ninth player in history to hit four homers in a game.) Then the road got bumpy again. The following day, he went hitless and made an error that allowed a run to score. He also went for the collar the next day and collided with Don Zimmer, both of them after a flyball. His batting average was .235.

Harry Craft, reigning "head coach" at the time, decided to switch Billy to leftfield for his next outing. He continued to show intermittent flashes of his hitting potential. On May 12, he broke up a six-inning no-hitter by Dodger ace Sandy Koufax with a sizzling double. On the 13th, the Cubs dropped their eighth straight game. Billy sat out the next two games, Bob Will replacing him in left. On May 17, he walloped a homer, and on the 21st, against the Cardinals, he regained more confidence by ripping a couple of Bob Gibson flaming fireballs for a double and a single.

Meanwhile, there was plenty of grumbling about the Cubs' dismal early-season performance—they'd lost 11 of their last 12 games and were hitting only .225 as a team. A strongly worded article by Edward Prell on May 21 echoed the recommendation that Boudreau had made at the end of the 1960 season: "SHIFTING OF BANKS TO 1ST BASE COULD CURE SOME OF CUB ILLS," it was headed.

He pointed out that five men had shuttled in and out at first without success; also that the trade on May 9 that had sent Frank Thomas to the Braves for first baseman Mel Roach wasn't producing any results, either. Nor had numerous switches in the outfield been effective.

Prell declared that Andre Rodgers or Jerry Kindall could fill Ernie's shoes at shortstop so that "First base definitely can be solved by switching Banks." He added: "And wouldn't the switch add length to his brilliant career?"

Obviously Prell's impassioned plea went unheeded. On May 23, Vedie Himsl, recalled for another stint as "head coach," announced that Banks was being moved . . . to leftfield!

Nevertheless, Billy promptly christened the occasion with a high, deep home-run shot in the first inning and repeated the act in the first the following day off "Vinegar Bend" Mizell.

The outfield experiments continued. Back in rightfield on May 26, Billy had a perfect day at the plate, with a double and three singles off "Toothpick Sam" Jones and Billy O'Dell in a 13-inning duel against the Giants. But he also made a wild throw that really hurt—it allowed a run to score, and San Francisco won, 3 to 2.

From then through the middle of June, Billy spent most of his time on the bench. In one stretch, he sat out completely for six straight games. However, he was called on to pinch-hit in eight games. *And how he pinch-hit!* He not only came through five times, a tremendous feat in itself, but the last five hits were consecutive. He had the final one on June 15, his 23d birthday, when the Cubs were on the West Coast playing against the Dodgers.

But because wheels were turning in his behalf, the best birthday present he could possibly have hoped for arrived the next day. Seeing how Billy responded to pressure with such icy calm and the rare ability to deliver in the clutch, John Holland took a hand in things. As Holland admitted in a recent interview, he was guilty of a little "front-office interference." He ordered that Billy be put in the starting line-up and stay there for 30 days.

On June 16, the Cubs opened a three-game series at San Francisco. Banks, who by his own admission had spent over 20 agonizing games in the outfield, was shifted to first base. Williams was sent to leftfield. Andre Rodgers was at short, Jerry Kindall at second, Santo at third, Richie Ashburn in centerfield, and George Altman in rightfield.

Seeing number "14" on first at last no doubt inspired Ed Prell to write one of the happiest stories he'd ever punched out:

"The Cubs moved Ernie Banks to first tonight to make room for Billy Williams in leftfield, and no rookie ever showed more grateful response.

"The 23-year-old southpaw slugger slammed a grand-slam home run [his second of the season] in the third inning and, thus inspired, the Cubs went on for a 12 to 6 smashing of the pennant-minded San Francisco Giants before a crowd of 20,622 in wind-swept Candlestick Park."

Billy doubled in the next game and went on a binge of 10 hits in his next 19 at-bats. And he didn't miss another inning in the rest of the season. Late in the season Billy ruined Warren Spahn's attempt to become one of only three pitchers since 1900 to throw three no-hitters. The Milwaukee Braves' southpaw ace had pitched his second no-hitter early in 1961. He blanked the Cubs on September 24 but had to settle for a two-hitter. Both hits were off Billy's bat.

His rookie record was one that many veteran ballplayers would happily settle for. He walloped 25 homers, highest ever for a Cub rookie, surpassing the 19 Banks hit in 1954 as a freshman. His batting average was .278, with 86 RBIs, 20 doubles, 7 triples, and 75 runs scored. The praise started pouring in.

"CUBS' WILLIAMS NATIONAL LEAGUE'S ROOKIE OF THE YEAR." Announcing his selection as the National League's Rookie of the Year, the story in the *Chicago Sun-Times* went on to say: "The star hitter won it by one of the biggest landslide votes since the baseball writers began giving the award in 1949. He received 10 of the votes, with Joe Torre of the Braves second with five, and Jack Curtis, the little Cub southpaw, receiving one vote. It was the first time a Cub freshman ever had gained the distinction, although Ron Santo was in the running last year when Frank Howard won the honor."

The article also called him "the most feared young hitter in the National League." *The Sporting News,* dubbing him the "Bruins' Blaster," stated: "If Williams had played the full season, he would have easily reached the 100 mark in RBIs." The same story described the young man from Whistler as having a "classic whiplash swing."

Billy was also the clear-cut choice for the Rookie of the Year Award from the Chicago Chapter of the Baseball Writers Association of America. Still painfully shy, he gave a one-sentence acceptance "speech," half-whispering that his goal for 1962 was to hit .300 and drive in 100 runs.

"That would give you the Sophomore of the Year Award," John Holland commented.

"I'm not thinking of that one at all," Billy smiled. "The next thing I'd like to win is the Most Valuable Player Award."

Although the 1961 rotating-coach plan didn't improve the club's position—the Cubs again finished seventh—they did manage to win four more games than they had in '60.

In 1962, the National League expanded to ten teams with a 162-game schedule as the American League had done a year earlier. Former Cub rotating coach, Harry Craft, was named to pilot the new Houston Astros, then called the Colt .45's. The Wrigleys, meanwhile, continued without a conventional manager—the "head coach" was first El Tappe, then Lou Klein, and, for the last 112 games of the season, Charlie Metro.

In May, the Cubs appointed the first Negro to coach a major league team, the same Buck O'Neil who had brought Williams back to San Antonio after Billy went AWOL. O'Neil's long impressive career included managing the Kansas City Monarchs, whose roster included future Cub stars Banks and George Altman.

Recalling the case of the homesick Sweet Swinger, O'Neil said, "I told him what a great future he had in baseball, and he decided to go back. I'm sure he would have gone back himself even if they hadn't sent me.

"The first time I ever saw him, he was just a toothpick. And, he hit everything to leftfield. But he always made contact, and you could tell right away that he was going to be a good hitter. Billy could have hit more home runs if he had tried, but with Banks and Santo around, he was satisfied just to get on base. He didn't try to hit the long ball much until Ernie was finishing up."

In the new season, Billy didn't pay much attention to the "sophomore jinx." He believes in hard work, not superstition. Besides, he was too intent on making himself the complete ballplayer. Billy was really bugged by his boots in '61—11 errors, highest in the league for an outfielder. "I got benched last year because I fouled up on grounders," he kept telling himself. "You miss a few, then you start gettin' shaky. I'm going to straighten *that* out!"

If he had bothered to look it up, he would have learned that even Willie Mays made nine errors in 1951, when he was the National League's Rookie of the Year, and made about the same in numerous other seasons. Their rookie year records follow:

	G	AB	R	H	2B	3B	HR	RBI	BA	E	FA
Mays	121	464	59	127	22	5	20	68	.274	9	.976
Williams	146	529	75	147	20	7	25	86	.278	11	.954

And, as usual, he was thinking ahead. Often the reason why many a rookie slumps at the plate in his second year is that a pitcher has discovered the hitter's weakness, the word gets around, and soon most everybody has a "book" on him. If the batter doesn't eliminate the weakness, or can't adjust, pitchers he used to clobber start getting him out.

But pitchers have weaknesses too. So, always a keen observer, Billy began to concentrate on getting his own "book" on them. Nearly everyone you talk to, starting with his former teammate Ron Santo, will tell you how Billy's always thinking ahead about the pitcher he's going to face. And he did this right at the start of his big-league career.

On the bench and in the on-deck circle, he never takes his eyes off the pitcher. It's important to know more than his best pitches—what's his best pitch *today?* When he gained more confidence that he could hit with the pitcher ahead of him by one or two strikes, he'd cross up a pitcher now and then by taking a pitch. Later, when the pitcher came in with the same kind of pitch, he'd go after it.

Another former teammate, Glenn Beckert, who joined the Cubs several years after Billy, put it this way: "Lots of times I'd be leading off an inning and I'd say 'What do you think, Billy?' He's remarkable in the way he knows pitchers and analyzes, and the ability he has to look for a certain pitch."

But "the thinking man's hitter" narrowly missed the goals he'd set for himself in his sophomore year, though he ended up among the team's top offensive leaders. Hitting around .300 most of the season— and .350 for a stretch—he might have finished with an average of .300 or more by sitting out the last couple of games, an opportunity that was offered him. But he turned it down: if he couldn't hit the magic figure legitimately, he didn't want it. Billy finished with .298. The only Cub with a higher average was Altman, with .318.

Appearing in all but three games, he hammered out 184 hits, most among the Cubs; led the team in runs scored, 94; was second to Banks in RBIs, with 92; and in homers, with 22 (tied with Altman); and he walked the most times, 70. Billy accumulated 288 total bases, not far behind the 307 by Ernie, who played his first full season at first base and after a subpar '61 came back with a brilliant year. Williams also had the Cubs' longest consecutive-game hitting streak, 17—the best since Walt Moryn's 19 in '57.

To Billy's great delight, he had been picked by National League manager Fred Hutchinson to appear in the second All-Star Game of the year, held at Wrigley Field July 30. Hard-nosed Hutch, the former gutsy pitcher who never had a losing season his last eight years with the Tigers, had been duly impressed by the young outfielder. According to the late Hutchinson: "He's just the best-looking hitter in the league. Mays overpowers the ball, but this fella is an artist with the bat."

Billy could hardly contain himself. He sat on the bench grinning from ear to ear. It isn't often a player with so little time in the majors gets to be on the same squad with such established stars as Most Valuable Player trophy winners Dick Groat, Maury Wills, Mays, Frank Robinson, and Roberto Clemente and such great pitchers as Johnny Podres, Art Mahaffey, Bob Gibson, and Juan Marichal.

"Billy had a lot of idols since he started playing baseball in Alabama," said Banks. "Two of his more recent ones were Stan Musial and Hank Aaron. I'll never forget the day they played on the same team. Billy made the National League All-Star team for the first time, and I was also on the squad. Neither of us started. About the middle of the game, I replaced Orlando Cepeda at first. And later, when Hutchinson told Billy to take over for Musial in leftfield, he was so excited he almost fell off the bench. His face lit up with a little surprised grin. And here comes Aaron over, and he starts wavin' a towel back and forth in front of Billy's face, and told him to 'keep cool'. Billy had replaced *one* of his idols, and *another* had come over to relieve him of some of his excitement and tension!"

But Billy bore up under it. He even got credit for an RBI on an infield out his lone time at bat. Banks belted a triple, to no avail. Paced by Tiger Rocky Colavito's four RBIs, the American League won, 9 to 4.

Some stellar-caliber Cub rookies climbed aboard in 1962—headed by future Cardinal superstar, outfielder Lou Brock, and second baseman Ken Hubbs. At St. Cloud in 1961, his first and only year in organized baseball before coming up to the majors, Brock had been a shoo-in for the Northern League's Rookie of the Year honors. He led the league in batting with a .361 average, 181 hits, 33 doubles, and 117 runs scored. With the Cubs, Brock hit a modest .263 but accounted for 24 doubles, 7 triples, 9 homers, and 16 stolen bases.

He also became the first lefthanded hitter ever to park a homer into the distant right centerfield bleachers in the Polo Grounds. Brock had one of the Cubs' two grand-slam homers of the season; Nelson Mathews, also a rookie, had the other.

Hubbs put on such an eye-popping performance, it was only logical that he follow Williams as the Cubs' second straight National League and Chicago Rookie of the Year. He shattered a pair of major league records for second basemen—playing 78 games without an error and handling 418 chances flawlessly. Working primarily with shortstop Andre Rodgers, he was the pivot man in 171 double-plays. Hubbs also rattled off 172 hits, drove in 49 runs, scored 90, and twice during the season, was the only Bruin to get 5 hits in a game.

Rookie righthander Cal Koonce had a 10–10 pitching record. So considering that the top winner on the staff was former Brave Bob Buhl with 12–13, it's easy to see how the Cubs finished in ninth place, suffering the extreme embarrassment of ending up six games behind the expansion Colt .45's and just one notch above the then "Miracle-less Mets," who won only 40 games all year and lost 120.

A number of players, among them Brock and Don Zimmer, were critical of the Cubs' rotating-coach system. Of his rookie year with the Cubs, Brock said later: "Coming from the minors and having 14 coaches around and you trying to please everybody can be tough on a guy at the age I was at the time."

Zimmer, later manager of the Padres, also had some unchoice words for the reigning-coach system. The favorite racetrack buddy of Rogers Hornsby in those days—they'd both take off right after the game for the track—Zimmer told how when El Tappe was in charge, as the Cubs' regular second baseman he played well enough to make the All-Star team in '61. When Lou Klein took over, Zimmer was benched the same day. When Tappe returned, Zimmer returned to the line-up. "I saw one coach wagging Santo to play deeper at third, and another motioning for him to come in farther. They were driving him crazy," concluded Zimmer.

Billy Hits His Stride

With the Cubs finishing in seventh place in 1961 and in ninth in 1962, it was obvious that the rotating-coach setup wasn't working. In any case, Bob Kennedy, who had played with Boudreau's 1948 World Champion Cleveland Indians, was named "head coach" for the entire 1963 season.

With a few bounces the other way, the club might have shot up high in the first division. Under Kennedy, the pitching—so pathetic the year before—was second in ERAs only to the fabulous mound corps of the pennant-winning Dodgers, led by Koufax.

Lefty Dick Ellsworth reversed his 1962 won-lost record of 9–20 to a remarkable 22–10 and the stingy ERA of 2.11. He was the first Bruin to post 20 wins since Hank Wyse had an identical record in 1945 and the first Cub southpaw to win 20 or more games since James ("Hippo") Vaughn in 1919. A pair of Cardinals acquired in a trade also had good years—Larry Jackson won 14, and fork-baller Lindy McDaniel, with 13–7, copped *The Sporting News* "Fireman of the Year" Award with 22 saves.

But the usually robust Cub hitting attack sputtered. Although Williams and Santo swung hot bats, Banks was hit with a blood infection and sub-clinical mumps, cutting his homers to 18 and his RBIs to 64. Brock still had not quite found himself at the plate but stole 24 bases, making him the top Cub base robber in 33 years. Hubbs, Rodgers, and catcher Dick Bertell all batted under .250. Hard-hitting George Altman had been traded.

In the season's most memorable game, McDaniel trudged from the bullpen in the ninth with the score tied, Giants on every base, and only one out. Lindy promptly became one of the few pitchers ever to pick off Willie Mays from second base. Then he struck out Ed Bailey to douse the rally. Leading off in the bottom of the ninth, McDaniel turned slugger, swatting a game-winning homer to give the Cubs a four-game sweep over San Francisco.

On September 22, 1963, veteran righthander Bob Buhl beat his former mates of Milwaukee, 7 to 3. It was the Cubs' tenth victory of the season over the Braves, and the first time they won a season series from Milwaukee since the Braves arrived from Boston in 1953.

Billy went hitless in five trips to the plate. He didn't suspect the significance of the game—he couldn't know that he would appear in 1,116 more games without missing one.

Williams and Santo provided the North-Siders one-two power punch. Billy continued to build a reputation as "Mr. Consistent." His average dipped slightly to .286, but he tied with Ron for the club leadership in homers, with 25; had 95 RBIs, 36 doubles, 9 triples; and was tops on the club with 87 runs, 304 total bases, .497 slugging percentage, and 68 bases on balls.

Santo bounced back from a mediocre '62 season to pace the Cubs with a .297 average and 99 RBIs, and he broke a 60-year-old NL record with 374 assists at third base. He also earned his first appearance in the All-Star Game.

Kennedy had the Cubs scrapping early, and they stayed up among the leaders over half the season, soaring to second place on July 19. But a pair of losing streaks—11 losses in 15 games in August and six straight in September—prevented a first division finish. Still and all, only six games separated the third-place Giants and the seventh-place Cubs.

It was the winningest Wrigley Field gang since 1946, and the fans responded. The season's attendance increased to about 980,000—a jump of over 369,000.

The Cubs won 82 games and lost 80—not bad, considering the magnificent pitching they faced all year. Juan Marichal of the Giants won 25 games, and Warren Spahn of the Braves and Jim Maloney of the Reds each won 23. The Pirates' Bob Friend and Roy Face, the Reds' Joe Nuxhall, and the Cards' Curt Simmons and Bob Gibson were other standouts. And then there were the Dodger hurlers.

Those who secretly agreed that the Bronx Bombers were "Damn Yankees" were delighted at the outcome of the unlikeliest World Series of them all. The Yankees went down to their most humiliating defeat ever; for the first time, they were eliminated in four straight games, victims of the Dodgers' "dream" pitching staff.

Spring training in 1964 opened on a sad note. Number "16" was missing. The warm, friendly, modest Cub second baseman, Ken Hubbs, had died tragically in a plane crash in February. The

Chicago sportswriters instituted an annual Ken Hubbs Memorial Award to the player who best exemplifies the life of Hubbs both on and off the field. The first to receive the honor was Ernie Banks.

All preseason indications were that the Cubs could hardly miss as contenders. There was even talk of a "dark horse" flag winner. They had improved considerably in 1963 under Bob Kennedy, and in 1964 he was again named "head coach."

In the spring drills, little clusters of baseball men would gather around the batting cage when Billy took his cuts, much like they used to do when Ted Williams went up to swing. One of them, Dodger executive Buzzy Bavasi, said, "I like to watch him swing a bat. He gets it around so fast, you'd think he's swinging a toothpick. But, when he connects, the ball really takes off. He'll be one of the greatest."

The '64 Cubs could boast more power than their 1929 "Murderers' Row" of Hornsby, Hack Wilson, Gabby Hartnett, Riggs Stephenson, and Kiki Cuyler. Williams, Santo, Banks, Rodgers, and Billy Cowan also promised to be more explosive than the '58 slugging crew of Banks, Walt Moryn, Dale Long, Bobby Thomson, and Lee Walls.

With such hitting and the nucleus of a good pitching staff, the Cubs felt that adding more front-line pitching could give them a real shot at the championship. So with the best of intentions, on June 15 they made what became one of the most regrettable trades in Cub history.

Lou Brock went to the Cards along with pitchers Jack Spring and Paul Toth for righthander Ernie Broglio and lefty Bobby Shantz and outfielder Doug Clemens. Broglio was an 18-game winner in '63 and had won 21 in '60 with St. Louis. Shantz had a 6–4 record in '63, but the little reliever also posted 11 saves.

Although Billy was a fast friend of Brock and had spent a lot of time helping Lou, he felt the trade could benefit the Cubs tremendously. Ironically, over in the other camp, Gibson agreed but looked at it differently. As he said in his book *From Ghetto to Glory:* "I remember telling a reporter that I didn't think too much of the trade, and I didn't. He [Broglio] was a good veteran pitcher and the one thing we could least afford to give up, it seemed to me, was pitching. Particularly for a player like Brock, who was hitting something like .250 for the Cubs. I wondered if we got enough in return for Broglio . . .

"Somebody on our team said . . . Lou would probably lead the league in hitting one day. I was doubtful. He never impressed me like that . . ." Gibson went on: "I am happy to say I was wrong . . . .

He was the missing link in our offense. Batting first, he always seemed to be on base when the big hitters came up. He began stealing bases and taking the extra base and upsetting the other teams with his speed and daring on the bases."

Speaking in the Cardinal clubhouse at Wrigley Field late in the 1973 season, Brock looked back and summed up how he felt when the trade took place. Looks like "the big one that got away" could be chalked up to the Cubs' revolutionary rotating-coach system in effect when Brock came up in 1962. Said Brock: "Too many chiefs and only one Indian as far as I was concerned. Having to satisfy so many people was very hard to do. I wasn't the kind of guy who could very well adapt to that. However, Billy did do it, and you have to give him a lot of credit for it. But some of us just couldn't make that adjustment, and I was one of them.

"In my opinion, it takes a ballplayer two or three years to make the adjustment in the big leagues. I don't think I was given ample time in Chicago to make that adjustment... I was in my third year when I got traded, and that happened to be the best year I ever had in baseball. So I think the Cardinals got the benefit of my maturing at that point, and the Cubs probably gave up a couple of weeks too soon."

The biggest thing Lou told me when he went over to the Cardinals was that their coaches said, "You're going to play for us. We're not going to try and change your style, we want you to play baseball." He was a lot more relaxed. Here, at times, he'd almost forgotten how to swing a bat, even though he hit over .350 at St. Cloud before joining our club. About every time he went up to bat, the coaches were telling him to bunt. I think the Cards gave him confidence by playing him, and letting Lou play pretty much his own type of game.

As the season wore on, things took some weird twists to say the least. The Cubs got an unexpected bonanza when Cardinal castoff, Larry Jackson, startled everybody by winning 24 games, losing only 11—tops in the majors and the best Cub performance since Charlie Root won 26 in 1927. Ellsworth won 14 but lost 18, Buhl was 15–14, ex-Brave Lew Burdette was 9–9, and McDaniel slipped to 1–7, though he had 15 saves.

Broglio, on the other hand, was a monumental disappointment. Sore-armed, he eked out only 4 wins, lost 7, and had one save.

As predicted, Cub sluggers bedeviled enemy pitchers, Williams spearheading the attack with 33 homers, including a grand-slammer.

Santo belted 30 round-trippers, Banks 23, Cowan 19, and Rodgers 12—the five of them alone accounting for 117.

Besides leading the team in hits (201), doubles (39), and runs scored (100), Billy had his highest major league average to date—.312, with 98 RBIs. And for the first time, he climbed among the leaders in the National League as well. He was second in homers, tied for third in hits, third in doubles, and third in total bases, with 343.

Williams and Santo combined to make up one of the game's most dynamic duos. Ron hit .313, drove in 114 runs, had 334 total bases, 13 triples, and a slugging average of .564.

Billy was named a starter in the All-Star Game and lined a long homer off Johnny Wyatt to give the Nationals their first run in a 7 to 4 victory. Because somebody somewhere pushed the wrong button, that exciting home run wasn't seen by the vast TV audience. He felt about the same as Lou Gehrig must have when the "Iron Horse" became the first modern-day ballplayer to hit four consecutive home runs in a game. It happened on June 3, 1932—the same day that Giant manager John McGraw abruptly announced his retirement, so Lou's prodigious feat was scarcely mentioned in the sports news.

Billy's scorching early-season ball-pounding not only made him the landslide winner of the NL Player of the Month Award for May, he also set three records—highest average, .455, most hits, 51, and most votes any player had received since the awards were initiated in '58. He capped the month with a homer, a double, and two singles in four trips to the plate against Milwaukee on May 30.

It won't be hard for Billy to remember his 100th homer. He hit it trying to help celebrate "Ernie Banks Day" on August 15, 1964. Over 23,000 fans and 2,000 youngsters in various baseball uniforms rocked Wrigley Field with thunderous cheers in affection for "Mr. Cub," who, at 33, was nearing his 11th full season in "the friendly confines."

The noncooperative Pirates put a damper on the day by getting off to an early three-run lead. But in the fourth, Joey Amalfitano opened with a single; then, with one out, Billy kissed one into the left-center bleachers. The guest of honor walked, and Billy Cowan belted another two-run homer to give the Cubs the lead. It was short-lived, however. Pittsburgh tied it up in the fifth and pushed over the winning run in the ninth. Adding insult to injury, they'd held Ol' Ern hitless.

Probably Billy's most satisfying honor of all in '64 was the one that recognized his enormous improvement as a defensive fielder. He was named leftfielder on both *The Sporting News* and the United Press International All-Star teams in the same outfield with Willie Mays and Roberto Clemente.

The Cubs, meanwhile, watched the meteoric progress of Brock, pop-eyed in disbelief, disgruntled at losing him. When Lou joined the Redbirds, they were in eighth place. Then the kid with the speed of a racehorse went to work. He led the Cardinals with .315– .348 since joining them—and for the season had 200 hits, including 30 doubles, 11 triples, and 14 homers; scored 111 runs; drove in 58 runs; and stole 43 bases. Against the Cubs he hit .418, with 10 RBIs.

With all their firepower, the Cubs wound up losing six more games than they had the previous year and sank into eighth place. But if the Cubs were unhappy over their poor finish, Gene Mauch and his Phillies were in a state of shock. After holding first place for 134 days, the Phils led by 6½ games—then with only 12 left to play, they lost 10 straight. The Cardinals took the pennant, sneaking in by only one game.

In the World Series, Larcenous Lou hit .300 and drove in five runs, then homered in the seventh game to help the Cardinals beat Yogi Berra's Yankees. Brock did not forget his former teammates. According to Williams, after the Series Lou sent a souvenir to the Cub clubhouse—the *box* his World Series ring came in!

It's a shame only 641,346 baseball fans came to Wrigley Field in 1965. Those who stayed away missed one of the most spectacular hitting onslaughts of all time as the flashing bat of Billy Williams boomed as never before.

Williams, Banks, and Santo made up the fiercest one-two-three attack in baseball. The Cubs were the only National League team with three hitters batting in more than 300 runs—Billy, 108; Ernie, 106; Ron, 101. Some say the crack of the bats could be heard out on Lake Michigan and as far away as the stockyards.

Billy was the only player that year to hit over .300, rap out over 200 hits, score more than 100 runs, hit over 30 homers, and drive in more than 100 runs. The only other Cubs ever to do the same were Rogers Hornsby and Hack Wilson.

He topped the Cubs in every offensive category, with 645 at-bats, 115 runs, 108 RBIs, 203 hits, 356 total bases, 39 doubles, 6 triples, and 34 homers—besting the team record for a lefthanded batsman formerly held by Bill ("Swish") Nicholson. In homers, he was third in the league, and although his .315 batting average was fourth in the NL—behind Clemente, Aaron, and Mays—he outstripped them all in runs produced. In other league standings, he was second in total bases, third in slugging, third in hits, second in doubles, and fourth in RBIs.

Had he been more flamboyant, received more nationwide press coverage, and/or been with a contender or pennant winner, he no doubt would have received far more than his 21 votes for Most Valuable Player. The award was won by Mays of the second-place Giants.

Despite their murderous stickwork, however, the Cubs were victims during the season not only of a 1 to 0 no-hitter but also of a 1 to 0 perfect game. On August 19, Jim Maloney of the Reds completely buffaloed the Bruins' batsmen in a ten-inning no-hitter, Cincinnati winning 1 to 0.

There had been only six perfect games since 1900, including Don Larsen's in the 1956 World Series. The seventh perfect game was pitched against the Cubs by Sandy Koufax on the night of September 9 in Los Angeles. It was one of the most exciting pitching duels in baseball history—a real heart-tugger for the Cubs' southpaw Bob Hendley, because in this outing he was almost Sandy's equal. Koufax, whose buzzing fastball could whistle through a car wash without getting wet, became the only pitcher ever to hurl four no-hitters. In this contest, it took an unearned run to do it. Sandy almost *had* to throw a no-hitter to win, because Hendley allowed only *one* hit, a bloop double by ex-Cub Lou Johnson that, most crushing of all, didn't figure in the scoring. The Dodgers got their lone run on a walk, a sacrifice, a stolen base, and an error by rookie catcher Chris Krug.

The game set two major league records: for fewest hits by both clubs—one—and for fewest men left on base by both clubs—one. Koufax was the master that night, striking out 14. He got Billy on called strikes the first two times up, went to 3 and 0 on him in the seventh, but came back with two strikes and then got Williams to fly out. Remembering the night, Billy commented:

Sandy threw only the fastball and the curve. Of course, his speed made him more effective with his breaking ball, and he threw everything hard. I think the most important thing that night was control.

Sandy's only problem sometimes was getting the ball over the plate. He was making good pitches that night.

Even if you knew a fastball was coming, Sandy was always awfully hard to hit. A lot of times with a pitcher who doesn't throw so hard, he can make a mistake and you might hit the ball out of the park. But guys like Gibson, Koufax, and Seaver—these guys throw so hard that when they do make a mistake, most of the time the ball's up. That's the kind of pitch you like to get off a mediocre fastball pitcher. But if a hard thrower gets a fastball up, you've got to lay off it because the ball's rising as it comes up to the plate. He gives you less chance to comprehend the mistake because you just don't have that much time to see the ball.

Five days later, September 14, the same two clubs and same two pitchers were dueling again—this time at Wrigley Field. And once more Sandy was holding on to a 1 to 0 lead late in the game. Billy, who hadn't taken his eyes off Koufax all during the game, had a glint in his eye as Glenn Beckert and he were heading for the on-deck circle.

Beckert was leading off the inning. And while we were waiting, I said, "Beck, I think I've got it figured out. The first three times up, he's started me off with fastballs away from me on the outside part of the plate. You get on base and we got a couple of runs." Almost apologetically, Billy went on:

Y'know, a lot of times a guy will say things like that, then doesn't do it. But Glenn got on base. Sandy comes back with the first pitch he started me off with before. He threw it in the same place, a belt-high fastball, outside away from me. I went to leftfield when I hit it. I wasn't trying to go that way, but because Koufax was the type of pitcher who threw the ball so hard, it was usually past you before you could react—so I went with it a little bit, and the ball flew over the leftfield wall, and we won that ballgame, 2 to 1.

No back-slapping, just the facts. That's Billy. What he didn't mention was that in '65 Koufax set a new major league strike-out record of 382 (broken by Nolan Ryan in '73, with 383) and won the Cy Young Award.

On the whole, the frustrating season was sadly reminiscent of the 1930 Phillies, who had a .315 team batting average yet finished in the basement.

"How could you finish last with such hitters?" somebody asked the Phils' manager, Barney Shotton.

"Have you seen my *pitching?*" he groaned.

Only two Bruin hurlers had winning records—Buhl, with 13–11, and reliever Bob Humphreys, with 2–0. Broglio was 1–6, Ellsworth 14–15, Jackson 14–21, and Koonce 7–9. Bill Faul, who claimed that he hypnotized himself before each game, was even up at 6–6. Newcomer Ted Abernathy, with his submarine ball, was 4–6, but he made 84 appearances, an all-time record, and led the league with 31 saves.

A pair of fine-looking rookies saw plenty of infield action in '65—second baseman Glenn Beckert and shortstop Don Kessinger. Beckert had the team's longest consecutive-hitting streak of the season—14 games. Both made a lot of errors, but left little doubt they had the makings of the league's premier double-play combination in future years.

Williams, Banks, with 28 homers and 106 RBIs, and Santo, with 33 homers and 101 RBIs, all made the All-Star team and helped beat the American League, 6 to 5. Ron and Billy also shared a new major league achievement by appearing in 164 games (there were two ties). And again, Billy was an honored guest at the Annual Diamond Dinner, this time to receive the Chicago Baseball Writers Major League Player of the Year Award.

Bob Kennedy, who'd been "head coach" for the last two seasons, was replaced by Lou Klein after 56 games. Klein finished out the year with 48 wins and 58 losses as the Cubs, with a 72–90 record, again finished eighth.

Before the 1966 season was launched, Phil Wrigley shot another bolt out of the blue—the new field boss would be the one and only Leo Durocher. The "Lip" lost no time in making it plain: he wasn't going to be the "head coach," he was to be The Manager.

In 1956, 18-year-old Billy gets his first taste of
organized baseball with Ponca City (Oklahoma)
Cubs. Not an auspicious start. He came to bat only
17 times in 13 games and hit .235. Billy's at the left,
middle row.

Billy Williams' personal collection

At 20 with the Bees of Burlington, Iowa, in his third
year of minor league ball. Billy hit .304 and earned
move up to San Antonio in 1959.

The Hawk-Eye, Burlington, Iowa

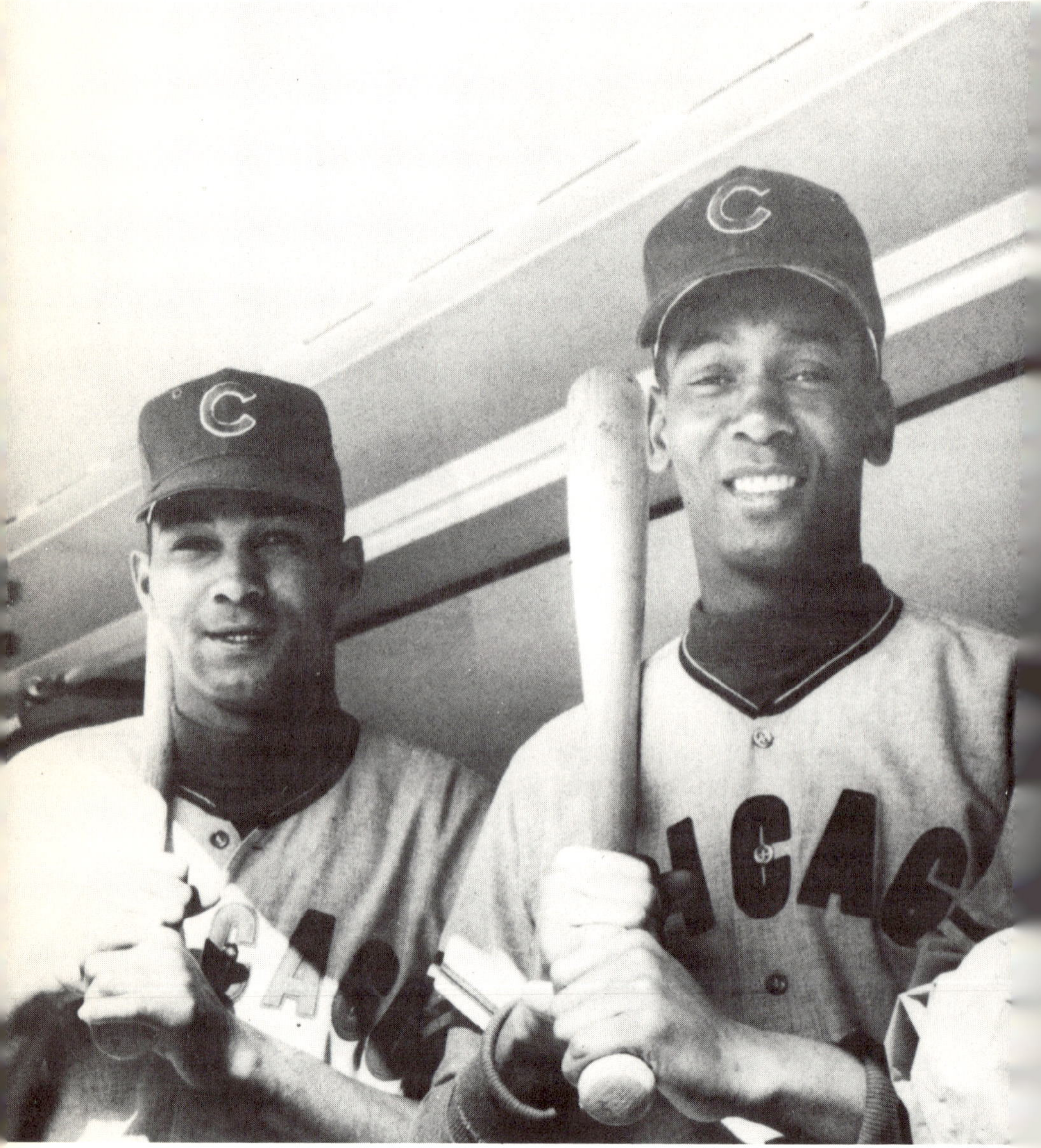

The most terrifying home-run trio in Chicago Cub history. They combined to put 1,225 out of the park. Ron Santo (right) hit 337 homers while with the Cubs, Ernie Banks (center) had a lifetime total of 512, and Billy slammed 376 through the 1973 season.

Chicago Tribune

Billy, the 1961 National League Rookie of the Year, the first Cub to receive the award. He batted .278, hit 25 homers, most of any Bruin rookie in history, had 20 doubles and 7 triples, and drove in 86 runs.
Chicago Cubs

The day he didn't play. Billy trots to broadcast booth for an interview after sitting out his first game in 1,117 on September 3, 1970, to establish the all-time "Iron Man" mark in the National League. His consecutive-game streak began September 22, 1963.
Chicago Tribune

Billy had to overcome "good hit-no field" tag early in career. Here ball bounces out of his glove in 1962. But, with hard work and sheer determination, he made himself one of the top outfielders in the game.
UPI

Icy eyes dare pitcher to put one by him. "But I've never seen the bat hit the ball," said Billy.
Chicago Tribune

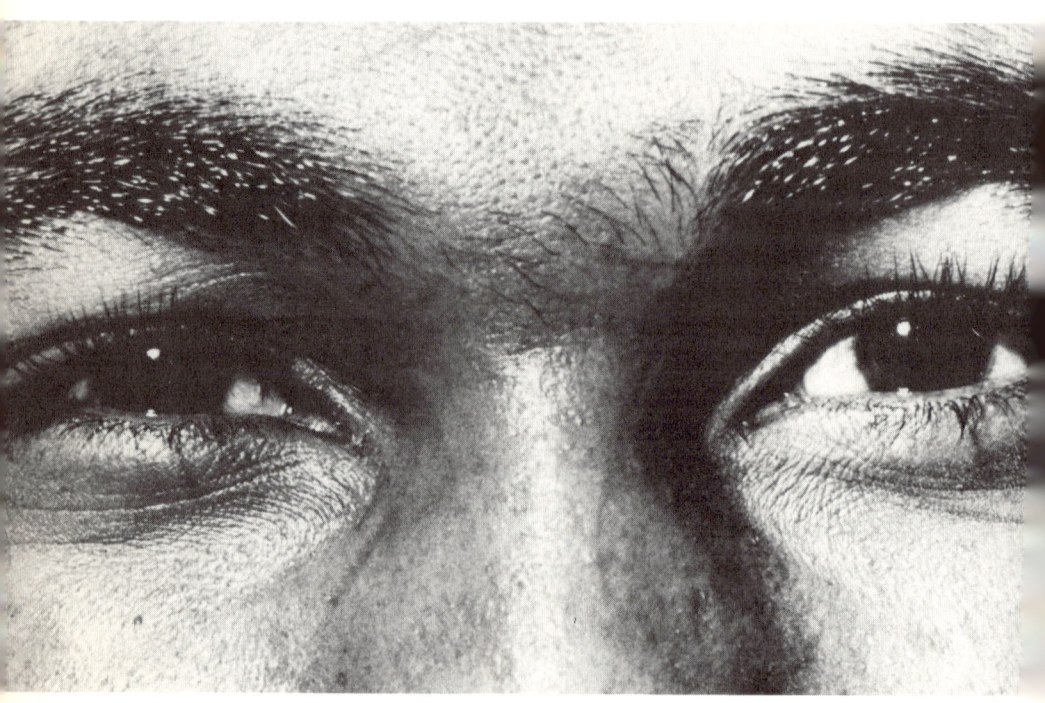

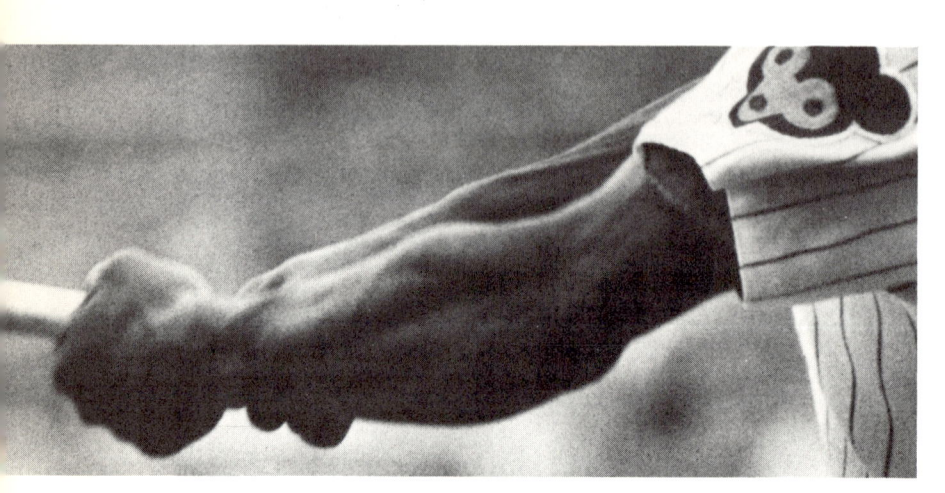

The raw, rippling power of the Classic Hitter, who ranks ninth among the all-time home-run kings of the National League—and still climbing. He did nothing special to develop his powerful wrists and arms, except for a lot of swimming in Eight Mile Creek back home in Whistler, Alabama.
Chicago Tribune

Billy shows the immense concentration and determination that have helped him produce more runs over a seven-year period (1967 thru 1973) than anyone else in the majors.
Chicago Tribune

Glenn Beckert and Billy admire results of a deep-sea fishing expedition in California.
Billy Williams' personal collection

"I just try to hit the ball hard someplace," says Billy. With this classic form and follow-through, he hit it hard enough and often enough to make him the only major leaguer to average over .300, 30 or more homers, 100 or more RBIs for the three years 1970 to 1972.

Chicago Tribune

When Bill North slips, Billy streaks out of nowhere to nab sinking liner and preserve a no-hitter by Milt Pappas against Padres September 2, 1972. Pappas retired 26 straight batters before walking Larry Stahl with two out in ninth to spoil his bid for a perfect game.
Chicago Tribune

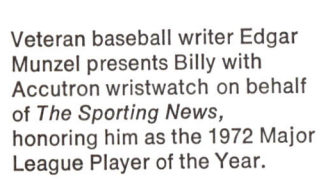

Veteran baseball writer Edgar Munzel presents Billy with Accutron wristwatch on behalf of *The Sporting News*, honoring him as the 1972 Major League Player of the Year.
Chicago Cubs

Billy and Richie Allen (right) of the White Sox, named Chicago Players of the Year for 1972, are guests of honor at the Annual Diamond Dinner of the Chicago Chapter of the Baseball Writers of America January 13, 1973. Allen was chosen American League MVP, while Billy came in second to Johnny Bench of Cincinnati (as he had in 1970) for MVP honors in the National League.
Chicago Cubs

ring the season, Billy stalks pitchers, and Jenkins
lks batters, but here they are enjoying one of their
orite off-season pursuits, a hunting trip in
wfoundland.
Williams' personal collection

In Billy's baptism at first base August 15, 1973, he leaps in vain for a wild heave as Paul Casanova beats out an infield hit and the Braves swamp the Cubs 15 to 1.

Chicago Tribune

He swings left but writes right, as the Classic Hitter shows an autograph-seeking hospitalized veteran.

Veterans Administration

Here's the Billy Williams grip on the coveted Silver Bat, awarded for his 1972 National League Batting Championship. His average of .333 was highest in the majors and made him only the third Cub in history to win the batting title.

Chicago Cubs

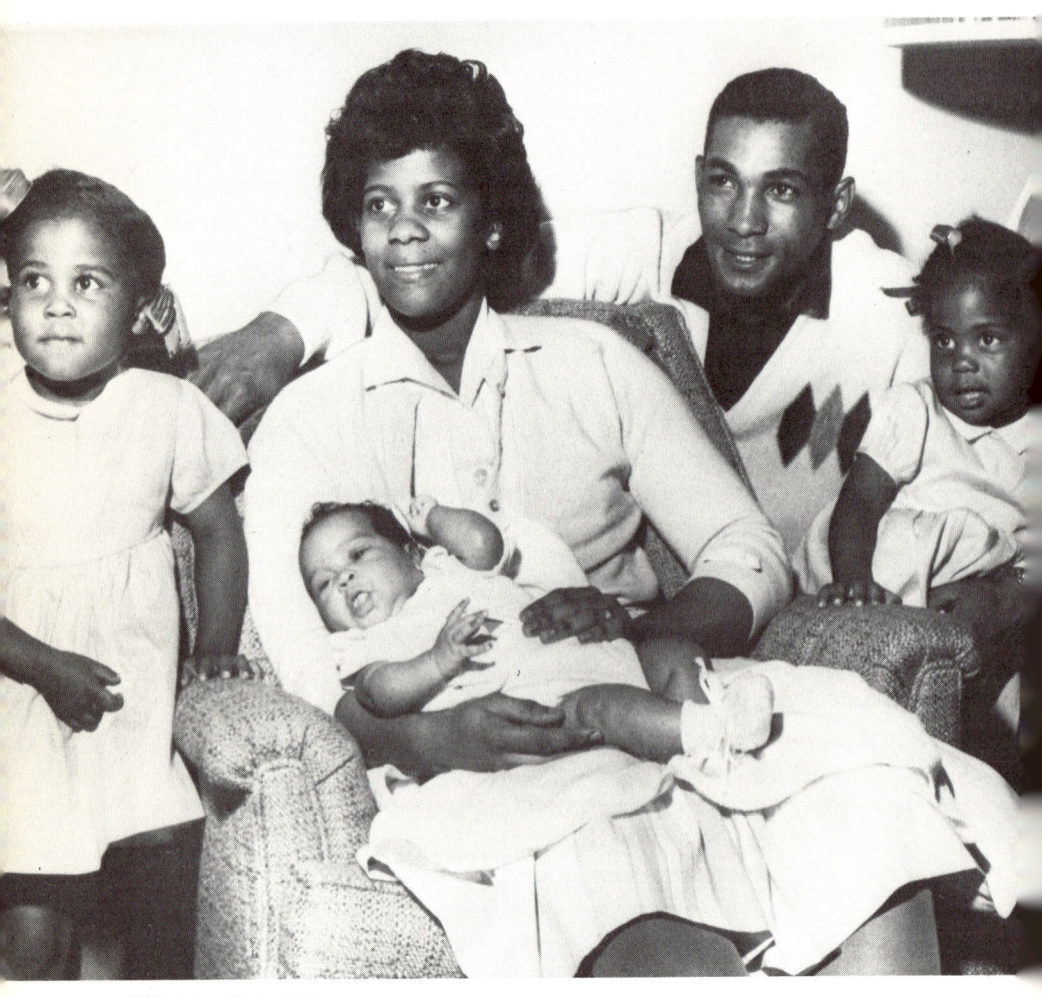

Billy's family in 1964. With Shirley and Billy, left to right, are Valarie, three years old, Julia, seven weeks, and Nina, two. A fourth daughter, Sandra, was born in 1968.

Chicago Tribune

On "Billy Williams Day," hunting and fishing pal Ferguson Jenkins gives Billy puppy from trainer Rich Milke. Quickly named "Lucky 26," the dog is now a husky 85 pounds and excellent at flushing out birds for Billy on one of his frequent hunting jaunts.

Chicago Cubs

Billy catches one right off his shoetops, making sure Maury Wills won't be on to steal a base.

Chicago Tribune

Billy celebrates his 34th birthday with two homers against Padres June 15, 1972. Here, manager Leo Durocher gives him "five" as he heads for home and his greatest season—National League Batting Champion with a .333 average, 37 homers, and 122 RBIs.
Chicago Cubs

National League President Warren Giles presents trophy to Billy on behalf of the Chicago Cubs, in commemoration of "Billy Williams Day," June 29, 1969 and in recognition of Billy's setting a new league record for consecutive games. Billy broke Stan Musial's string of 895 on his "day" and went on to make it 1,117 straight.
Chicago Cubs

The Early Durocher Era

How could a sometimes suave, glowing, intriguing, or captivating, sometimes snarling, caustic, irascible, belligerent, glib, biting, or grating man like Leo Durocher *help* but inject a gargantuan flood of color, clamor, and excitement into the somewhat subdued, sedate surroundings of beautiful Wrigley Field? And Chicago ate it up.

If anyone rates the word "inimitable," it's Durocher. He'd feuded and fought with the best of them—including Babe Ruth, Frankie Frisch, Casey Stengel, and the commissioner of baseball. As their captain, he coined the phrase the "Gashouse Gang" for the hell-for-leather Cardinals of the 1930s.

Durocher's raucous, running battles with the little, hard-boiled umpire, Jocko Conlan, have become treasures of baseball lore. During one of his diatribes, Leo asked Conlan if he thought anybody ever paid to see Jocko umpire.

"No," Conlan snapped back, "but if you don't shut up and get back in the dugout, anybody who paid to see *you* is gonna be disappointed!"

Most everybody knows that the expression "nice guys finish last" is generally attributed to "Lippy," the name given to him by Will Wedge, baseball writer for the *New York Sun* when Durocher was a rookie shortstop with the New York Yankees. Whether he ever actually said those exact words is a matter for debate, but the same idea is reflected in this statement allegedly made by Leo: "I've known a lot of nice guys, but I never saw a nice guy who was any good when you needed him. The nice guys are all in the second division."

According to Edwin Pope in *Baseball's Greatest Managers:* "Any final analysis of Durocher as a manager is not difficult if one can block out the vision of his overwhelming personality.

"He was superb at keeping 'hot' players going, but impatient and subsequently mediocre at handling youngsters.

"He could do more than most with a fast team that lent itself to his hit-and-run, squeeze-play system.

"On the other hand, he got less than most managers out of innately sluggish squads."

Nevertheless, Leo the Lion was named Manager of the Year three times by *The Sporting News*—in 1939, when he led the Dodgers to third place from sixth the previous year; in 1941, when his Brooklyn "Bums" won their first pennant in 21 years; and in 1954, when he piloted the New York Giants to the pennant and the World Championship.

He worked miracles—and saw them worked against him. The 1941 Dodgers lost the World Series to the Yankees. His '51 Giants made one of the most stirring stretch drives in history. On July 20 that season, the Giants had lost four straight and slipped to third place behind the Cards. From then on, they won 52 of their next 70 games, including a 16-game winning streak, and 37 victories in their last 44 games, forcing the famous three-game playoff against the Dodgers. In the World Series, Casey Stengel's Yankees whipped the Giants four games to two.

On the other hand, Durocher's last championship team, the 1954 Giants, astonished millions—not necessarily because they beat the Cleveland Indians, who supposedly had the most unbeatable pitching corps in baseball and who had set the all-time American League record by posting 111 victories (only 43 losses). The startling fact was that, sparked by the pinch-hitting of Dusty Rhodes, Leo's Giants crushed the Indians in four straight games.

So this was the Durocher who swept into the Cub picture, effervescent with enthusiasm as boss man after four years as coach with the Dodgers, during which time there were periodic rumors about his second-guessing of manager Walter Alston, especially in two of the years Los Angeles ended up in second place.

With him came some characteristic "Durocher-isms" that quickly became part of the Windy City's baseball vocabulary—"he came to play," "he's some kind of ballplayer," "no way," and one that was to haunt him later—"Back Up the Truck!"

And in an early press conference, bubbling with confidence, he made the remark few will ever let him forget.

"This isn't an eighth-place club!" he exclaimed. The 1966 Cubs sank into tenth place, the sorriest record ever suffered by a Cub team—59 wins, 103 losses.

But it would take more than that to demoralize the man who got himself fired by owner Larry MacPhail the same day the Dodgers won the '41 pennant. With about 30,000 fans waiting at Grand Central Station to welcome their conquering heroes, Durocher ordered the train to skip a stop on the way. It turned out that MacPhail and Branch Rickey were *waiting* at that stop to hop aboard and personally congratulate the "Bums." Of course, the hot-tempered, unpredictable MacPhail rehired the fired Leo the next day.

In Durocher's freshman year, the Cubs as usual were no "patsies" at the plate. But the pitching staff took an even bigger nose-dive than in '65. Rookie and part-time college student Ken Holtzman, a southpaw Leo hailed as another Koufax, topped the staff with 11 wins. Another newcomer, Bill Hands, was 8–13, Koonce 5–5, and Ellsworth, who had won 22 in '63, *lost 22*.

But Leo found a real "sleeper" in an April trade with Philadelphia that brought relief pitcher Ferguson Jenkins along with outfielder Adolfo Phillips for Larry Jackson and Bob Buhl. Fergie captured the hearts of Cub fans in his debut. And what a debut! Coming out of the bullpen, he held the Dodgers scoreless for $5\frac{1}{3}$ innings. The lanky six-foot-five Canadian also clouted a homer and a single to drive in the only two runs that won the game.

Watching him, Durocher no doubt got to thinking, "No way this guy's a relief pitcher. He's my kinda starter!" So the same man who had switched outfielder Whitey Lockman to first and centerfielder Bobby Thomson to third back in 1951 converted Jenkins from reliever to starter. In nine starts, Fergie won six; he also picked up five saves, and posted the best ERA among Cub pitchers, 3.31.

The Cubs also trotted out their best all-round catcher since Hartnett, acquiring Randy Hundley from San Francisco in a deal that also included Hands in exchange for Don Landrum and Lindy McDaniel. The "Rebel," from Martinsville, Virginia, hit 19 homers, set a new league record for most games by a rookie backstop—149—and, for a catcher who'd had only eight starts before joining the club, displayed a rare, "take-charge" attitude to get the most out of the hurlers.

With Banks off to a slow start, winding up with 15 homers and 75 RBIs, Santo, Beckert, and Williams carried the brunt of the hitting attack. Glenn, with the second highest batting average—.287—on the club, led the team in hits, 188. Ronnie had 175 hits, with 30 homers, and the team's highest average—.312; Billy, who had 179 hits, with 29 homers, ended up with a .276 average.

If Jimmy (the "Greek") Snyder ever has time, he might figure the odds first on a player hitting for "the cycle"—a single, a double, a triple, and a homer in the same game—and then the odds of cranking them out in that *exact order*. Whatever figures he'd come up with, they'd have to be astronomical. Billy accomplished this extremely rare and astounding feat—and off three different pitchers—in the second game of a doubleheader at St. Louis, July 17, 1966.

He had two hits and a pair of RBIs in the opener, which the Cubs lost. The Cards tied the game 3 to 3 on a wild pitch by Billy Hoeft in the 10th and won it in the 11th on a lead-off homer by Curt Flood off Bob Hendley's first pitch in relief.

Williams made sure there'd be no such nonsense in game two. Billy singled in the first off Art Mahaffey, doubled off Don Dennis in the third, and rifled a triple off Dennis in the fifth. In the seventh, lefty Hal Woodeshick was on the mound. As Billy rummaged in the rack for his bat, Durocher told him, "Go out there and hit one out." Always easy to get along with, Billy followed orders. What made his accomplishment more remarkable was that his round-tripper came in the Cardinals' new Busch Memorial Stadium, where, Torre claims, "Hitting a homer is like trying to drive one out of the Grand Canyon."

Quite a day for Billy—six hits in nine at-bats, four RBIs, and four runs scored. Only five previous Cubs had ever hit for the cycle.

At the end of '66, Billy's string of consecutive-game appearances reached 493. But what gave him equal satisfaction was his vastly improved throwing. He ranked among the top three in the league for double-plays by an outfielder.

The names of the players who came and went during Durocher's first turbulent years at the helm would probably fill a column or two in the phone book, but Leo was starting to build "my kind of team."

From tenth in 1966, the Cubs vaulted all the way to third in 1967, the first time they finished out of the second division since '47. And when they kept clawing and hustling among the leaders—even holding first place for a few hours and tied for first July 24—some delirious followers dreamed of a miracle a la the Philadelphia "Whiz Kids," who, finishing 16 games behind the leaders in 1949, won the pennant in 1950. Why not? The really impossible had happened before. What about George Stallings' "Miracle Braves" of 1914? Dead last on July 19, 11 games off the pace, the Braves stormed on to win the pennant. Not in a photo-finish, or even in a tight battle in the stretch—but by a 10½-game margin. And then, in probably the greatest upset in Series history, they not only beat Connie Mack's Philadelphia A's, but they won four straight, the first team to do so.

(A doctor told Stallings he had an unusually bad heart, and asked him if he knew of any way to account for it. "Bases on balls, you bleeping so-and-so . . . bases on balls!" the fiery Stallings told him.)

Cub fans began clambering out of their cocoons—or wherever else they'd hidden during the dreary second-division days. Home attendance swelled to 978,000, an increase of more than 340,000 over the previous year. It was back in fashion to *admit* being a Cub fan, especially when confronting any sassy, smug fan of the White Sox, then headed by Durocher's old pal, Eddie Stanky.

And the fans had something to cheer about. They could happily babble about how the Wrigleys tied for second in the league for pitching efficiency, were first in fielding, tops in runs scored (702), second in RBIs (642), and were shut out the fewest times (6).

Jenkins bloomed into a superb starter. His 20 wins were bettered only by Mike McCormick of the Giants, with 22. He was second in the NL with 236 strike-outs—the most ever by a Cub—and his 20 complete games topped the league.

Holtzman was fantastic. Pitching mostly on weekends on leave from the Army, he won nine games, losing none. Young Rich Nye was 13–10, Joe Niekro 10–7, Hands 7–8, and reliever Chuck ("Twiggy") Hartenstein 9–5 with 10 saves, and Ray Culp 8–11.

Billy's broad contributions to the team became increasingly obvious in '67. And yet, he could still carry his press clippings in a match box, especially since news media outside the Chicagoland area virtually ignored him. Figures showed he'd been the Cubs' deadliest clutch hitter with a .419 average, and .347 in advancing runners in the clutch. No platooning necessary for the whiplasher from Whistler, either; he hit lefties and righties almost exactly the same percentage wise.

On August 3, Billy appeared in his 600th consecutive game. By coincidence, on that same date, a column by Bill Gleason in the *Chicago Sun-Times* showed that Billy's other talents weren't going entirely unnoticed.

"There is much about Williams that escapes the eye. Fans tend to think of him as Billy the Hitter. They seldom mention Williams the Fielder. It is as though he were a one-dimensional ballplayer, a sort of Smoky Burgess of the younger set.

"There probably is no outfielder in the majors who has improved as much as Williams in the last three or four years. Billy has made himself a competent defensive player by working hard at that phase of his trade. And he has done it as he does everything else. Quietly."

Gleason went on to mention that according to coach Joe Amalfitano, Billy had developed a much more accurate, stronger throwing arm, and that Joey said: "Billy is one of the very few hitters whose fielding isn't affected when his batting average drops. He still gives you a good job in the outfield."

Then, quoting Durocher, "Sure, he throws better. Billy does everything better. He's improved like hell since I saw him the first time. He's thinking ahead. He knows what he's doing. This year I'd say he has thrown to the right base 99 percent of the time. I wish all our guys were thinking ahead the way he is."

Meanwhile, Chicago Cub diehards again were cursing the Broglio-Brock deal that let "the big one get away" to the Cardinals. Brock had his greatest year since '64. In the World Series, between Boston and St. Louis, Lou went wild. He helped the Cards take the championship in seven games, blasting Red Sox pitching for 12 hits, including two doubles, a triple, and a home run for a .414 average, and stole seven bases.

Lou could now *really* give his pal Billy the needle if Williams happened to ask Brock to see his World Series ring. Lou'd just flash his impish grin and reply, "Sure, Billy ... which one?"

After the upward surge in '67, anyone but the most cockeyed optimist had to wonder whether the Cubs "were for real." That question was put to the acid test in 1968, the "Year of the Pitcher."

Suspicions arose that somebody had removed the rabbit from the baseball throughout the majors. Team batting averages plunged to the lowest ever, to a skimpy .237. There were more shutouts and more 1 to 0 games. There were also fewer homers: 300 fewer than in '67, 700 fewer than in '66, and over 1,000 fewer than in '62.

It was the year Detroit's pitcher-playboy Denny McLain won 31 and lost only 6—surpassing Dizzy Dean's 30–7 string that had been tops since 1934. Flame-throwing Cardinal Bob Gibson yielded the stingiest ERA ever for a righthander, 1.12. Jenkins of the Cubs won 20 games but was hard to find in the cluster of top winners. Six other NL hurlers excelled. Juan Marichal of the Giants had 26 wins, Gibson 22, while Nelson Briles of St. Louis, Chris Short of the Phils, and Jerry Koosman of the Mets all won 19.

Then, too, Fergie could have qualified for the "Unluckiest Man of the Year" award had there been one. Even though he was the only Cub to win 20 or more games for two straight seasons since Lon Warneke in '34-'35 and topped his own club strike-out record with 260, he lost five games by scores of 1 to 0. Moreover, the king-sized righthander whose trademark is to run, not walk, to the mound, had the misfortune to start nine games in which the Cubs were shut out!

The Cubs blasted more home runs off the stingy pitchers than any other National League club, with 130—32 by the seemingly ageless Banks, 30 by Billy, and 26 by Santo. They ranked second in the league in RBIs (576), second in runs (612), third in triples (43), and second in total bases (2,008). They also led the NL clubs in fielding.

Billy wasted little time chalking up new milestones. In an icebox of a Crosley Field at Cincinnati April 11, he lined a three-run homer off Mel Queen—number 199 in his career—and then clipped Bill Kelso with a solo shot for his 200th. At the end of the year, his fifth straight season without missing a game, he rose to third place among all-time Cub homer hitters, with 228.

On May 11, Billy broke Richie Ashburn's record of 694 consecutive games for an outfielder, and on June 18, he appeared in his 718th game, to establish the new Cub record for longevity, moving ahead of Banks.

Sunday September 8 was a long-awaited day for Cub management. Some 15,800 fans showed up to push attendance past the million mark, the greatest season turnout since 1952. Too bad more weren't on hand—Billy's bat had been smoking. He'd hit safely in ten straight games and pounded a pair of round-trippers in each of two other Sunday contests. In the second inning of this game, he gave one of Woodie Fryman's deliveries a good, long Sunday drive into the seats for three RBIs and tagged another off Jeff James in the fifth. And by the eighth inning, he'd bombed Philly pitching for a double and a single as well, giving him 4-for-4. But next time up, he flied to center.

That was the best pitch I got all day, Billy recalled. *But I saw it so good, I tried to kill it and jammed myself. Guess if you want that fifth hit, you've just got to go up there and swing normally.*

Following a round-tripper by Banks in the same game, Billy, grinning and making sure Ernie could hear him, commented:

Ernie may go on forever. He conserves all his energy by hitting homers . . . 472 times is a lot of times to go round the bases without runnin' hard!

After the game, Cub batting coach Pete Reiser said, "Billy's tired, but he won't admit it. He never complains, never gets angry, at least visibly, and he hits the ball hard almost every time." Overhearing him, Billy chimed in:

The only time I get tired is when I stop to think I've been in 803 games in a row.

Fortunately, Monday was a day off. The Mets were in on Tuesday, September 10, but it was such a tooth-chattering day, only 1,501 fans witnessed Billy's blistering performance. Against Dick Selma, he smacked a two-run homer, blasted another with a man on, and finally, sent one of Nolan Ryan's smokers out of sight. That last one did it: Billy had tied the major league mark for most homers—five—in two straight games. It had happened only seven times before. Joe Adcock of the Braves had been the last one to do it, in 1954. What's more, Billy had rapped seven hits in his last nine at-bats, ten in his last fourteen.

After one of Billy's circuit clouts, Kessinger, nudging Banks on the bench, said to him: "Better wake up—he's gonna catch you." With that, Banks hit the first ball pitched to him for his 31st homer of the year to remain two ahead of Williams.

Durocher just shook his head. "That Banks is the damnedest man I've ever seen. His reflexes should be getting slow at his age [37]. But his are speeding up." Durocher threw up his hands. "And every time he gets on first, he's lookin' for the steal sign. Can you beat that!"

About his trio of four-baggers, Billy confessed:

The first two homers weren't really hit that well. But, that's a good sign for me because I was jammed on both of them and was still able to stay with the pitch. That day off helped too. I felt strong today.

Billy's binge lifted his runs batted in total to 94, highest in the league at the time. He increased his RBIs to 98, but "snake-bit" the last two weeks of the season, he couldn't buy another. McCovey, meanwhile, drove in ten runs to pace the league with 105.

That figure alone proved that pitching was more brutal than

ever—it was the lowest tally to win an RBI championship in the National League since the "dead-ball" era. Santo tied with Billy for second, with 98. But "Mr. Smooth," as George Langford called Billy, beat out his Alabama "neighbor" Aaron for the league high in total bases. He had 321 to Henry's 302.

"Everything about Billy Williams is smooth," wrote Langford, "from the easy, flowing rhythm of his batting swing to his calm, cool temperament and quiet voice. Yet, when the Cubs' 'Mr. Smooth' makes contact with a baseball, all the gentleness and serenity is shattered. The Cubs argue Williams even hits into the 'hardest outs' in the league."

Billy was third in the league in slugging, with .500, while leading the club with 30 doubles, 8 triples, and 7 sacrifice flies. He was second in Cub homers with 30. Ron, Ernie, and Billy all hit grand-slam homers in '68—and, in a vote among Cub fans, all three were voted "Greatest Cubs Ever," Williams getting the nod over Riggs Stephenson for the leftfield position.

Williams, Santo, and the now-stellar shortstop, Kessinger, played in the first indoor All-Star Game in the Houston Astrodome. Pitching was so overpowering, the Nationals won in the only 1 to 0 game since the series began at Chicago's Comiskey Park in 1933.

A couple of exciting new heroes joined the fold in April. From Los Angeles came outfielder Jim Hickman, one of the original Mets and the first on that team to hit three homers in a game, and ice-blooded reliever Phil Regan.

Nicknamed the "Vulture" by Koufax because he finished off so many rivals, Regan had umpires asking themselves, "Does he or doesn't he" . . . throw the spitter? And they frequently frisked him trying to find some "greasy kid's stuff." Despite the harassment, he was 10–5 and earned the most saves in the majors, 25 (21 with Chicago), and his second "Fireman of the Year" Award.

Hickman came up to the Cubs late in May, and though his batting average was only .223, he demonstrated plenty of power-hitting ability. Pinch-hitter Willie Smith and ex-Brave Al Spangler quickly became favorites too, and the scrappy-go-lucky, sparkling second baseman, Beckert, really came into his own.

Glenn had the league's longest hitting streak (27 games), led the Cubs in batting average (.294), topped the league in runs scored (98), and was the NL's "Toughest to Strike Out" for his third straight year, with only 20 whiffs in 643 at-bats. He won the Golden Glove as the league's best defensive second baseman, and both major wire services saluted him by selecting him for the honorary

All-Star team, while the Chicago Baseball Writers Association named him the city's Player of the Year.

Williams made the best showing of his career in the voting for Most Valuable Player. Earning only six points in '64 and 21 in '65, he received 48 points in '68, eighth among National Leaguers. For the first time since the Baseball Writers Association of America took over the annual selections in 1931, the MVPs in both leagues were pitchers—Gibson of the Cards in the National, McLain of the Tigers in the American. Each also received the Cy Young Award.

Meanwhile, the 1968 Cubs, watching the fall classic on TV—a seesaw battle between St. Louis and Detroit—entertained high hopes that the Cards and/or Tigers would be watching *them* in the 1969 World Series.

1969—The Big Year

The 1969 Cubs whipped their fans into a frenzy right from the opening day, extra-inning game against Philadelphia at Wrigley Field. There were two out and one on in the bottom of the 11th with the Phils leading, 6 to 5, when pinch-hitter Willie Smith swung the bat.

Up in the WGN Radio booth, exuberant, excitable Vince Lloyd sprang to his feet, nearly knocking over his play-by-play partner Lou Boudreau, and began bellowing, "Willie hits one! High! Deep rightfield! This *could* be! . . . This *is* a home run! *A home run for Willie Smith and the Cubs win! Holy Mackerel!*"

Right next door, in the WGN-TV booth, Jack Brickhouse was torturing his tonsils too—shouting his famous, jubilant "Hey! Hey!" as he does every time the Cubs hit a homer.

The pet expressions of three of the radio and TV "voices" on Cub broadcasts—Brickhouse's, Lloyd's, and Boudreau's, who usually echoed Vince's reference to a great play or a real wallop with a soft, sincere "No doubt about it"—inspired advertising man Irv Haag to write a song about the Cubs back in '67. Several years later, Haag, who also wrote lyrics for musical radio commercials, asked composer John Frigo to set it to music.

A highly talented musician, composer, and arranger, Frigo—also a staunch Cub fan—wrote the music shortly before the '69 season began. The composers gave The Chicago Cubs' Song, "Hey, Hey! Holy Mackerel!" to the club as a gift from two die-hard Cub fans, though it was never the official Chicago Cub song.

"Hey, Hey! Holy Mackerel!" was played after every Cub victory for the crowds at Wrigley Field. It blared on radio, TV, and jukeboxes and was spinning virtually nonstop at Ray's Bleachers—a cozy, noisy, neighborhood tavern in the shadow of Wrigley Field's leftfield bleachers and headquarters for the first famous, then infamous "Bleacher Bums." Records and sheet music were snatched up by fans throughout the Midwest, deliriously happy when the Cubs moved far ahead of the pack.

The song boomed from the loudspeaker in the Cub clubhouse— "Hey, Hey! Holy Mackerel! No doubt about it!... The Cubs have come to play... The Cubs are on their way!—Hey, Hey!" it went—was sung by the team and the "Bleacher Bums" on road trips, and was publicized by local and out-of-town papers, as well as publications like *The Sporting News*. The *Chicago Tribune* ran a picture of a cute dog, with Cub cap and pennant, and the caption "Hey, Hey! Howly Mackerel!"

The day after the Cubs' pulse-quickening triumph in the first game of the season in Wrigley Field Billy tattooed the pitchers mercilessly to tie another major league record—four doubles off four different hurlers, pacing an 11 to 3 rout of the Phils. Two were opposite-field blows, all off sliders and curves—a hitting barrage not seen in the senior loop since 1954. After the game, partly joking but mostly in earnest, Billy told reporters who were interviewing him:

I'm a label man. They always label a player when he first comes up to the majors, and I was labeled quiet. You say I haven't gotten the publicity I deserve over the years, and that I'm an underrated ballplayer. Well, that's up to you guys. I can't write about myself.

Then Banks jumped into the confab. "It's too bad that a lot of things Billy does are overlooked. He's a tremendous asset to the team. He gets so many big hits, makes so many great plays, and yet he's the most underestimated player in the game. He loves the game as much as any of us. He just has a different way of expressin' it. Some guys like me go around hollerin', but he quietly does it all."

Thus launched, the Cubs really went into orbit, winning 9 of their next 10 games and 32 of their first 48. The scripts were often thrillers and featured a wide cast of heroes. In May, Banks sank San Diego with seven RBIs as Dick Selma won a 19 to 0 three-hit shutout, the Cubs' third straight shutout. Also that month, Holtzman chalked up 33 scoreless innings in a 7 to 0 whitewash of the Dodgers, and Ernie belted his 12th career grand-slam homer. On May 31, Chicago led Pittsburgh by 7½ games, and the Mets by 9.

By June 10, Holtzman had become the first major league pitcher to win ten games. Five days later, shortstop Kessinger completed his 54th errorless game, a new major league mark.

On Sunday, June 29, it looked as if every fan who ever rooted for the Cubs was trying to squeeze into Wrigley Field. They'd come to roar their affection for the "toothpick" from Whistler, who once wept, frustrated and heartsick, in the tunnel behind the Cubs' dugout, after being benched his rookie year for failing to do what he thought he'd do best—hit a baseball.

Today he'd weep again. An overflow, standing-room-only crowd of 41,060, the season's largest, refused to let a heavy morning rain keep them from celebrating "Billy Williams Day" and watching a big doubleheader against the Cardinals. The fans knew too that they would see a brand-new page go into National League history.

Billy was on the threshold of breaking Stan Musial's National League record of 895 consecutive games. When he was asked by columnist Robert Markus of the *Chicago Tribune* what it takes to play that many games in a row, Billy answered:

Desire and ability. You have to want to be in there every day to help the team. And you have to be a good-enough hitter so they're not going to take you out against lefthanders.

Wrote Markus: "There can be little doubt about Billy's desire to play. He has played with hurts. A bruised shin, courtesy of a Mets pitcher's fastball, in New York. An aching back from sleeping on a soft mattress in Atlanta. And, of course, more recently, a painful instep after fouling a ball onto his foot in Cincinnati." Markus also pointed out the Sweet Swinger's success against southpaw hurlers. To this comment, Billy modestly replied:

I saw a lot of lefthanded pitching in Triple-A ball, and quite a bit of it up here. The trouble with a lot of lefthanded hitters is that they don't see enough lefthanded pitching to get used to it. A righthanded hitter will see a lot more righthanded pitchers. Lefthanded or righthanded, it takes a while to get used to pitchers' motions.

In his column that Sunday in the *Tribune*, Banks also paid tribute to his teammate: "The most fascinating thing about Billy is that despite all his records and tremendous success, it hasn't changed him as a man. He's still the same guy he was the day he walked into beautiful Wrigley Field for the first time, back in 1959. Billy often says, 'I want to do the best job possible each day I play and each season I play'."

Billy tied Musial's record with the first game. With the second, he became the new NL endurance champion, having played in 896 games without a miss. Only two other major leaguers surpassed

Billy's consecutive-game streak: the Yankees' Lou Gehrig, with 2,130, and the Boston Braves' Deacon Scott, who also saw some service with the Yankees, with 1,307.

Signs like "Win Two for Billy," "Trump the Cards, Billy!" and "Give 'Em the Billy Club, Billy" were sprinkled throughout the stands. But for 7½ innings of the first game, there wasn't much hitting to yell about. Gibson and Jenkins were locked in a scoreless tie. The crowd came to life, saluting the guest of honor each time he stepped into the batter's box. And in the bottom of the eighth, Billy came through. As he does so often, he swung the bat behind his shoulders and flexed his back, then pat-pat-patted the top of his batting helmet, and glared at Gibson. "Hoot" reared back and fired. Billy electrified the crowd with a whistling double to lead off. The crowd went bananas when Banks followed with a single to send Billy in for the first run of the game and raised a still more boisterous hullabaloo when Willie Smith shot a two-run homer into the seats to ice it for Fergie.

The ceremonies honoring Billy began with a deafening standing ovation for the Cub leftfielder. Billy, his wife Shirley, daughters Valarie, Nina, Sandra, and Julie watched and listened with wide, sometimes misty, eyes. The compliments and cheers just kept coming. So did the gifts.

Among them were a new car from the Cubs; a washer and dryer combination; a pool table; a watch; checks for the Billy Williams scholarship at Mobile County Training School from WGN and the Chicago Chapter of the Baseball Writers Association of America; numerous other miscellaneous contributions and proceeds from the advance sale of "Billy Williams Day" buttons; a deep-sea fishing rod from the local baseball writers, who share a great fondness for Billy; and, wheeled out last, a boat and motor from his teammates.

Choked up, toweling away tears from his eyes as the gifts were presented, Billy's turn finally came at the field microphone. He thanked God for giving him the ability to play baseball, and expressed his deep gratitude to all who'd made his years in Chicago so rewarding.

I got emotionally upset up there when they were presenting me everything. Nothing like this had ever happened to me before. The standing ovations, the applause really got to me. I really didn't know quite what to say. Before the second game started, I kept telling myself to simmer down, cool it, but I was still nervous.

The Cubs wasted no time putting the crowd back into a hysterical mood, bombing Cardinal Jim Grant with four runs in the first inning of the second game. Paul Popovich, Williams, and Santo hung one run on the board with three straight singles. Then Ernie repaid Billy—who had homered on "Ernie Banks Day"—with a three-run blast into the riotous "Bleacher Bum" section in leftfield. From then on, almost every Cub contributed to the celebration, among them pitcher Dick Selma, whose voluntary duties in '69 included leading the "Bleacher Bums'" cheering section. The former Met gave up only four hits.

And Billy kept thanking the huge turnout with his bat. He doubled in the second, tripled in the fifth, and hit another three-bagger in the sixth. Santo had a double and a homer to drive in five runs. Popovich doubled, and Hundley parked one in the seats.

With the Cubs leading 12 to 1, Billy, already 4-for-4, came up for his final appearance. Somebody reminded him that all he needed for another "cycle" was a homer. Since they were that far in front, Billy admitted he was going for the distance. You can guess the rest. He struck out. But as he tossed his batting helmet aside, the crowd rose for another thunderous standing ovation.

I guess it was my day. We hadn't won a doubleheader all year, and here they give me a doubleheader! Still smiling, shaking his head, trying to believe all this had happened to him, Billy went on: *I had to repay all those people some way. Never before had so many people paid so much attention to me. Radio, television, pictures, interviews, handshakes . . . I never realized so many folks knew about this little boy from Alabama. I've got to be the luckiest man in baseball. No injuries, no long slumps, just good health to let me play every day. I'm happy the way everything came out, but I'm happier that it's all over, and I can go back to being just plain Billy Williams.*

As part of the festivities on "Billy Williams Day," a large band played a stirring arrangement of "Hey, Hey! Holy Mackerel!" with much of the crowd joining the "Bleacher Bums" in a giant sing-along. They had little reason not to believe every word of it, particularly the lines, "No doubt about it! The Cubs are on their way!—Hey, Hey!" By the end of June, the Cubs had won 49 of their first 76 games and led the Eastern Division by seven games over the Mets, who had slipped past Pittsburgh into second place.

In July, they had a chance to spurt away and become virtually uncatchable—scheduled for six head-on clashes with the Mets in nine days. Jenkins pitched a one-hit masterpiece in the first game at Shea Stadium July 8 and was holding a 3 to 1 lead when the Mets came to bat in the last of the ninth. Then, catastrophe. Rookie centerfielder Don Young couldn't handle two flyballs, one a blooping single, the other a drive to the wall. Billy recalled the game.

After Don missed the first ball—he was trying too hard—I got him to one side and told him "You can only give 100 percent. You can't do any more." But next time, he must have had in his mind the thought "Wherever this ball's going, I'm gonna catch it." If the ball had been hit over the fence, he would have tried to catch it. He made a fantastic play to try and get it but banged into the wall and the ball bounced out of his glove.

The Mets greedily accepted the extra at-bats and rallied to win, 4 to 3. In the clubhouse after the disheartening turn of events, Leo the Lion roared and Santo steamed—spouting off in earshot of reporters, blaming Young for the defeat. The incident was blown sky-high.

Among the bitter words attributed to Leo were: "That kid in centerfield. Two little flyballs. He just stands there watching one and he gives up on the other. It's a disgrace." And the papers quoted Santo: "He had a bad day at bat, so he's got his head down. He's worrying about his average and not the team. Alright, he can keep his head down and keep right on going—out of sight for all I care. We don't need that sort of thing."

But there's one story the writers didn't get. Billy revealed what happened the next day after reading about the furor.

I came downstairs and Santo's sitting in the lobby, and he's looking sad 'cause Santo's the type of guy who says a lot of things he doesn't mean. I sat down and we got talking. I've been playing with Ron since 1958 in San Antonio, and I know a lot of his ways. When a person first meets him, the impression is he's a hard-nosed guy who looks like he doesn't want to be bothered. But I think if you'd get to know Ron, you'd like him. He's an aggressive-type ballplayer and he goes out and wants to do the job so bad that sometimes he winds up not doing it.

At times when he comes into the clubhouse, he might want to make a statement. So once in a while, I kind of go over it with him and say, "Do you think this is right?"

Anyway, down there in the hotel lobby, I said to him, "Why don't you call all the writers in and have a press conference. Tell 'em you said things you didn't really mean because of the heat of the pennant race."

Shortly afterward, the remorseful Cub captain contacted the writers and made a public apology to Young.

Buoyed by their dramatic victory, the Mets—and especially starting pitcher Tom Seaver—came out ten feet tall for the next game. Young was on the bench, replaced in centerfield by another rookie, Jimmy Qualls.

Going into the game, Seaver had won 13 of 16 decisions, and proceeded to prove why. He completely mystified the Cub batters and retired 24 straight. Ironically, Seaver himself drove in the only run he would have needed after errors by Santo and Kessinger. In the top of the ninth, he threw out Hundley trying a surprise bunt. And now he was just two outs away from achieving only the ninth perfect game since 1900. But Qualls earned the undying hatred of the breathless Metso-maniacs by lining a clean single to left center. Seaver had to settle for a one-hitter, winning 4 to 0, Holtzman taking the loss. The Cubs salvaged the third game, 6 to 2.

Seaver was practically untouchable again the next time the two clubs met, on July 14, to open a three-game set at Wrigley Field. But so was Bill Hands. With the game still scoreless in the sixth, the Cubs jumped on one of the few opportunities Seaver gave them all day. Kessinger bunted for a hit to lead off, then Beckert hit the next pitch toward second, putting Don in scoring position for Williams. Billy also hit to the opposite field, over short, to send Kessinger home. That was the winning run. Hands shut out the Mets the rest of the way.

After the game, Seaver said he was amazed the Cubs hit either of the pitches. About the game-winner by Billy, he shrugged: "It was a good pitch, but Williams fought it off. He hit it off his fists."

But the next day, the Mets rebounded, winning 5 to 4, and also gave a sneak preview of the preposterous miracle to come. First, Al Weis, who'd hit only one homer in four years, hit his second, to give the Mets their fourth run. Then, Ken Boswell, who had only three homers all season, put one out for the winning run. The real killer, though, came in an eighth-inning Cub rally. Kessinger opened with a single and Beckert rammed a "sure hit" right up the middle—except that Boswell unexplainably was in perfect position to grab the ball and erase both runners on a fast double-play. Thus, when Billy blasted Gary Gentry's next pitch far over the centerfield wall, it was worth only one run and not three, which would have won the game.

New York flexed newly found muscles to win the next day too, 9 to 5, Weis throwing fresh iodine into the cut by sending another one out of the park—his last for the season.

So instead of moving further out front, the Cubs suffered four games in the important loss column and played only one game over .500 for the month. The Mets, meanwhile, won 12 of their first 17 in July, including seven straight from top contenders. But they finished the month with a four-game losing streak, Houston humiliating them three times—16 to 3, 11 to 5, and 2 to 0.

On July 31, the Cubs were still six games ahead of the Mets. And to help swell the rising tide of pennant fever, the Cubs were winning the kind of games they used to lose. On July 28, for example, they beat the Giants' pitching ace, Juan Marichal, who had won every game he pitched in Wrigley Field since 1966, Billy banging out the hit that chased in the winning run.

In addition to their final game in July, the Cubs won nine of the first ten in August. The superstitious among the fans may have considered it a bad omen on August 13 when the new expansion club, San Diego, turned a hot smash by Billy into a lightninglike triple-play. Still, the Cubs did win, 4 to 2, and standings the next day showed them 8½ games ahead of St. Louis, who had moved into second, and 9½ ahead of the Mets, who had slipped to third.

After the game on August 19, it would have been considered heresy in Cub Country to express the tiniest doubt that *this* year was the *next* year they were always looking for. Santo homered with two on to give Kenny Holtzman a three-run lead in the first inning, and Kenny had a no-hitter going against Atlanta as he faced Hank Aaron in the seventh. Aaron connected. As the ball started to rise, Vince Lloyd's voice began to sink in the radio booth.

"That baby is hit ... look out. It's way back there in leftfield, Billy Williams's back to the bleachers, back to the corner ... He grabs it! Holy Mackerel!"

Billy had retreated all the way into the farthest corner of the wall where it curves about 70 feet from the foul line and, with his back up against the vines and both hands over his head, managed to snare the ball as it fluttered down, just before it hit the bricks.

Interviewed in August of '73, Aaron recalled the wallop that came so close to bringing him one homer closer to Babe Ruth's record. Hank smiled. "Oh yeah. I remember that one. That was a home run but the wind blew it back into the ballpark. Billy jumped up and made a great catch on the ball. Every ball he gets to, he catches. I've seen him make more good catches in leftfield than any left-fielder I've played against. And Wrigley Field isn't really the easiest place in the world to play those flyballs."

Holtzman bore down and continued to hold the Braves hitless. With two gone in the ninth, he got Hammerin' Hank to ground to second. Beckert, who'd made two sensational stops earlier in the game, gave the crowd heart failure, momentarily bobbling the ball, but then recovered in time to make the final put-out. Over 37,000 happy fans hailed the first Cub no-hitter since Don Cardwell's in 1960 against St. Louis. Oddly, using mostly fastballs, Ken had failed to strike out anybody, and walked three.

The win over the Braves, who went on to capture the Western Division title, put the Cubs 7½ games ahead of the Mets and 9 in front of the Cards. But after they were beaten by the Astros for their ninth straight loss on August 13, the Mets started to become Hodges' "Houdinis," winning 12 of their next 13 games for a torrid pace of 21–10 for the month. The Mets were starting to make their move.

Meanwhile, a big blow-up by Durocher in August may have helped to put a few square wheels on the Cub "pennant express." Leo, who had the reputation of driving a winning team harder than a loser, was determined to use his best men in every position, every game if possible. He rarely went to his bench unless he had to. Dick Dozer of the *Chicago Tribune* unexpectedly caught the Lion's wrath in the clubhouse one day by asking Durocher if he planned to rest the regulars. Instead of answering the question, Leo angrily stopped shaving and stomped away, leading Dozer and the other writers present up to the players, and demanded that he, Dozer, ask *them* that "silly" question.

Billy reminisced about that incident in '69 and commented on other memories of the Durocher Era.

It was really sort of a childish thing. Maybe it would have been better if Leo had taken the players aside and discussed with them whether they were tired, instead of bringing writers in on it. A lot of us were tired but nobody was going to admit it. There was sort of a barrier. When Leo had this ball club, people were actually afraid to go and talk to him. A lot of times, a fella might have been hurt, but wouldn't go up and tell him he didn't want to play that game. I think a lot of the coaches were afraid to make decisions. They had ideas on working with certain ballplayers, but wouldn't express them. Leo's attitude was "I'm running the ball club, I know what's going on," so they wouldn't express their ideas.

When he first took over the ball club, a lot of the guys knew about Leo from the past, that he was an aggressive-type manager. He got on a few fellas. He got on Kessinger for his fielding. It seems to me he made Kessinger a better ballplayer. At the time, Don wasn't a switch-hitter. He was just hitting from the right side. He made himself a good hitter by switch-hitting, and now he's a better hitter from the left side. Same thing with Popovich. Paul was a right-handed hitter all the way, and he became a switch-hitter under Durocher. It was Leo's suggestion that Fergie go into the starting rotation. And for six years, he really started!

A manager has a team with 25 different personalities, and his responsibility is to seek out the guys who might need a pat on the back rather than a kick in the rear. A big example is Santo. He'd respond to a pat on the back. Then there are the guys you have to yell at.

I think the younger kids felt they had to be perfect all the time, due to the impression Leo gave them in meetings. He's not a manager who'll sit around and wait for a ballplayer to develop. We had several ballplayers who weren't developing as fast as he wanted them to. So eventually he got rid of them. A guy like Oscar Gamble. Leo felt he didn't develop fast enough. Take a fella like Joe Decker. When he got out on the mound, he became a little tight and tense. A guy by the name of Ray Culp. The type of pitcher Culp was he'd throw a ball, then a strike, then another ball, another strike, and usually get to three strikes before four balls. Leo didn't want Ray to pitch that way. He said he was too cautious. But it was kind of hard for Ray to change. Several guys who came through this organization went on to become good ballplayers because other managers weren't impatient.

One time, for example, we needed a pinch-hitter. So Lee Thomas went up to the plate. And Leo said, "I don't know why I sent him up there. He can't hit, he can't field, he can't do anything. Watch him pop up." And Thomas pops up. So the next day we needed a pinch-hitter again, and he told Ted Savage to go up to the plate. And Ted's kind of skeptical about goin' up because he's wondering what Leo would say about him. It really doesn't help a ballplayer sitting on the bench to hear stuff like that. I think he [Leo] would show up one guy and hope the others would learn by example.

Sometimes, kids would ask me to go and talk to Durocher about them. And I'd say, "You go up there and see him. He said his door's always open. Tell him how you feel." But they wouldn't do it. They were afraid.

Despite the surge by the Mets, the Cubs still led by five games as they met the Pirates at Wrigley Field on September 5. That day saw a couple of the most cockeyed twists of any game in any pennant race.

The Pirates started their winningest pitcher, Steve Blass, and he held every Cub hitless except Williams! Billy tied a major league record for getting all of his club's hits in a game and went 4-for-4, including two homers and two doubles as Pittsburgh bombed Chicago, 9 to 2. Stranger still, in five at-bats, Blass also collected four hits, one of them a three-run homer off Holtzman.

Later, reminded about Billy's 12 total bases for the day, Blass said, "I'm glad I didn't have to face him a fifth time. I ran out of pitches." According to Blass, Williams got his doubles on fastballs, his first homer on a change-up curve, and his second on a slider.

Pittsburgh's manager, Larry Shepard, joining in the conversation, said about Billy, "If he isn't the best in the league, I'd like to see who is. And the beautiful thing is that he plays every day."

Blass then threw in a parting shot. "Billy's invited me to his house for the rest of our stay here. He doesn't want anything to happen to me!"

The Cubs weren't laughing. It was their 13th straight loss to Pittsburgh at Wrigley Field. And when the Mets also won, the Cub lead dropped to only four games. In the next two days the Pirates ran their victory string to 15 straight—the final game the real backbreaker. With two out in the ninth, Stargell belted a tape-measure shot way out of the park to tie the score, 5 to 5, and the Bucs won it in the eleventh, 7 to 5. Meanwhile, the onrushing Mets dumped Philadelphia twice, so when the Cubs arrived at Shea Stadium on September 8, they nursed only a 2½-game lead, which the Mets promptly cut down to 1½.

When the Cubs lost their seventh straight game on September 10, the Mets beat Montreal in 12 innings to slip into first place by half a game. It was the first time the Cubs were out of the lead in 155 games. And the Mets never let go.

What a turnabout for a team about which they used to tell jokes like this:

"Hey, did ya hear? The Mets scored 16 runs today!"

"Yeah? Who won the game?"

They didn't walk on water, but then no one *asked* them to. From

September 10 to the end of the season, the Mets won 18 of 23 games. The Cubs won 8 out of 20. There's no question that the Cubs became unglued seemingly all at once in pitching, in defense, and, except for Billy's bat, in hitting. He batted .304 in September while the rest of the team's average was a puny .219 for the month, compared with .253 earlier in the season.

The '69 Mets' pennant drive was unbelievable. How else can you describe a race won by a team that could survive a record-setting 19 strike-outs by the Cardinals' Steve Carlton and still win the game? Or a team that could hold the murderous, free-swinging Pirates scoreless for 18 straight innings, winning both games, 1 to 0, and in both games, a Met pitcher driving in the winning run? And what pitching! The Mets' Tom Seaver won his last ten games in a row, finishing 25–7, the most wins in the majors.

Baseball had seen nothing like it since Durocher's '51 Giants started 13½ games behind Brooklyn and won 37 of their last 44 games to tie the Dodgers and force the historic playoff for the pennant. The Mets won 38 of their last 49 games. The New Yorkers "Mets-merized" the Atlanta Braves in the division playoffs, winning three straight, despite three homers and seven RBIs by Aaron. The "smart money" was on the Orioles to put down the upstarts in the World Series. But after Earl Weaver's American Leaguers unseated them in the opening game, the Mets walloped Baltimore four straight.

Surprisingly, the Cubs, who played only two games over .500 against Eastern Division clubs, held a whopping 46–26 margin over Western Division teams. Unfortunately for the Cubs, their "patsies" weren't there to kick around in the fatal September. All but three games during the month were against Eastern Division clubs. Winning a few more "two-gamers"—that is, a game between close rivals where a win is worth both a full game in the win column and a full game in the loss column—especially in the final month would have helped tremendously also.

Instead, the Cubs lost three of their last four games with the Mets, five out of six to the Pirates, and four out of six to the Cardinals. They even lost three out of four to the Phils and two out of three to the expansion Expos. The Pirate "hex" really hurt too, the Bucs beating the Cubs 11 out of 18. The Mets held the season edge on the Cubs, taking 10 out of 18, while the Cardinals broke even.

Postmortem examinations revealed theories on all sorts of possible reasons for the Cubs' decline—overconfidence, symbolized by Santo's heel-clicking; too many off-field money-making activities by the

Cubs for everybody's benefit in the players' pool; cracking under the pressure of the team's first real pennant race; early season pop-offs about the Mets that led the Cubs to underrate their nemesis; and the unsavory antics of the "Bleacher Bums," which riled up their opponents.

Durocher's failure to rest his regulars was thought by many, including some of the players, to be a major factor in the Cubs' September collapse. As Beckert remarked, "We learned that eight men can't win a pennant. Guys can play every day if they have to, but with today's travel and mixed up schedules, I can't see that a player can be up to his full capability. We tried in '69, but fell apart the last month and a half."

The Cubs got excellent "mileage" out of their established stars, but even as Durocher himself said, maybe they did run out of gas—especially since most of the other clubs were platooning.

In such vital positions as catcher, today's game demands not just a back-up catcher, but a top-quality back-up man. The experience with Randy Hundley is a good example of how the "iron man" philosophy of a manager can seriously harm a ball club. Billy commented on this a few years later:

When Leo was with the ball club, Randy, for example, would go to spring training weighing 195, and he was used in so many ballgames that he weighed about 165 at the end of the season. So it was a case of letting another catcher sit on the bench because you're concentrating on this one man. Then when Randy got hurt [in 1970] *and we had to go to somebody else, the other man wasn't ready. He had experience, but he wasn't ready ... he hadn't played all year.*

The song "Hey, Hey! Holy Mackerel!" came in for its share of the blame too. Many Cub loyalists had the notion that the line "The Cubs are on their way" meant on their way to a *pennant* in 1969, which of course was not the writer's idea at all. Nonetheless, it was considered a "jinx" if not *the* "jinx." And so today, a record and a copy of the sheet music of "Hey, Hey! Holy Mackerel!" the song that symbolizes the Cubs' '69 season, rest in peace in the Hall of Fame, among other mementos of baseball lore.

In retrospect, however, it was not so much that the Cubs "blew" the pennant but that the eye-popping performance of the Mets made it impossible for anyone else to win it.

Though certainly no substitute for a pennant to their shattered fans, the Cubs provided a season throbbing with excitement and an almost perpetual World Series atmosphere and came up with their best won-lost record (92–70) since the 1945 league champions and numerous unforgettable individual performances and achievements.

As usual, Billy's season-long performance was rock-steady. He paced the team with a .293 batting average, in hits (188), in total bases (304), and in triples (10). He also scored 103 runs, hit 21 homers, and drove in 95 runs.

At 38, though nursing a bad knee most of the year, Ernie Banks drove in 106 runs and belted 23 homers. Ron Santo chased in a career high of 123 RBIs, second only to the 126 by Willie McCovey, the NL's MVP. The stellar third baseman also led the club with 29 homers. Former Met Jim Hickman played "Mr. Fireworks," with 21 round-trippers; Hundley also hit 18.

For the first time since Bill Lee and Lon Warneke did it in 1935, a pair of Cub pitchers won 20 or more games, Fergie, with 21–15—his third straight season with at least 20 victories—and Hands, with 20–14. Holtzman won his highest number of games, 17. Regan, whose record was 12–6, with 17 saves, was deadly against the Mets, winning two, losing none, and earning a pair of saves.

The entire Cub infield—Banks, Beckert, Kessinger, and Santo—and Hundley were named to the NL All-Star team that swamped the American Leaguers, 9 to 3. Home attendance skyrocketed to 1,674,993, an all-time high, far surpassing the previous home gate record of 1929.

One thing can be said about Cub fans. They may never forget the deeds and misdeeds of their team, but they always forgive. You couldn't chase 'em away with Sherman tanks in 1970. And a good thing too... in 1970, to borrow a "Durocher-ism," Billy was going to have "some kind of year!"

The NL's New "Iron Man"

"There's no known cure for 'Cub-ism'." So said WGN's Bill Berg, former sportscaster and presently one of Chicago's favorite talk-show hosts. True to tradition, the crushed fans dried their crying towels from 1969 and swarmed back in near-record numbers in 1970. And their heroes amply rewarded them. Especially Billy. Williams celebrated his tenth full major league season, blistering the ball as he'd never done before.

The Cubs started off by scoring only five runs to lose three of their first four games. But then they launched their longest winning streak—11 games—since 1945.

And they were still flying high when they opened at Atlanta on April 30. As Billy emerged from the dugout, the Braves' scoreboard suddenly flashed, "CONGRATULATIONS, BILLY!" and the crowd gave him a warm, standing ovation. He was appearing in his 1,000th consecutive game, extending his own National League record. No such Southern hospitality from the Atlanta players, however—they held Billy hitless and shelled Jenkins to win, 9 to 2.

When the Braves came to Wrigley Field on May 12, it was Ernie's turn to doff his cap to a timber-rattling ovation. Banks uncorked his 500th career home run off Pat Jarvis. Billy also hit for the distance—his 12th of the young season—as the Cubs went all out to "win one for Ol' Ern" in 11 innings, 4 to 3.

The Cubs topped the division or were tied for first through most of June, then came down with a thud—losing 12 straight. Worst of all, the losses were all to top contenders: five to the Mets, four to the Cards, and three to the Pirates. Jenkins finally stopped the slide with a 5 to 0 shutout at St. Louis.

Back in the "friendly confines," Billy led a 14-run barrage against Pittsburgh with a grand-slam homer off lefty Joe Gibbon but, as Boudreau says so often, "You never have enough runs against the Pirates." The Bucs staggered the Cubs with a maddening 16 to 14 victory and took the next two games as well. But the Cubs battled back into contention again. On September 2, they pummeled Philadelphia, 17 to 2, banging out 20 hits, 4 homers, and 8 runs in the fourth inning. All without Billy's bat, however. He went hitless in the big inning and had failed his last 12 times at bat.

By now, the race had really tightened up. You could cover the first three teams with a wad of Wrigley's finest. Pittsburgh was in first by just half a game over the Cubs and only one game ahead of the third-place Mets. Since Chicago had another game with the Phils before the Mets came in—what better time to give the "Iron Man" a rest?

Durocher had scratched Billy's name from the starting line-up long before game time on September 3. If necessary, he could still call on Williams to pinch-hit, as he'd done other times that season, and keep Billy's consecutive-game streak alive. But the Cubs removed the need for that fast, romping to win again, 7 to 2, behind a four-hitter by Fergie. In the late innings, the home crowd kept chanting, "We want Billy!" He didn't hear them. Billy had nerves of jello forcing himself to sit it out as a spectator after appearing in every game since September 22, 1963. Finally, he hid in the clubhouse and heard the rest of the game on the radio.

"I was concentrating on pitching," remarked Jenkins, "but I half expected him to come out there in the ninth inning. I looked and he wasn't there, and I knew it was over."

The end of Billy's streak after 1,117 consecutive games, the all-time National League record, was one of two headline stories on September 3, 1970. The other announced that Vince Lombardi had died of cancer. Those who knew him found it hard to believe that the steel-tough, tireless, demanding coach who had made the Green Bay Packers one of pro football's mightiest dynasties was gone—that the man who put "Winning isn't everything, it's the *only* thing" into the language could ever lose a battle.

I want to make it clear this was my decision. Leo knew I wanted the streak over with, Billy told reporters huddled around him after the game. He went on to explain that coach Joey Amalfitano had told him he wasn't in the line-up, but that Herman Franks assured him Leo'd put him back in if he wanted to play.

I just wasn't performing, and the strain was there, physical, mental, or both. All I know is, if I start a new streak tomorrow, I want to include some World Series games. Right now, I have mixed emotions, part sad, part relief.

Billy's feat is extra significant because he had to contend with situations the old-timers never had to face—rigorous coast-to-coast travel and all the effects of the routine-ruining time differences, plus a 162-game schedule. And something else that the huge, amiable Pirate slugger, Willie Stargell, brought up in an interview.

Stargell especially marveled at how Billy could stand up so well and perform so consistently, playing so many games without a miss under the hot sun at Wrigley Field. "And you can't take a Billy Williams out and replace him with someone else," said Stargell. "It's got to affect the ball club. We actually have what amounts to two teams where we can take someone out and someone else will come in and do an outstanding job. When they talk about ballplayers 'doin' it all', the first person that always comes to your mind is Billy Williams."

One of the greatest tributes paid Billy when his streak ended came from syndicated columnist Jim Murray. In his column, under the heading "BILLY WILLIAMS: MR. DEPENDABLE" that appeared in the *Sarasota Herald Tribune*, Murray wrote, in part:

"There are two kinds of ballplayers in the big leagues, those who play for the record books and those who play for the team. Or, put another way, some are trying for the pennant and others are trying for the Hall of Fame.

"Look in any locker room and check the guy whistling in the shower even though his team got lumped, 10 to 4. Chances are he hit for the cycle. Too bad about the team but, what the hell, you win a few, you lose a few, right?

"Which brings me to the reluctant record-setter, Billy Leo Williams, of the Whistler, Alabama, Williamses.

"Williams comes from a long line of people who show up for work every day. Like all such, Billy was quiet, steady, dependable as a railroad watch. Every employer should have one. They give him a watch at the end of 50 years, and the boss' son, who inherited the business, notes at the banquet, 'He never missed a day at the lathe in his life'.

"Williams was born to hit a baseball. He had that short sweet stroke, the beautiful uncoiling of the body that only a couple dozen hitters had in the history of baseball—all of them, it sometimes seems, named 'Williams'. It was like a Dempsey left hook. It only traveled a few inches through the hitting area but the velocity was such and the ball was struck so hard that Billy Williams sometimes needed his speed to reach first base before the ball bounced off the outfield wall back to shortstop.

"Williams was so conscientious, he went to manager Leo Durocher after a particularly fatiguing afternoon and announced, 'It's bugging me. Sit me down for a game'. Hotter heads prevailed, and Billy was coaxed into logging at least 1,000 games (April 30, 1970)

"One day in Philadelphia, he settled himself in the dugout, determined to get rid of the incubus of fame once and for all. The game, of course, went into a tie. In the late innings, with the bases loaded, Billy Williams had to keep his record going. He went to the plate, not for the record, but for the win. He rapped a double off Chris Short.

"Sixty-odd games later, it was September 3, 1970—1,117 consecutive appearances in all. That day, Billy sat in the dugout. Wild horses couldn't drag him out. Nor wild pitchers. The next day, he started his string all over again. He played in 161 games in '70.

" 'Do you think you will regret it?' I asked Billy. 'I mean after all, it would be a shame to play in, like 1,999 out of a possible 2,000 games some day'. Billy shook his head.

" 'When a record gets in the way of performance, the choice is pretty clear'."

Jenkins, probably the man closest to Billy, gave his slant on Billy's achievement in his book, *Like Nobody Else.*

"It didn't take a superman to accomplish it; it took character and dedication. Even when he was hurt, Billy made sure he was in the line-up. Occasionally, he had the flu. Other times, he could hardly walk because he had bruised his ankle with a foul ball. He always told himself, 'If I have to crawl out to my position, I'll be out there because I think I owe something to my ball club, and I can contribute something'."

Fergie concluded with a supreme compliment. "Billy has inspired me to try to become as consistent as he is."

What if Billy had it to do all over again—would he still play that many games? Billy answered that question and commented on other aspects of the streak after the 1973 season.

No. I don't think so. I really don't think so. How I got myself involved in it, when I first came up to the big leagues, probably is because I was concerned about one thing. I wanted to play baseball. In '61 I got a chance to play, but wasn't doing the job I was doing in Triple-A baseball. All of a sudden, I'm sitting on the bench, and Bob Will is playing leftfield. It's not that I wanted to play all those games but, back in my mind, I was saying to myself "I don't want to sit on the bench—on the field is where you make money."

Besides, I was concerned about somebody coming up to take my job, the way I did when I came up. I made up my mind that nobody was going to get me out of that line-up for a long, long time if I had anything to do with it. Later on, you get to a certain point where you're close to a record. And in baseball, y'know, I guess we live by records. So, you want to try and break it. Let's see. First I had to get by Richie Ashburn's [694 games], then it was Ernie's [Cub mark of 717 straight games], and then, Stan Musial's [895]. You kind of get swept along with it. Then after you break it, you want to establish a record of your own, one you're pretty sure no one else will reach.

I don't know whether it hurt me physically or not. But they say you're as young as you feel, and I'm feeling pretty good. It was an advantage in a way. By me being so determined to stay in the line-up, I was able to hit over 275 homers and I forget how many RBIs at the time the streak ended. Y'know, individual records. But as far as playing and helping the ball club, there were times I went out and wasn't capable of giving 100 percent. I knew it, and they knew it. I always tried to give everything I had, but maybe sometimes I just didn't have as much to give as I would if I'd got some rest now and then.

A lot of times, a ballplayer gets caught up in individual records, and players should be concerned with winning. Your greatest reward is when your team wins, not when you have an individual record.

Then there are other things you have to deal with if you're a good ballplayer. I remember when a team like Philadelphia was coming into town. I went up to the office that morning and told Leo I wanted out of the line-up because I was tired. He told me that Mr. Wrigley wanted me to play against the Eastern Division teams, and I could take off against the Western Division teams. I couldn't see where it made any difference. You've got to play all the ball clubs to win.

I can remember times when my back was hurting. A doctor comes in and he's going to treat me. He really treated me. He sticks a big needle in me, a cortisone shot. So I went out and played that day—got a home run, a double, and a triple.

And if you get hurt, it's not like you're a mediocre ballplayer, because the management and the manager want you in the line-up. But a ballplayer who's capable of doing more than an average job, he's going to find himself back in the line-up before he's fully healed. That's why you see so many good ballplayers who just don't have it in their later years. Take football, for example. They tried to bring Gale Sayers back as soon as he could get back. Guys like him, they don't get to sit out long enough to get healed.

After I played in 1,000 ballgames, I made this trip to Coopers-

town, the Hall of Fame. They'd sent for the scorecard of my 1,000th game. Nobody there could find it. It was misplaced. At that point, I felt that this particular record didn't mean a helluva lot. The only thing you had to show for it was the wear and tear of your body.

The Cubs and Pirates were now virtually tied for first place, the Mets 1½ games behind Chicago. Billy's usually hot as a pistol after a day off, and on September 4, he had two hits and scored twice to help beat New York, 7 to 4.

Pennant fever was just starting to build up on the North Side, when, on September 12, the Pirates beat the Cubs to grab a two-game lead. But the following game, on Sunday September 13, provided one of those finishes that brought a surge of hope to the die-hards among the fans.

Bone-chilling dampness and the gloomy prospect that another pennant drive might end in a fizzle held the Wrigley Field crowd to only 22,567. The Pirates led, 2 to 1, with two out in the last of the ninth. Many fans had given up and left. Thousands more were streaming for the exits as Willie Smith faced Steve Blass, who had allowed the Cubs only a bunt single since the second inning.

Up in the WGN Radio booth, a frustrated Vince Lloyd said it all. "There's a swing ... and a high flyball. This game is going to be over. Coming in is Matty Alou ... coming on ... he reaches out ... and *drops the ball!* The wind kept carrying it in ... and the Cubs get a break! *Willie Smith reaches second!"* The crowd roared in anticipation—the tying run was on second. Moments later, Rudolph raced in to score when Kessinger kissed the next pitch into right.

The winning run was on. Beckert was up, Billy on deck. Glenn lined the first pitch to center, sending Kessinger to second. That brought out Pirate manager, Danny Murtaugh. He wanted a lefty, George Brunet, to pitch to Williams. Brunet missed with his first pitch. But Billy didn't miss the next one. He laced a liner into left, scoring Kessinger, and the Cubs were mobbing Billy with hysterical delight.

"Beautiful, just beautiful!" chanted Billy at his locker. Smith was wondering out loud what his life would have been worth had he failed to run it out when Alou moved in for the "sure" catch. "I'd have *kept on* running," he laughed, "right to the parking lot. Heck, I might have run right over the centerfield bleachers!"

Had Durocher ever seen such a fantastic turnabout?

"Yeah," retorted a happy Leo, "in 1951."

The Cubs were definitely still in it, and, already, drums were starting to beat for Billy as the National League's Most Valuable Player. With ten games still to play, *Chicago Sun-Times* writer Jerome Holtzman took up the charge.

"Doff the chapeau, please, for Billy Williams of the Cubs. The Sweet Swinger is having some kind of year—42 homers, 125 RBIs, and 196 hits—but that isn't all. Here's the biggest surprise; he has already scored more runs than any National Leaguer in the last 23 years [136]. If you're not impressed, consider this: Willie Mays, Maury Wills, and Frank Robinson, to name a few, never scored that many runs in any single season.

"There's no question that Williams, after all these years as one of baseball's strongest and most consistent hitters, is finally emerging into what could be genuine superstar status. He might even pass Santo and Ernie Banks on the Cub pay scale and ask and get a new contract at $100,000 per year.

"The biggest trouble with Billy, in a sense, is that he hasn't had the big-time publicity. He's been sandwiched between Banks and Santo all these years, taken for granted."

Holtzman went on to say that with luck Billy might beat out Cincinnati's Johnny Bench for the MVP award, depending on whether or not the Cubs captured the National League East.

But the Cubs, after winning the next game at St. Louis, dropped the following two, and for the rest of the season were 8–9. Not good enough. The Pirates, who hit their stride after September 13 with a 12–5 pace, rolled on to take the division title.

The Cubs weren't eliminated until September 27, but second place was still up for grabs on the final day of the season. On October 1, with the Cubs and Mets tied, Chicago beat New York, 4 to 1, behind Jenkins to clinch the runner-up spot. Looking back at the '70 Cubs, it's difficult to see how they could have failed.

Power? Billy, Santo, and Hickman were the league's most explosive batting trio. Each hit 25 or more homers and drove in over 100 runs. Hickman won the "Comeback of the Year" Award with his best season—a .315 batting average, 32 homers, and 115 RBIs. Santo drilled 26 homers and chased in 114 runs.

Former Yankee, Joe Pepitone, who came to the Cubs from Houston late in July—complete with wigs, hair dryers, zany gags, and an active war-club—contributed 12 round-trippers and 44 RBIs. (In one of his rare, serious moments, in response to a remark that Billy was "dull," the controversial Joe minced no words. "If Billy's dull, then so was Joe DiMaggio. The more I see of Billy, the more I realize he's more like DiMaggio than any player of our time.")

Elsewhere in the power department, there was Johnny Callison, who swatted 19 homers to help bring the Cubs' season total to 179—second only to the Reds in the National League—and just three shy of their all-time mark of 182 in 1958. And the Bruins were second in RBIs, with 761, and runs, with 806.

Pitching? No other NL team had three pitchers who won 15 or more games. Fergie paced the staff with 22-16, his fourth straight season with 20 or more wins. Hands was 18-15, Holtzman 17-11, and newcomer and veteran righthander Milt Pappas, purchased from Atlanta, contributed ten victories.

True, there were injuries. Hundley was able to play in only 73 games, and knee trouble benched Banks for over half the season. And the bullpen was ineffective in relief. Winning just a few more "two-gamers" might have brought them in, but the Cubs failed miserably in handling other contenders, with only 7-11 records against both the Mets and Cards, 8-10 against the Pirates, and exactly .500 against the Phils. Surprisingly, they won 7 out of 12 from the Reds, who romped to the Western Division title by 14½ games.

What's more, the Cub failure to win the division title probably was the body blow to Billy's chances for the MVP award. Despite his spectacular performance, he was snubbed for the All-Star Game, missing out on the nationwide exposure that might have made a difference in the voting. And like that "other" Williams, Billy happened to have his greatest year in the same season as another superstar, but one whose club took the division championship.

Ted Williams was the last hitter to bat over .400—his average was .406 in 1941—but that was the year Joe DiMaggio reeled off his 56-game hitting streak, and Joe was named MVP. In 1947, the "Splendid Splinter" won the Triple Crown but lost the MVP by one point, again to the "Yankee Clipper," whose record that year, by the way, was pale in comparison to Billy's in 1970. Except for the .406 batting average, Billy topped Ted's overall offense in 1941, and in 1947 Ted bettered him in doubles and triples only. Apparently, too, Billy's having set the new NL "Iron Man" mark counted for little among the members of the Baseball Writers Association.

The Classic Hitter led or was high among NL leaders in most offensive categories in 1970. His league-leading 137 runs scored was the highest since 1947 when Johnny Mize also tallied 137. He tied Pete Rose for most hits in the NL, with 205; was second in homers, with 42; topped the league in total bases, with 373; tied for second in RBIs, with 129; and his .322 average was fourth in the league.

Billy also hung up the new Cub record for homers by a leftfielder, beating Hank Sauer's old mark of 37 in 1952, the year ex-Cub Sauer was named MVP, a decision that churned up some bitter controversy. The only Cubs ever to hit more homers in a season than Billy were Banks and Hack Wilson.

Along the way, Billy not only led the team in batting average, runs, RBIs, homers, doubles, and total bases but he also tied an NL record for most years—nine—with 600 or more at-bats.

Scarcely noticed was Billy's brilliant defensive work—with only three errors in 161 games, he was second in the league.

Bench, the catching and hitting wizard of the Western Division champion Reds, who at 22 became the youngest in history to win the MVP, received all but two of the 24 possible first-place votes and piled up an overwhelming majority of 326 points over Billy's 218 for second place. The 1970 records for Bench and Williams follow:

	AB	R	H	2B	3B	HR	RBI	BA	RP	TB	SO	SA
Bench	605	97	177	35	4	45	148	.293	200	355	102	.587
Williams	636	137	205	34	4	42	129	.322	224	373	65	.586

How did Billy feel about losing out?

I was hurt, but really didn't feel all that bad about it, even though I would have liked to win the Most Valuable Player Award. I knew that another ballplayer, Bench, had an equally good year and that I had maybe a fifty-fifty chance of winning it. And he was in the playoffs. I wasn't. I've learned to accept it when somebody else does something as good or better than you do and you sometimes have to concede to the other guy. Well, not really concede, but give him credit too. I was disappointed, sure, but I wasn't bitter about it.

One who didn't go along with the crowd was *Baseball Digest*, the game's only monthly magazine for over 30 years. About choosing Williams as "*Baseball Digest* Player of the Year," editor John Kuenster wrote, "Mickey Cochrane, Hall of Fame catcher for the old Philadelphia A's and the Detroit Tigers, was sitting behind the screen at Wrigley Field one day some years ago, watching a slender, young, lefthander taking his rips during batting practice.

"'He's going to be a good one', said Mickey. 'He's got those quick wrists, and I don't think the pitchers will fool him too much with the curve ball'.

"The year was 1961 and Iron Mike predicted a great major league future for Billy Williams. Of all the major league players in 1970, there wasn't one who had a better season than Williams. And for that reason, *Baseball Digest* is happy to choose him as its 'Player of the Year', an honor that went to Tom Seaver of the Mets in 1969.

"Perhaps we'll get a little flack from fans of Johnny Bench, Bob Gibson, and Manny Sanguillen, who also turned in superb performances. But there was no way we could overlook the day-to-day superiority of Williams—as a hitter, base runner, and fielder. He excelled in all departments, and without him, the Cubs would have never been able to challenge for the National League's East Division title."

Bud Burns also took a strong pro-Billy stand in the *Nashville Tennessean*. "Understandably," he said, "a player having a year such as Bench did is going to grab a lot of votes. Let's face it, no catcher in baseball throws better, bats better, or catches better than Johnny. And, they say, a spot is already reserved at Cooperstown for him. But for consistency, there was no ballplayer in either league better than Williams... There are some who believe Cincinnati would have won the West Division and entered the Series with someone other than Bench catching.

"Bench had quite a supporting cast—Pete Rose, Lee May, Tony Perez, and Bobby Tolen, to mention a few. He was far more fortunate than Williams, whose Windy City crew finished another disappointing season.

"Howls are expected from irate fans and more are expected from members of the writing fraternity who prefer not to have anyone disagree with them. Meanwhile, give Sweet Swinging Billy the credit due him."

Zanger and Kaplan's *Major League Baseball 1971* was more outspoken. "Johnny Who? Of the Big Red What? Had the Cubs, not the Reds, won the pennant, Williams and not Bench would have been the NL's Most Valuable Player. At 32, Billy has established himself as one of the Cubs' all-time great stars—and 'great' is a word that should not be used lightly. He hits for average, hits with power, and hits in the clutch."

Edgar Munzel of the *Chicago Sun-Times* took quite a different approach. "Johnny Bench was voted Player of the Year honors in most sectors last season. Billy undoubtedly would have been accorded that honor everywhere [offensively] because he had the greatest all-round batting record in baseball, based on hitting for percentage, power, and run production. Many baseball observers believe that the best measure of a player's offensive value is in runs-responsible-for which includes the combination of RBIs and runs scored. By this yardstick, Williams topped the majors with 224 on 129 RBIs and 137 runs scored, minus the duplication of 42 homers. Bench had 200 runs produced, Tony Perez 196 runs produced. Highest in the American League was Carl Yastrzemski's 187."

Billy's performance didn't go totally unrecognized. He was named to the All-Star teams selected by *The Sporting News* and the Associated Press and was named Chicago Player of the Year by the Windy City's Baseball Writers Association.

In November, Billy took his first swing at "show biz." Joining Banks, Santo, and Pepitone, he appeared for a short run with the "Thief of Gagbad," Milton Berle, at the Mill Run Theater in Chicago's northwest suburbs. They took turns dishing out the corn with Berle. Billy also did some singing.

It was a lot of fun, said Billy. *I've sung in the church choir and Sunday School and enjoyed it. But being on the stage was a new experience.*

Early in February, Billy was honored as the Major League Player of the Year by the Braves 400 Club in Atlanta. Hank Aaron, slated to receive the club's Milestone Award, couldn't attend because of a previous commitment. But Hammerin' Hank grinned when he heard about Billy's award. "Great, just great. I'd sure like to put in my plug for Billy. He's one of the greatest outfielders I ever played against. It just seems to be Billy's 'thing' to be an all-time, unsung ballplayer. People like Willie Mays and me, and even Cleon Jones and Tommie Agee, who all came from around Mobile, get quite a bit of publicity, but they always seem to bypass Billy in spite of how great he is.

"I guess it's partly because Billy is quiet," Aaron went on. "He goes about his job quietly and they take him for granted. They expect so much out of a guy like him, and they just think he'll go out and do it every day. Really, it amazes me the kind of ball he plays day in and day out."

Just before spring training rolled around, the Cub management showed how it valued Billy's contribution to the club—in a tangible way. Late in February, Billy became the first Cub to sign a contract in the $100,000 bracket. Even more gratifying to Williams was that Phil Wrigley dispelled any doubts about Billy having him over a barrel in granting the precedent-making salary—flatly stating that Billy deserved it both by his deeds on the field and by his loyalty to the team. Declared Billy:

The big man paid me a tremendous compliment. I'd like to have his statement and a copy of the contract framed for my home. It's something you pray for and pray will happen to you.

Hard-nosed Rick Talley of *Chicago Today*, who seldom writes anything mild if there's a chance to tackle a subject that will start a fight, put the situation in a nutshell: "Billy Williams gets his $100,000. That's class. If the Cubs had balked at Billy's asking price just because of a 'policy' against paying $100,000 to anyone, it would have been unfortunate. Everyone, including Vice-President John Holland, knew Billy deserved $100,000—at least in light of the skyrocketing salaries other major league players are receiving. He would get it with any team in baseball.

"I can understand, tho, why Holland didn't want to pay the six figures. It opens the door. The Cubs already have the highest payroll in the National League—and maybe in the major leagues." Talley, who was later to make Durocher—he called him "Whatshisname"—his favorite dart board, added, "You can see, then, why the Cubs' management is apprehensive. What happens if the Cubs win it all this year? Zooooom! The salaries will go out of sight!"

"Mutiny on the Wrigley"

Billy likes to recall a time he and the "other" Williams, Ted, were having a long chat about batting.

When you talk hitting with Ted, he talks about the fine points, I mean the really fine points, of what it takes to hit a baseball. Like he told me that the hitting space on your bat is just 2 to 2½ inches long and about as big around as your finger. If you hit under that space you hit the ball on the ground. If you hit above, you pop it up. And if you hit it "right there," you get a line drive.

Whatever and wherever that space is, Billy found it to the delight of over 39,000 opening-day celebrants at Wrigley Field in 1971. He hammered a homer in the tenth to rescue Fergie and beat Bob Gibson of the Cardinals, 2 to 1. He also "hit the spot" for the distance in each of the next two games for the Cubs' longest consecutive-game home-run streak of 1971. That, however, was about all the excitement the team whipped up in April, the Cubs playing a dismal 8–13. But they won eight of their first ten in May, including seven straight.

During that streak, on May 15, Billy gave Yosh Kawano an extra chore. Yosh, who Billy claims has been "Cub clubhouse manager for about 100 years it seems," usually commemorates a special game or feat by marking up a new baseball for a player's collection.

This time the ball was a memento of Billy's 300th career home run. He hit it off Tom Phoebus of San Diego, again in support of Fergie, who also belted a two-run homer, one of six the rangy right-hander clubbed in '71. Billy's blast made him the 31st major leaguer to slug 300 round-trippers, tied him with ex-Cub Chuck Klein, and put him only two behind his hitting instructor Hornsby.

Four days later, he pulled even with the "Rajah," scuttling San Francisco with two homers and a triple for six RBIs, most by a Cub in a single game all that year. (Billy had two homers in a game five times in '71.)

After the game, Billy made a confession you'd hardly expect from a man who, by the end of the season, would rank 28th on the all-time home-run list.

I don't consider myself a home-run hitter. I can't get up to the plate thinking home run. If I get into that habit, I'm in trouble. That's what happened last month. I hit homers in three straight games, and started thinking I was a home-run hitter I guess. Shaking his head, he went on: *I didn't drive in a run the next three weeks! I better consider myself just a line-drive hitter. Remember the day they gave me in '69? In the second game, I had a couple of singles, a double, and a triple my first four times up. If I could homer the next time, I'd go for the cycle again. Since we were winning by 10 or 11 runs, I figured, "What the heck, I'll try for one." You know the rest—I struck out! 'Course that day they gave me a standing ovation.* Then, in mock anger, *I don't want any more standing ovations* that *way.*

You'd figure that when Billy hits a homer or gets his first hit of the day, he'd stick with that same bat, right? Wrong. Unlike most ballplayers, Billy claims he's not superstitious. He even tempts fate. He always has several of his favorite model bats—the S-2 "Vern Stephens" 32-ounce Louisville Slugger—in the dugout and others in the clubhouse. Next time he comes up, he'll grab any one of them. If Billy happens to break a bat, it doesn't bother him, he just replaces it with another, though he does feel the older the bat, the better.

(Not at all like DiMaggio. Joe was almost in a panic when a fan stole the same 36-ounce bat he'd used during the first 41 games of his 56-game hitting streak in 1941. DiMag borrowed a similar one from Tommy Henrich and kept the streak going, but felt uneasy, shaken. About a week later, Joe's famous black-looking bat came back—and so did Joe's confidence. He hit the first pitch for a 420-foot homer the first time he swung it!)

Rookies naturally like to borrow Billy's bat, hoping some of that sweet-swinging magic will rub off on them. Billy doesn't object for a few swings, but if it's a righthanded hitter, he'll retrieve the bat because smacking the ball from both right and left sides damages the hitting surface. If the borrower still wants to use Billy's model, he'll give him one from his reserve supply.

Billy shrugs off superstition with "What you're supposed to get, you'll get, and whatever happens is for the best." Despite this assertion, he goes through some preliminary motions almost habitually. When he trots in from the outfield, knowing he'll hit that inning, he pops about half a stick of gum into his mouth. More often than not, as he goes around the catcher to step into the batter's box, he'll spit out the tiny wad of gum and take a cut and try to hit it with his bat.

I guess I figure if I can hit that little piece of gum, I oughta be able to hit that great big baseball. Of course here at home, we get all the gum we want!

Billy almost invariably will reach up and pat-pat-pat his batting helmet too as he squares away to face the pitcher. He starts his swing with his bottom hand wrapped around the knob of the bat. But after he swings, his hands are an inch or two above the knob.

He's not concerned about his glove. In fact, he used to hurl his glove into the stands after the last game of the season "to make some kid happy." He prefers to break in a new glove during spring training. In more recent years, he's turned his glove over to Fergie, who collects discarded equipment to distribute to needy youngsters. But not the bats! Those Billy holds over till the next year.

And he gets "lucky" feelings, he says. One of his favorite places to hit is Cincinnati.

It seems I almost always get a home run there, if not the first game in a series, the second or third.

"Yeah, Billy, except they recently switched to a *new* ballpark, Riverfront Stadium."

It doesn't make that much difference. I thought it would, but it didn't. Lots of things in baseball are psychological. That's probably the case with me against this ball club. It's something you don't predict, just something you feel *will happen.*

"You mean *superstition,* Billy?"

Grinning. *No, no . . . intuition! Like one time I was on the bench next to Pepitone and here it's the third game of the series and I still don't have a home run. And I said to Pepi, "Well, guess it's about time for me to hit a home run 'cause I always hit one here." Sure enough, I went up and it went out-the-ballpark.*

One who'll verify Billy's roughness on the Reds is Pete Rose, whose *shoes* probably run for an extra base when he takes them off. The 1973 National League's MVP, a marvel of consistency with three batting championships, who considers Billy the best natural hitter he's ever seen, said: "He's got a beautiful stroke—he's picturesque as hell."

Pete told of one extra-prodigious home run slammed out by Billy at Riverfront Stadium, only the second he recalled ever being hit onto the canvas way up in straightaway centerfield where it's 404 feet just to the wall.

The one time Billy didn't hit for the distance at Cincinnati in '71 was on June 3. He didn't have to. Holtzman issued four walks in the first four innings, then started throwing mostly fastballs to throttle the hard-hitting Reds for his second no-hitter. The crafty southpaw, who reportedly got a $65,000 bonus for signing with the Cubs in 1965, also scored the game's only run—unearned—to spoil a fine shutout performance by Gary Nolan. Firing in to rookie catcher Danny Breeden, Kenny retired the last 11 Reds in order and fanned the last two.

However, the "Good Ship Wrigley" was wallowing around fourth and fifth place in May and June, and angry undercurrents began banging at her hull. Some of the crew were grousing about the tyranny and rantings of the flint-hearted skipper, Durocher, convinced he would run the ship aground. The veteran of many other storms at sea adamantly refused to change his course, flirting with a mutiny that might break out at any time. Still, the ship picked up steam and slipped into second place on July 24. But pennant hopes were dim. The Pirates were cruising way out in front by 11½ games.

The All-Star Game came and went, and despite his sensational 1970 performance, Billy was overlooked his third straight year.

Suddenly in August the Cubs—winning seven of their first nine games in the month—began closing the gap on the Pirates, who started to flounder. Highlighting the surge, Billy treated over 43,000 at Wrigley Field to the mightiest one-day explosion by a Cub all season, clobbering Giant pitching for three homers and seven RBIs in a doubleheader on August 8. Why, incidentally, does Billy seem to victimize the Giants so often? His answer was modestly matter-of-fact.

I think it's because we get to see their pitchers in games during spring training. And, when you boil it all down, good hitting is a matter of knowing the pitchers.

Number "26" jumped into another exclusive bracket at Atlanta on August 17. Billy punched out two hits, one of them the 2,000th of his career. By the end of '71, only 122 other major leaguers had ever reached that level, and Billy was 116 on the list, with 2,040 base hits—more, for example, than the powerful lefthanded slugger and premier pinch-hitter, Johnny Mize.

On August 20, the Cubs opened a long home stand by beating Houston twice as the still-stalled Pirates lost. The Cubs were now only 4½ games back. Then they blew a great chance to move even closer. The Pirates lost their next two but so did the Cubs, the last one a 4 to 3 heartbreaker when Doug Rader homered off Pappas. Even so, with 12 more games scheduled in the "friendly confines," here was the hottest opportunity all season to overtake the leaders. This was the situation on August 23, when the crew decided to hash things out with the skipper. Here's how Billy recalled it:

The players called the meeting with Leo because we were slumping a little bit. Everybody wanted to win, and we were trying to iron out any difficulties. When the meeting started, Leo said something like, "Alright boys, let's do things just as if I'm a player, not the manager. We're all in this together." That's probably why the guys really opened up to him, feeling that if anybody had a grudge, they could sit there and talk it over, work things out.

Pepi was sort of the spokesman because he'd been involved with Leo quite some time and knew his ways. And he had experience with the Yankees when they won the pennant and he'd tell about it, what to look for, and so forth, hoping it would be helpful to the other ballplayers.

The meeting started out tamely enough. Players aired various gripes, a lot of them critical of Durocher's handling of the club. Eventually, they hit one big bone of contention. The veterans thought it would be a good idea to spot-rest some of the regulars here and there but wanted to be sure the guys coming off the bench could be relaxed and confident enough to do an adequate job to keep the club winning. But, as it was, they felt Leo had the "kids" too tensed-up, afraid they'd make a mistake. The give and take got warmer, and Durocher was starting to bristle when he got a chance to get in his licks.

There's one thing that might have stirred it up. Leo brought it up to Joe, Ronnie, or somebody—I can't remember exactly who—about not taking batting practice. Then they threw it on me. "Billy didn't hit!" That's true. I didn't. Everybody has his own way of doing things. After the first half of the season, I take very little batting practice, unless of course I'm not going well. At the time I was hitting around .310 or .315, and felt I had my stroke down, meeting the ball good. I'd go out about twice a week and take some swings. But after playing all those games and a lot more coming up, I was trying to keep my strength and timing instead of wasting everything in batting practice.

Then the skipper switched his attack to Pappas and accused him of grooving the 2-0 pitch Rader hit for a homer instead of wasting one on the outside corner, which Milt firmly denied, some other players backing him up. Next, Durocher took a verbal slap at Santo, claiming that at contract time Ron had asked for the "Day" (like the ones held for Ernie and Billy) that was scheduled for the next weekend. Santo fumed, furiously disputed the charge, and demanded that somebody phone John Holland to come down to the clubhouse right away and set the story straight.

When Holland arrived and said he couldn't recall whether he or Santo brought it up, it had the same effect on Ron as dumping kerosene on red-hot coals. Then, as the raging continued, Durocher suddenly ripped off his uniform, barked he was quitting as manager, and stormed up to his office, possibly to phone Wrigley. Most of the players yelled, "Let him go!"

As long as I've been in baseball, I've never seen anything like it. I knew Ronnie, and I was trying to restrain him because at one point he wanted to go up into the office and go nose to nose. I don't know what he would have done, but he was really upset, and could have done something he probably would have regretted the rest of his life.

You take a ball club like Oakland. They've won the last couple of years. It seems like a ball club can't win unless they have a few fights— y'know, get mad at the manager or each other. I guess some managers have to do this with different ballplayers to try to get the best out of them.

But for us, for all this to come up at that time, I don't think it was right. The timing was terrible. We still had a good chance to win. In fact, it was wrong anyway. I think after that most of the ballplayers looked at Leo as a manager who probed into their personal lives, things that had nothing to do with playing baseball. It seemed he tried to command respect that day, but he didn't get it.

Holland persuaded Leo to stay, and the Cubs settled down enough to beat the Reds that afternoon. Despite efforts to keep the mini-mutiny hush-hush, the press got wind of it and started firing their big guns, demanding, in essence, that the owner speedily try the case and hang the guilty parties from the yardarm.

Anti-Durocherites seized the chance to lambast the skipper for a variety of sins—"blowing the pennant in '69" by failing to rest his regulars, always playing for the big inning, rarely sacrificing, failing to lift starting pitchers in time to avert disaster, his impatience with youngsters, ruptured press relations, lack of rapport with the players, and tactical blunders.

Durocher's defenders said the players were prima donnas coddled in a "country-club" atmosphere, trying to shift responsibility for their failures to Leo, and compared the Cubs to the "cry-babies" of the 1940 Cleveland Indians who had asked the front office to fire their manager, Oscar Vitt. Vitt stayed, however, and Cleveland lost the pennant to Detroit by just one game.

Billy almost prevented the Braves from spoiling "Ron Santo Day" on August 28 as 34,988 fans swarmed into Wrigley Field to honor number "10," who'd patrolled third base ever since being brought up by Boudreau late in June of 1960.

The Braves led 4 to 3 in the last of the ninth, but, with a man on, Durocher had Beckert hit away instead of bunting. The strategy backfired. Glenn rapped into a double-play. Billy then followed with his second hit that could have scored the tying run with only one out.

In acknowledging the numerous gifts and the accolades, the Cub captain concluded with "This wasn't a day—it was a lifetime." "Billy told me you get a lump in the throat and he was right," said Ron after the game.

The press kept firing away as the Cubs lost seven of their next ten games after the rhubarb and fell into third place, nine games behind Pittsburgh on September 2. Then, out of a clear-blue sky, Phil Wrigley did as expected—the totally *unexpected*. He wrote a newspaper ad that appeared in all four Chicago papers on September 3. The verdict: the *players* would swing from the yardarm!

THIS IS FOR CUB FANS
AND ANYONE ELSE WHO IS INTERESTED

It is no secret that in the closing days of a season that held great possibilities the Cub organization is at sixes and sevens and somebody has to do something. So, as head of the corporation, the responsibility falls on me . . . .

Many people seem to have forgotten, but I have not, that after many years of successful seasons . . . and five league pennants, the Cubs went into the doldrums and for a quarter of a century were perennial dwellers of the second division in spite of everything we could think of to try and do . . .

We figured out what we thought was needed to make a lot of potential talent into a contending team, and we settled on Leo Durocher who had the baseball knowledge to build a contender and win pennants, and also knowing he had always been a controversial figure . . . particularly with the press because he just never was cut out to be a diplomat. He accepted the job at less than he was making because he considered it to be a challenge, and Leo thrives on challenges.

In his first year we ended in the cellar, but from then on came steadily up, knocking on the door for the top.

Each near miss has caused more and more criticism, and this year there has been a constant campaign to dump Durocher that has even affected the players, but just as there has to be someone to make final decisions for the corporation, there has to be someone in charge on the field to make the final decisions on the spur of the moment, and right or wrong, that's it.

All this preamble is to say that after . . . consultation with my baseball people, Leo is the team manager and the "Dump Durocher Clique" might as well give up. He is running the team, and if some of the players do not like it and lie down on the job, during the off season we will see what we can do to find them happier homes.

PHIL WRIGLEY, PRESIDENT
CHICAGO NATIONAL LEAGUE BALL CLUB, INC.

P. S.   If only we could find more team players like Ernie Banks.

You had ballplayers out there, trying to win, giving 100 percent, doing everything they could to win. When this ad came out, a lot of ballplayers were hurt, a lot of them dropped their chin, and felt unappreciated. Most of them felt our owner didn't think we were giving 100 percent, and we were dejected that he'd say this at this particular time. We still had a chance. When he mentioned we needed more players like Ernie Banks, it gave the idea we weren't capable of winning, and that others weren't contributing. I think many of the players felt—if we win, good. If we don't, what the hell, we won't be appreciated anyway. Ernie probably felt like a sore thumb standing out. He didn't know the ad was coming. There wasn't anything he could do—he just had to accept it. If he [Mr. Wrigley] had it to do over again, I wonder whether he'd do it or not.

Holtzman, one who accepted the offer in the ad to ask for a "happier home" and went to Oakland for Rick Monday, told why he wanted to be traded.

"The immediate cause was the statement Wrigley made in the newspapers that the only player who was trying all out to win was Ernie Banks, that the rest of us weren't giving our best. That hit me like a ton of bricks. I couldn't understand how he could say that. Every time I went out on the mound, I was a fanatic about winning. I couldn't believe he could say that. It damaged me so much it wasn't funny."

The ad hardly hypoed the Cubs' spirit. They lost nine of their next eleven games and ended up 12–16 for the month. Even though they beat the Mets five out of six times in September, they tied with New York for third place.

Still and all, a Cub rookie pitcher and a veteran gave fans an unforgettable September 21st. "Knuckle-curve" artist Burt Hooton outdueled Seaver and the Mets with a two-hitter, and Santo cranked out his 300th career home run. The burly righthander struck out 15 Mets, tying the Cubs' one-game record set by Dick Drott in 1957.

Billy again was the overall offensive leader of the club, with a .301 average, 300 total bases, 28 homers, 27 doubles, 93 RBIs, and 86 runs. And though playing the fewest games since 1962, had 179 hits, second only to Beckert's 181. Billy also took over the home-run leadership among active Cubs, with 319.

"Mr. Cub" reached the saddest of all days, calling it a career after appearing in 2,528 games. Before bowing out, Ernie stroked three homers, boosting his lifetime total to 512, tying with Eddie Mathews, and surpassing other all-time greats Mel Ott (511), Lou Gehrig (493), and Stan Musial (475).

Jenkins and Pappas were the only shining lights among the pitchers. Fergie opened his famous "envelope"—he seals it and tapes it on his locker at the start of every season. He'd set his won-loss goal at 25–9. The lanky ex-reliever finished '71 with 24–13, best in the league, making him the first Cub winner of the coveted Cy

Young Award. Fergie also notched his fifth straight 20-or-more victory season, broke the club record for all-time strike-outs (1,454), topped the league with 30 complete games and 325 innings pitched, and twice struck out 14 in a game, his career high.

Pappas won the most games of his career (17), but none after September 4, while usually dependable Hands and Holtzman slumped to 12–18 and 9–15 respectively.

In addition to the internal strife, injuries hit the Cubs hard, especially the loss of take-charge catcher Hundley, who was out for the season after only nine games. Pepitone, Beckert, and Hickman spent a lot of time in sick bay too.

The best the Cubs could do was try to forget their worst record (83–79) since 1966, heal the wounded bodies and bruised egos, grit their teeth watching another World Series on TV, and set their sights on "next year." For Billy Williams, "next year" was to be spectacular, the climax of a three-year record unmatched by anybody in baseball.

The Batting Champ

A "funny thing" happened on the way to the season's opener in 1972—the players went on strike. Baseball's only general strike, it delayed action ten days—until April 15—and canceled a total of 86 games.

The Cubs won two of their first three games, then dropped nine of their next eleven, including eight straight. Maybe it would have been better for them if the strike had continued, at least through April. Except for Sunday, April 16. A wet, chilly day kept all but the bravest fans home in front of their TV sets while 22-year-old Burt Hooton hurled a no-hitter over the Phils in only his fourth major league start.

Thank heavens the Cubs still had Cincinnati to kick around. On April 28, Billy cut loose with five hits to help Chicago outlast the Reds, 10 to 8, and give Jenkins his first win. Despite the abbreviated season, Fergie went on to a 20–12 mark—the first major leaguer since Warren Spahn to hit the charmed circle six straight years.

Billy's five-hit barrage was only one of three similar batting binges for the year. No other batter in baseball had more than one—and the slender swatsmith also collected three four-hit games, causing one shell-shocked hurler to mutter, "If Williams likes fishing so much, tell him I'll buy his license and the best equipment in the world if he'll start fishing full-time right through the season. Otherwise, the way he keeps hitting me, it won't be long before I'm fishin' full-time myself!"

Hits continued to crackle off Billy's bat, yet the Cubs finished May in third place, eight games back, but managed to close the gap to only 3½ at the end of June. Billy's bat was hot all through the month of July too. He won the National League Player of the Month Award in a walk—hitting .438 and driving in 29 runs in 31 games.

Still, the Bruins dropped seven out of eleven games and tied one in the first twelve games in July. A good share of the writers were convinced the only solution for the Cubs' slump was to get rid of that raspy-voiced rascal Durocher. In fact, one—Ray Sons of the *Chicago Daily News*—got so exasperated, he turned one of Leo's own phrases into a hotly worded article, suggesting they "back up the truck" and make Durocher its first (and only) passenger.

In Houston, on July 11, Billy became the only active player to get eight hits in a doubleheader, plus a sacrifice fly his only other time at bat to complete a perfect day. In the first game, he homered, slapped two singles, and hit a sacrifice fly, but the Cubs lost, 6 to 5. In the nightcap, he cleared the wall, doubled, and hit three singles. Yet, the Cubs also needed a three-run blast by Pepitone and two homers by Rick Monday to defeat Houston, 9 to 5.

When the fans began voting for the All-Star Game and the results were starting to be posted, it's amazing Billy didn't switch to playing horseshoes—at least, that's one game where close counts. When he was running sixth for an outfield spot, an irritated Leo Noonan of the *Los Angeles Herald-Examiner* lashed out at the fans.

Noonan wrote, "Baseball, being a simple game, attracts that type fan: the simplest folks to be found this side of the first grade. There aren't many scholars in the stands. How else can the career-long snub of Billy Williams be explained? With the possible exception of Roberto Clemente of Pittsburgh, there is not an outfielder in all of baseball as consistently productive as Billy Williams. (Put an asterisk by Henry Aaron who now is a full-time first baseman.)

"The Cubs' leftfielder was named Rookie of the Year in 1961. Then his name was placed in a secret box and everyone forgot about him. Oh, he has made the All-Star team three times, but that is like remembering Babe Ruth for his pitching.

"He won't make it this time, either, except as extra baggage. Quiet, noncontroversial Williams is sixth in the semifinal balloting for outfielders for the National League All-Stars later this month in Atlanta. That alone is reason enough to pull back the voting from the fans.

"Williams should be a cinch for the Hall of Fame when he retires. But, if no one is aware of him now, and there is a mandatory five-year wait after retirement to be eligible for the Hall, he may not make it.

"Williams, who went 8-for-8 in a Tuesday doubleheader, extended it to 10-for-13 in yesterday's 10–6 loss to Houston when he hit his fourth homer in two days and drove in his fifth, sixth, and seventh runs. His average is up to .329, and his home run total is up to an imposing 19." Billy finished fourth in the fans' ballot. Pittsburgh's

Murtaugh, however, thought enough of Williams to name him to the NL squad.

But while Billy, Santo, Kessinger, and Jenkins were in Atlanta for the game, big headlines hit Chicago's sports pages. Durocher had "stepped aside," and the new Cub manager was the star first baseman of Leo's '51 Giants, Carroll ("Whitey") Lockman. Whitey inherited a 46–44 record at the All-Star break, with the Cubs in fourth place, ten games off the pace.

Following the announcement, Wrigley issued a statement—really a two-edged sword—first referring to the scorn some players felt for Lippy, but also giving Durocher his due, then hurling a challenge to the Cubs to prove they were pennant contenders under a new leader.

Billy, who maintained his title of "Mr. Consistent" under 12 different managers and/or rotating head coaches in his 13 full seasons with the Cubs, had this to say about Leo and the role of manager in general:

Managers don't make ballplayers. I feel a manager just calls the shots. A good manager knows how to handle his men, get the best results from everybody, and keep the men on the bench happy. But the ballplayers themselves should be responsible for whether they want to win or lose.

Fellas in the big leagues know, or should know, what they have to do to win. It should be left up to the players. If they're not real major leaguers or aren't ready yet, then you have to go right up to the top, to the people who brought them into the big leagues.

I can remember only one time I had any trouble with Leo, an incident at St. Louis. It was a matter of going from first to third on a ball hit to Curt Flood. Flood was supposed to have a sore arm, and he didn't look like he was throwing well in practice. But sometimes when the game starts, under game conditions, things don't hurt anymore. Anyway, I took off when the ball was hit and Flood charged it fast, so after I rounded second, I held up instead of trying for third.

When I got back to the dugout, of course, Leo lets me know about it pretty good. Right then, I'm steamin' too because I know I messed up. When I do something wrong on a baseball field, I'm hurt more than anybody else, and this is on my mind. When somebody starts reviewing the whole thing, like it's news to me, that's when I'll speak up and give him something back. I guess with me, it's just a case of leaving me alone and letting me play baseball. Leo got it off his chest and so did I. Nothing violent, just one of those things. He never brought it up again and neither did I. That was the only little personality difficulty we had.

Going back to '69, I don't think it would have hurt any for Leo to give the regulars some rest, especially while we still held a good lead in the race. It seems to me that this has been a problem with our ball club over the years. You have guys playing good baseball and then in August and the first part of September, the bottom kind of drops out. Playing in so many day games, with that hot sun beaming down on you, it's hard to stay as strong as you'd like—and that's when everybody has to be at their best, in the stretch.

Here's where I wonder about my consecutive-game streak. Maybe it would have been better to sit out a few games, rather than extending it into the next year when I finally did end it. Whether it would have made any difference, I don't know. [Billy played every game in 1969, Santo 160, Kessinger 158, Banks 155, and Hundley 151. Williams hit .304 in September while the rest of the team batting faded to only .219, 34 points lower than their season average of .253. After the season, Durocher admitted, "Maybe we did run out of gas. But if the Mets had played only .500 ball, we still could have hung on. But they just kept winning, winning, winning."]

Then too I can see how Durocher probably figured. He wanted to win the same as we did, and could have been afraid to put guys in he thought weren't ready, that it might hurt the ball club. A lot of the players on the bench hadn't seen much action and needed some experience. So with the pressure on, Leo could have just decided to go with the guys he thought he could count on. It didn't work out.

Leo had his own ways, like everybody else. Like one time I remember, Fergie was out on the mound, chewing a big wad of bubble gum. And, as he'd get the ball back and be looking for the sign or be a little riled up at some calls, he'd speed up the chewing. Probably not even thinking about it, he'd also blow some big bubbles. That's why you've got to be careful of what you do out there—you never know when they put that closeup TV camera on you. They must have done that to Fergie that game. Anyway, the next day during a meeting, Leo brought it up, and mentioned that Mr. Wrigley watches television every day and we're not advertising bubble gum. Most of the fellas took it as a joke. But not Fergie. He got pretty annoyed. After that, though, he chewed Wrigley's gum!

Under Lockman, the Cubs finished July in third place, ten games behind the pace-setting Pirates, three behind the Mets. A 16–12 pace enabled them to overtake the Mets, but by August 31, the Bucs had opened an 11-game bulge. Billy continued to terrorize rival pitchers—and he had to have at least one field day against the Giants. It came August 26, another of his five-hit days. He smashed two homers and three singles to drive in four runs, allowing the Cubs to sneak by San Francisco, 10 to 9, in ten innings.

The Cubs finished with a strong September, a rarity for them, and, in the process, gave new pilot Lockman one of the top thrills in his 30-year career in baseball. Especially Milt Pappas and Billy. On September 2, Pappas came even closer to a perfect game than Seaver had against the Cubs in '69. Eight innings and 24 outs. In the ninth, lead-off man John Jeter dumped a blooping fly into short center. Centerfielder Bill North slipped and fell when he charged in for the ball. Seeing him go down, Pappas mentally kissed the no-hitter goodbye. But he didn't see Billy, who came out of nowhere to make the catch. Now he'd retired 25 in a row. A grounder to Kessinger, 26 in a row. Then pinch-hitter Larry Stahl swung and missed two of Milt's next three pitches. One more strike and Pappas would have the first perfect game ever thrown by a Cub and one of only nine since 1900. Milt's next three deliveries were close enough to swing at but not close enough to be called strikes. Stahl refused to bite, finally trotting to first with a pass. It was only the second time in the game Pappas went to a three-ball count. He got the next batter to pop to Carmen Fanzone to preserve the no-hitter.

It was the first time Lockman had been with a team that won a no-hitter. For Pappas, it was delicious frosting on the cake. His 17 victories for the year equaled his career high, and his 2.77 ERA topped the Cubs' staff.

Billy found the range against Steve Renko at Montreal on September 27 for his seventh career grand-slam homer, to tie him with Mel Ott. It was far more than the Cubs needed as rookie pitcher Rick Reuschel posted his fourth shutout in ten victories.

Under Durocher, the Cubs had a 46–44 record; under Lockman, a sparkling 39–26. The season total of 85–70 (.548) gave them their third second-place finish in four years, 11 games behind the Bucs, who made a shambles of the division with a sizzling 41–26 pace.

Again, the Cubs were the Pirates' "patsies." How can you figure it? The last few years, the Pirates murder the Cubs who murder the Reds who murder the Pirates. In 1972, the Pirates were 12–3 over the Cubs, the Cubs 8–4 over the Reds, and the Reds 8–4 over the Pirates. Then in the playoffs, the Reds win their second NL flag in three years, and at the expense of *their* "patsies," the Pirates!

Meanwhile, unaccustomed as he was, Billy had to blink and take bows under the national spotlight that finally focused on him. When baseball's final statistics were in, his record was awesome.

Billy's .333 average as National League batting champion was also the highest in both leagues. He led the majors both in total bases (348) and in slugging percentage (.606), and was second in RBIs (122). He was third in the National League in homers (37), in doubles (34), and in hits (191). Billy also topped everyone in the American League in hits, total bases, doubles, and slugging. His homers tied Richie Allen, home-run leader and overwhelming choice for MVP in the AL. And he committed only four errors.

The guy who once balked at his dad's efforts to make him a switch-hitter when hardly as tall as a bat himself and said, "Daddy, I got to bat *my* way," was just three RBIs and three homers shy of becoming only the 14th Triple Crown winner in baseball history.

Before the balloting for the big postseason honors began, Bill Gleason of the *Chicago Sun-Times* wrote an article on the Cub left-fielder in *Baseball Digest*. About Billy's chances for the MVP:

"The only rap that can be put on Billy in the competition for Most Valuable Player is the canard about not being colorful. One wonders about that word 'colorful'. Was Paul Waner colorful? Did Stan Musial ever bring uproar to baseball except when he was batting or running the bases? Is Harmon Killebrew a character? How about Hank Sauer, another Cub who was MVP for a club that didn't win anything?"

Gleason then gave Billy's hitting marks for the season, concluding, "Those figures ought to be colorful enough for anybody. Especially opposing pitchers."

The Sporting News featured a handsome color photo of Billy on the front page of its October 21, 1972, issue, naming him its Player of the Year. Comments by Jerome Holtzman included, "He has been in the major leagues 12 full seasons and has just about done it all.... Nonetheless, he has had less publicity than any of the other major league stars. Several years ago, in a rare magazine story about him, he was described as 'a mechanical man'. He read the story in disgust and threw it away."

Reviewing some of Billy's bush-league days, Holtzman added: "Williams still is remembered at Ponca City. He finished the 1956 season there and returned in '57, immediately showing signs of his ability and endurance. He led the league in games played, 126 (he has led the N.L. five times in this category), also led in doubles with 40, drove in 95 runs and hit .310.

"He also is remembered as the fellow who hit the equivalent of a grand-slam homer while striking out with the bases loaded.

"'I don't remember the details', Williams said. 'The ball got away from the catcher and must have ricocheted all over the place. All I remember is that everybody scored'."

Then came the bad news. In November, the Baseball Writers Association of America announced that for the second time in three years, Johnny Bench had been selected the National League's Most Valuable Player.

This was shocking enough to many who felt that Billy deserved the award for his spectacular, all-round offensive performance—regardless of the Cubs' finish. Even more incredible was that one of the voters didn't even list Billy among the *top ten* players on the ballot! With eleven first-place votes to Billy's five, Bench won with 263 points, Billy was second with 211, Willie Stargell third with 201. Their records and Richie Allen's, the AL's MVP, follow:

	G	AB	R	H	2B	3B	HR
Williams	150	574	95	191	34	6	37
Bench	147	538	87	145	22	2	40*
Allen	148	506	90	156	28	5	37†
Stargell	138	495	75	145	28	2	33

	RBI	BA	TB	SO	SA	RP
Williams	122	.333*	348*	59	.606*	180
Bench	125*	.270	291	84	.541	172
Allen	113†	.308	305	126	.603	166
Stargell	112	.293	276	129	.558	154

* Tops in majors   † Tops in league

In his *Sporting News* column on November 18, Jack Lang wrote: "Williams, regarded by many managers as just about the best all-round player in the league, got strong support for the MVP after winning the batting title with a .333 average. However, the fact that he was playing for a second-place club obviously hurt his chances." Lang also said he was surprised that Stargell received only two first-place votes after leading the Pirates to the title in the East, adding, "All votes for the MVP were cast before the playoffs began."

Earl Lawson made some significant points in his review of the Reds' 1972 season in the 1973 *Sporting News Baseball Guide*.

"Johnny Bench won the National League's Most Valuable Player Award for the second time within a three-year span. It's another way of saying that the Reds also won their second National League pennant within a three-year span. Bench, though, was anything but a one-man gang. The Reds' all-star catcher received plenty of help from his teammates, especially from the three who preceded him in the batting order."

Lawson noted that Rose led the league with 198 hits; Joe Morgan hit .292, drew 115 walks, led the NL in runs with 122, and swiped 58 bases to rank fourth in the MVP voting; and Bobby Tolan hit .283 and had 42 stolen bases. He added: "Altogether Rose, Morgan, and Tolan reached base safely 781 times, which, as one can see, gave Bench many an opportunity to drive in runs."

The MVP vote caused even Billy Williams to run out of cheeks to turn.

I think I was done an injustice by the Baseball Writers of America. I really felt I should have won it. When I read about the voting and how it turned out, and especially that one didn't even put me on the ballot, I was so disgusted, I just stopped reading. Nobody likes to finish second and this was the second time I did. I was bitter about not winning it, and bitter about baseball in general for a while. Looking back, I think the only way I could have got it was to win the Triple Crown, or if the Cubs had won the pennant.

But no question about who was No. 1 in Mobile. A committee went to work on a gala celebration to hail the superstar from nearby Whistler, and the mayor proclaimed Saturday, November 25, 1972, "Billy Williams Day" in Mobile. Shirley, daughters Nina, Julie, Valarie, and Sandy, and Billy's parents were the honored guests at a parade, a reception, and a luncheon at the Admiral Semmes Hotel. Billy was overwhelmed.

This is really great . . . what a wonderful feeling for my hometown to do this for me, set a day aside and say it belongs to you.

He told the gathering that the event and the day held for him at Wrigley Field in 1969 were the highlights of his career.

Numerous congratulatory telegrams arrived, including one from Governor George Wallace; another, calling him "a true superstar of the majors and a fine example for our nation," was signed Richard M. Nixon, President of the United States.

Among those attending the ceremonies were other major leaguers who'd come from around Mobile, including Frank Bolling and Henry and Tommy Aaron, and the former White Sox manager, then coach of Alabama South, Eddie Stanky.

Hank Aaron told the crowd he felt Williams should have been

voted the National League's Most Valuable Player. "I have nothing against Johnny Bench," said Hank, then, looking at Billy, "but this guy had a heck of a season. I was disappointed when Billy didn't get it. Surely, he is one of the greatest players I have ever played against."

Billy also received top recognition in other circles, being named to the All-Star teams selected by the Associated Press and *The Sporting News* and, along with Richie Allen of the White Sox, was chosen Player of the Year by the Chicago Baseball Writers. During the off-season, Billy was also honored at eight baseball dinners around the nation; he was presented with the Tris Speaker Award in Houston as Major League Player of the Year and was saluted as National League Player of the Year at Kansas City.

But his bitterness was still smoldering. In one address over the winter, he stated:

I felt I was given the shaft—plain and simple. This is the most disappointing thing that has happened to me in my baseball career. I have nothing against Bench. He's a good ballplayer, a great receiver, and a fine all-around player. It's just that I consider myself a good ballplayer too.

Had I batted .230 or .240 in 1971 and then come back in 1972 with the kind of year I had, maybe I would have gotten it [the MVP award]. *That's what I get for being so consistent every year. I want to win the MVP. I've set goals for 12 years. And now, for 1973, I'm setting that one.*

As talk about the coming season intensified, there was little chance of dousing cold water on the white-hot Cub hopes, now that the Eastern Division "bridesmaids" since 1969 had apparently found the winning combination with Lockman's leadership, which had resulted in a .600, pennant-winning pace after he took over from Durocher in '72. Who could blame the Cubs and their followers if they could hardly bear to "wait till next year?"

"It Wasn't Durocher, After All!"

"We were awed when Philip K. Wrigley kept the price of chewing gum at a nickel for so many years. Then P.K. surpassed himself." The writer was David Condon, whose words in the *Chicago Tribune* often hum with wry humor and subtle sarcasm. "The owner of the Chicago Cubs topped all previous business coups by getting Billy Williams' signature on a one-year contract for the coolie salary of $150,000," Condon went on. "We were absolutely overwhelmed at this bargain for baseball's most generous owner. P.K. certainly beat the price. Particularly since Billy Williams, with seniority and loyalty and Hall of Fame credentials, sought a three-year pact."

The *Tribune* columnist mentioned how such bargainers could have bought Manhattan Island from the Indians "without that $24 front money," and told what the ex-Yankee pitching star Lefty Gomez had said about Billy. Gomez, one of the game's flippest characters, who often attributed his success to "clean living and a fast outfield," wasn't reaching for laughs when he called Billy one of the all-time greats.

"It's sad that so few people seem to know it. I'll guarantee, though, that the Cubs have to know how great Billy is if they've ever looked at all the games he wins for 'em over the years. Billy minds his own business, quiet-like. Otherwise, he might be a national legend."

Mentioning that Williams had to settle for a one-year pact and that the White Sox later announced they'd given Richie Allen a three-year contract at $225,000 a season, Condon added, "If I were wearing Billy Williams' cleats, I'd have kicked myself for not having asked P.K. Wrigley for Catalina Island."

The Cubs were in spring training when George Vass made his annual pick of winners for *Baseball Digest*. First he quoted Lockman: "We've got the best team we've ever had. I don't see any weakness anywhere. We've got the best pitching staff in the league with five starters (including young Bill Bonham) and a much improved bullpen." Then, pointing out that the Cubs had a solid veteran at every position, Vass selected them to finish first in the Eastern Division.

Billy showed up at the Cubs' training headquarters in Scottsdale, Arizona, late in February, and since he'd been only the third Cub in history to win a National League batting title, the topic naturally turned to hitting.

I think knowing your pitchers is about 10 percent of your batting average, Billy mentioned. *Watch them from year to year and you soon find out they're throwing the same stuff. But, you can also guess too much. Sometimes you look for a curve and get a fastball. Other times with two strikes, you might think he might waste one. But he doesn't.*

The Cub who was reported to have signed for the highest salary of any previous North-Sider also got more off his chest about the resentment he still felt over winding up second to Bench for MVP honors twice in three years.

I've just realized that most of the things written about me over the years haven't helped me. All these stories make it sound like my good seasons should be taken for granted. For 13 years, every story written about me starts off "Billy Williams, the quiet man of the Cubs," but I'm not going to be quiet anymore. He went on to claim it had cost him a lot of money in endorsements. *If you're well known and popping off, it doesn't make much difference what you're saying or whether you're right or wrong. You get your name in the papers and that's the name of the game, I guess. It shouldn't be this way, but that's the system. If you can't beat the system, you join it. No more of that "nice guy" stuff for me.*

But Billy wasn't fooling anybody with his new image. The words were there, but the venom wasn't. Jerome Holtzman asked him if he really thought he could change.

Maybe I can't. I've been quiet all these years, so everybody takes me for granted. I can hit a few homers or go 8-for-8 in a doubleheader and nothing much happens. But I say one word that's controversial, and there's a big headline and picture—"Williams Erupts." [He was talking about a story that came out after he rapped the baseball writers for denying him the award he felt he had earned.]

They shouldn't pick the MVP on what your club does, but what you do for your club. It's unfair to players like myself who don't play on pennant winners.

But, to those who've been around him much of his career, Billy's attempt to become baseball's new "Mr. Mean" was totally out of character.

You're right. It's not my nature to be mean or to pop off. That's not the way I was brought up. But I'm glad I did because people have always put a label on me as somebody who'd accept everything that came along. Now they know I won't. And that I'm not a machine. It wasn't like me to be more concerned with what happened in the past instead of looking at the future. I'd get it pretty much out of my mind, but then friends, writers, and other players would come up and tell me I should have won the MVP—not just guys on our own team, but on other teams. The result was, I think, that I became more determined. I wanted to have a good year so badly just to see what would happen in '73.

I haven't changed my opinions on voting for Most Valuable Player. There's no consistent pattern. Maybe the writers ought to sit down and decide just what "Most Valuable" is or should be. Lots of times, in fact, most times, the winner is the best or nearly the best all-round hitter in the league, no matter how his team finishes. In '65, Willie Mays won it. He led in one department, homers, 52, but the Dodgers won the pennant. In '69, the Mets won, but Willie McCovey won it. He led in homers and RBIs. In '71, Joe Torre of the Cards got it, even though Pittsburgh won the pennant. Joe deserved it too because he led in hits, 230, RBIs, 137, average, .363, and also had 24 homers.

Take Banks. He won it twice, in '58 and '59, and should have. Even though the Cubs finished tied for fifth, he had such great marks those years, there was no question that he should win.

If they decide the winner should be the guy with the best hitting record, fine. Then everybody understands it. If they arrive at some kind of formula for rating players with some other way of judging, even better—then there's no question about it. A player will win on his record, regardless of where his club finishes, and whether he's quiet like me or a pop-off. All I say is, it should be the same for everybody. If they want it to stay the biggest, most important award in baseball, it can't become a popularity contest, and it shouldn't cause suspicion or controversy. That's what the players and fans deserve—a way to do it with no ifs, ands, or buts.

Another thing. They say the votes are in before the playoffs and World Series are played. If so, why don't they announce the winners right away so nobody gets the idea the way a player performs in those games has any effect on the voting?

By the way, I don't think pitchers should be included in voting for MVP. It's a different thing entirely. The Cy Young Award should represent the best pitcher and mean as much to pitchers as the MVP to players in other positions. If those guidelines aren't clear enough now, then they ought to be, so that whoever wins it deserves it most.

That out of his system, the Sweet Swinger went through his usual spring training routine, breaking in a new glove, feeling the knob of the bat bite deep into his hand till it was raw and painful, then the gradual healing and toughening up again after the winter of tenderizing.

Billy paced the club in the exhibition schedule, leading in RBIs and homers, and hit .318 as the Cubs won 12, lost 11. As a whole, the club hit an impressive .292.

April 6: Cubs win opener over the Expos, 3 to 2, before biggest opening-day crowd—40,273—at Wrigley Field since 1969.

April 21: Wrigleys have home crowd blinking in disbelief. They rattle off eight straight hits in first inning against chief tormentors, the Pirates. Take 10 to 4 lead, but Pirates pull to within 2 runs. Game suspended after six innings because of darkness.

April 30: Cubs now 11–8, including three wins over pesky Mets, and hold second, half a game behind New Yorkers.

May 5: Holtzman points out in *The Sporting News* that Cubs' first eight victories were by eight different pitchers, and that "Under Lockman, No Cub Player Rusts on Bench."

May 18: Billy slams 361st homer of his career to tie Joe DiMaggio on all-time homer list and also scores his 1,200th run.

May 19: In a surprise move, Cubs trade first baseman Joe Pepitone to Atlanta. Bring up Pat Bourque, who in '72 had 20 homers, 87 RBIs in 119 games at Wichita. He gets off to a fast start, with four homers in first 46 official trips to the plate, clubbing the ball at around .300.

Santo, meanwhile, is stinging the ball at .381, second highest average in National League.

May 23: Billy's surprised. Can't believe he's hitting .301.

My timing's all wrong. I'm taking too long a stride. I'm too far out in front and just pushing at the ball with my arms. It all started at the end of '72. We had second place clinched, and I was going after the Triple Crown. I needed a few more homers and got myself fouled up going after outside pitches they were feeding me. Tried to pull 'em . . . . . I'm really hitting .301? That's scufflin', real scufflin'!

Nonetheless, the reigning batting champ leads club with 24 RBIs.

May 28: The Sweet Swinger jolts Reds' ace Jack Billingham for his 362d homer to beat DiMaggio's lifetime output and move to 22d on all-time list. Cubs really winging with 16 wins in last 25 games. With 27–17 record, now lead division by five games over second-place Mets.

May 31: Cubs wage one of weirdest rallies in baseball history against Durocher's Astros. It's first time Leo's back in Chicago. In third game of series, with two out in first, Billy singles. Cubs score ten runs, just two shy of major league record.

June 8: Jenkins, Hooton, and Reuschel all have 6 wins. Billy's average is up to .321, and he's fifth in league with 35 RBIs. Monday, with only 11 homers in '72, already has 12.

June 15: Billy's 35th birthday. He makes the occasion easy to remember by drilling career hit number 2,300, topping former Cubs Charlie Grimm and Kiki Cuyler (both with 2,299) and far beyond other fine hitters of the past, including Yogi Berra, Joe Cronin, and Joe DiMaggio.

June 17: Cubs have won 12 out of 17 one-run decisions thus far.

June 25: Miracle finish by Cubs over Mets, who are sliding into last place. Held by Jon Matlack to only two hits and no runs in eight innings, Cubs rally for three runs in ninth after a walk, a single by Billy, and another walk loads the bases. Tying runs score on double by Santo, winning run by Kessinger off reliever Tug McGraw.

June 28: Somebody apparently spikes coffee of *Chicago Today* Sports Editor Rick Talley. No doubt sensing his personal vendetta to dislodge Durocher is a prime factor in the Cub runaway, he exudes a rare confidence in a column headed "IT'S CLEAR THIS IS CUBS' FLAG YEAR." Among his remarks: "Many of the Cubs will hate me for this, but I really don't see how we can put it off much longer. It's time to get excited . . . . It's the memory of 1969 that keeps the Cubs subdued these days. But, this year, folks, it's going to be different . . . . Why will this season be different? First and foremost, Leo Durocher is gone. The ramifications of that statement are many and varied, and I'll not clog your mind with them. Just believe me when I say it matters."

After praising the individual players and Lockman for making his bench strong by having faith in it, Talley concluded: "Sorry, fellas. What am I supposed to say... that you can't make it?"

June 29: Cubs coasting out front now by 7½ games, but look who's climbed into second—Gene Mauch's surprising Expos. Mets in last place, 10½ games back. Wrigleys now boast 45–31 mark for season, the only club in division playing .500 or over, with .592.

July 4: Will same old jinx repeat? Billy Goat the Twelfth, accompanied by Sam Sianis, is refused admission to Wrigley Field though his keeper has a pair of box seat tickets. Billy Goat the First was denied entry to 1945 World Series, and maybe the animal hexed the Cubs. They lost the Series. A disappointed Sam sadly leads Billy Goat away, muttering something about keeping the hex "on" and/or switching to the White Sox.

July 5: Jimmy (the "Greek") Snyder makes Cubs 1–5 favorites in NL East and tabs Mets at 50–1. Jenkins makes a startling remark. Disappointed with his performance (8–6) and giving up 23 homers in 20 starts, he says, "I just don't feel like coming out to the park anymore. I haven't lost my zest for the game. I just don't like coming out here."

Billy's also worried about slump—only six hits in last 32 at-bats in ten game home stand, which Cubs split 5–5. Santo still hot, with .325, as Cubs leave for eight games on West Coast.

July 6: Owner Wrigley sets a precedent by offering to pick up tabs for wives and children to accompany players on California junket. It's met with mixed emotions, *until* they return.

July 16: Cubs return home scorched and smarting from loss of six out of eight on coast and see their lead slashed to only two games over the surging Cardinals.

According to Jerome Holtzman, the idea of taking wives and kids along at least once during the year came from player rep, Milt Pappas.

Bouton, the irreverent author of *Ball Four*, which hardly described a ballplayer's road trips as family affairs, was heard to comment, "The Cub players ought to impeach Pappas."

Former American League umpire Bill Valentine added this one-liner: "Next trip, the Cubs ought to bring the wives and leave the players at home."

Billy's family was unable to make the trip. Shirley was busy with the chores of moving into their new home.

Carmen Fanzone, one of the most sought-after bachelors in Chicagoland, cracked, "I should have been allowed to bring a broad along."

Lockman, who was accompanied by his wife and four children, didn't see how the families' being along hampered the club's play, they'd been in a slump before leaving.

"That we lost six out of eight games... had nothing to do with our wives being with us," said Whitey.

And, presumably after burning his column of June 28, Rick Talley returned to form as "Rick the Ripper." Quoting in part from his *Chicago Today* story: "What happened to Our Heroes in California shouldn't happen to any team that is serious about playing major league baseball.... The Cubs' situation is far more serious than whether or not somebody visited Disneyland with his family.... The Cubs have become a team which cannot live with success.

"Talk to any man in baseball about the Cub line-up and he will tell you they should win because they have the best talent. But give the Cubs a lead and a little pennant heat and they run for cover .... Until now Whitey's job has been relatively simple. He did all the things Durocher didn't do, and the Cubs responded by winning baseball games.... What will Whitey do to change the oh-oh-we're-gonna-get-beat-again-attitude? Quite frankly, I hope he'll do something drastic.... I vote for a spanking. Over the head with a two-by-four."

July 22: *Whoops!* Cubs tumble into second place. Their loss to Giants in final game before the All-Star Game break is 9th defeat in last 10 contests, 15th in the last 20. Cardinals now top the division with 51–45 record, Cubs are 51–46, half a game back.

Billy and Santo are the only Cubs chosen to start for the National League in All-Star classic July 24 at Kansas City.

July 24: "CUBS, WILLIAMS, JENKINS DIP BELOW EXPECTED LEVEL." This was headline of a story by George Langford in the *Chicago Tribune* the morning of the All-Star Game. Langford began: "Long after the disappointed thousands had abandoned Wrigley Field Sunday, a black cat strayed thru the litter... in the box seats near home plate. The cat was alone in the stands and it was a prophetic sight, the scrawny animal strolling thru the arena where a July disaster had just reduced the Cubs to a second-place organization after 74 days at the top. A superstitious sort would blame the cat. But the Cubs' run of luck has a more concrete basis. It has to do with the matter of skill—its quality and quantity. And timing.

"EXHIBIT NUMBER ONE is Billy Williams, for the previous three years combined, the most productive hitter in the major leagues, the only player during the time to average more than 100 RBIs, 30 home runs, and a .315 batting mark.

"Suddenly, after 13 remarkable seasons that have been taken for granted simply because of his quiet nature and effortless ability, Williams is not producing at the expected rate. His swing isn't the flawless weapon of beauty it has always been before.

"He is 35 years old, a fact that nags and raises questions that even fans feel compelled to whisper. It can't be age. It just couldn't be. It's just a slump. His worst slump. At the worst time.

"Williams and Jenkins have fallen below their expected level, and, not unexpectedly, so have the Cubs."

Shirley's comment: "If people know me as Shirley Williams, then sometimes it's rough. But when I'm Mrs. Billy Williams, then I get the royal-carpet treatment. They give me that 'Are you *the* Mrs. Billy Williams?' It was a lot different in '73. In previous years, they'd ask what's wrong with the team. In '73, they'd ask what's wrong with Billy, how come he isn't doing what he did last year. I say, 'He's only human, he can't do it all the time. Can you be perfect in *your* job all the time?' They expect perfection all the time from a ballplayer. They can't have a position like a human being. They have to be superhuman."

July 24 (evening): Billy trots out to be introduced before the TV cameras at new Royals Stadium in Kansas City, and his face lights up with a grin that says it all. It's the sixth time he's appeared in the All-Star clash. All other times he's been picked by the players and managers, a fine tribute to a ballplayers' ballplayer, but not until this season had the fans voted the long-overlooked superstar into a starting position. Only Pete Rose received more outfield ballots, Billy collecting 889,669. To make the event even more gratifying, a poll taken among players on their choices agreed with the fans, at least in Billy's case. The players would have preferred Bobby Bonds of the Giants and Willie Stargell of the Pirates instead of Rose and Cesar Cedeno of Houston. For the first time, Billy had achieved full recognition. Santo topped the Cards' Joe Torre for third base and, like Billy, was the choice of the players as well.

Both repaid their backers. Billy got the Nationals' first hit, a savage smash up the middle that disabled the American League's starting pitcher Jim ("Catfish") Hunter of the A's, who stabbed at the ball with his bare hand and fractured a thumb; Santo had the second hit as the NL routed the AL 7 to 1.

July 26: Billy receives Silver Bat in recognition of his National League batting championship, with a .333 average, in 1972. League President Chub Feeney is at Wrigley Field to make the presentation.

Cubs squeak out 10–9 win over Pirates in completion of game suspended in April, then drop second game 3–2 despite ten strikeouts by Reuschel.

July 27, 28: Cubs lose to Pirates and Cards. Now 2½ games out.

July 29: Billy rams a two-run homer, but Cards take the first game of a doubleheader, 5 to 4. Cubs split as Billy drives in the deciding run in the nightcap, another 5 to 4 nail-biter.

Sportswriters and fans alike are prepared for the worst, as indicated in this comment by Edgar Munzel in *The Sporting News.*

"Remember the collapse of the Cubs in 1969? In recent weeks, Chicago fans have been reminded of it again in all its horror because they're seeing it happen all over again. Only this time it has come earlier.

"On June 29, the Cubs were out in front . . . with a margin of eight games over the Cardinals. But suddenly the bottom fell out. By July 22, the day before the All-Star interlude, the Cardinals had taken over first place and the Cubs never have been back. Primary reason for the big plunge was a dismal team batting slump."

July 30: Williams raps out two hits and an RBI to beat Cards and Gibson, 3 to 1, and cut St. Louis' lead to 1½ games. Cards' lone run scores when Lou Brock walks and steals his 600th base. This prompts sarcastic remark in press box as Chuck Shriver announces the Cubs will present the base to Brock as a memento. Recalling the trade that sent Brock to Cards for sore-armed Ernie Broglio in '64, somebody cracks, "Why not? They've been *giving* it to him for years!"

July 31 (morning): "WHAT WILL CUBS' EXCUSE BE THIS TIME?" Robert Markus heads his column in the *Chicago Tribune.* "When Durocher left, I warned the players that they hadn't begun to know what pressure is. There'd be no more Leo Durocher to kick around and blame for their failure. . . . They have the kind of manager they said they wanted. The regulars are getting plenty of rest, the reserves are seeing plenty of action. . . . The seven-game home stand just completed against the Pirates and Cardinals was billed as crucial. It was no such thing. The seven games are over and the Cubs lost more than they won. They're still in position to challenge.

"The season is 162 games long and will be decided by the team that wins the most games over that span, not just in a 'crucial' seven-game period. The Cubs have never seemed to understand that if the Cardinals beat you three out of four this week, you can knock over the Phillies three out of four next week and be right back where you were. Now would be a pretty good time for them to learn it. If they don't, it's going to be the same old story on Chicago's North Side. But this time there won't be any Durocher to blame." Billy comments:

I think this had to happen sooner or later. It all started in 1971 when the team and Durocher had that big blow-up, when Durocher quit, then was persuaded to stay. And Mr. Wrigley backed him up with the ad he ran in the newspapers. We didn't do well after that at all. Then Leo started out with us in '72, and we still couldn't seem to get going. Mr. Wrigley apparently thought the best thing to do at the time was let Leo go or let him "step aside." I'm not sure how it worked. But anyway, when Wrigley announced that Leo'd be leaving and that Whitey'd be taking over, he gave the idea he wasn't too happy about losing Leo, and that it was up to the players to prove we were able to win with another manager. We finished up great in '72 with Whitey, and the writers and just about everybody figured we'd win in '73, especially after we got off to such a good start and a big lead. But after we started to slip, the stories began coming out that if we don't do it this year, it's nobody's fault but the players'.

It wasn't any surprise to me. I could hear the fans chanting in the stands. "It wasn't Durocher after all .... We want Durocher back."

July 31 (evening): Billy drives in two runs, one the winning tally, to beat Phils in first game of twin-bill. Pinch-hitting in second game, chases in another run, but Cubs lose.

August 1: Lockman explodes. Monday explodes. Even Billy explodes! According to Fergie, it's the first time he ever saw Billy really hot. It happened at Philadelphia. There's no score in the sixth but the Cubs have a golden opportunity. Monday doubles, Kessinger walks, and Billy comes to bat with one out. Philly pitcher Wayne Twitchell's first pitch to Billy hits him on the right foot. Billy starts for first but is called back. Seeing the ball bounce at the plate, Monday streaks for third. The catcher's throw arrives in time and Rick's called out, but starts ranting that he hasn't been tagged. Meanwhile, Billy's barking at plate umpire, Jerry Dale, trying to show him where the ball hit his foot. Dale of course goes deaf, and Lockman is livid. Monday's ruled out, Billy's sent back to the plate, and instead of a bases-loaded, one-out situation, it's two outs with a man on first. Monday and Lockman are ejected, the Cubs fail to score, and the Phils win, 2 to 0.

Fergie's right. I was really burning. The important thing is I felt this guy knew he was wrong, and yet he wouldn't admit to it. If a guy knows he's wrong and beats around the bush instead of admitting it, that's what gets me. No, I couldn't believe the call, especially when I never get into an argument with an umpire. Because I live by the book, I guess I feel everybody else should live by the book.

August 4, 5, 6, 7, 8: Cubs lose three to Expos, two to Reds. Talley writes, "OUR CUBS HAVE DONE IT AGAIN." Among Rick's barbs: "Have you heard about the Cubs being sold to a group of businessmen in the Philippines?"

"Naaahhh, really?"

"Yeah... they're gonna move the team to the Philippines and rename them the Manila Folders."

"The records show that this 1973 Collapse has been even more complete than the Collapse of 1969, Collapse of 1970, Collapse of 1971, or Collapse of 1972.

"You can leave town with that same comfortable feeling you've had for the last five years. You won't be missing a thing at Wrigley Field. The Cubs have done it again."

August 9: Cub owner Phil Wrigley isn't giving up, announces: "All we need is for lightning to strike again like it did in 1935 when we won 21 games in a row, and the pennant."

August 10, 11, 12: Cubs drop three to Astros. In his column, Robert Markus of the *Chicago Tribune* notes that he reminded Billy that his .281 batting average would look pretty good to a lot of hitters.

But more's expected of me. After all, I did win the batting championship last year. I don't know what's wrong. All I know is there are only two things to look at. You do. Or you don't. There's no in-between and no excuses.

Markus then told how he felt about the situation. "One of the reasons opposing clubs can afford to pitch around Billy Williams is that there's nobody up behind him. Ron Santo, who used to hit in the fourth spot, has been batting No. 5 all year. I'm told it's to take the pressure off him. But nobody's taking it off Williams. For the most part, the fourth spot has been filled by Pat Bourque, who's under .200 with seven home runs, or by Jim Hickman, who has only three homers and never has hit well in a utility role like the one he's been employed in this year. Williams won't use that as an excuse, but I think there's plenty of evidence that it's one good reason he's having an off year."

August 13: Bill Gleason of the *Chicago Sun-Times* gets off one of his scathing bits as Cubs' losing streak continues, and they slip into fourth place, 4½ games behind the Cards. "Our North Side nine is one of the few championship contenders in history that has managed to lose ground while the team it was chasing endured six straight defeats. The Cubs non-accomplished this extraordinary feat by losing eight straight."

August 14: Braves knock Jenkins out of the box. After being relieved, Fergie throws tantrum in dugout—and four bats out onto field, one close to umpire Jerry Dale. Cooler heads get him to the clubhouse. Rico Carty makes first appearance as pinch-hitter.

August 15: To get Carty's bat in line-up, Lockman puts Rico in left and Billy plays his first major league game at first base. Braves clobber Cubs, 15 to 1, the Cubs' tenth straight loss. Vince Lloyd sadly wraps up story of the massacre for radio audience, then adds, "The starting pitcher tomorrow for the Cubs will be Milt Pappas, *if* they can talk him into it."

August 16: Pappas and Bob Locker stymie Braves for seven innings and have 2 to 0 shutout going. But in eighth, Braves explode for nine runs, including what 17,682 customers came to see—Hank Aaron's career homer number 702, a 425-foot blast. It's Hank's 29th of the year and 49th at Wrigley Field, where he's hit more homers than in any other park on the road. Cubs' losing string reaches 11 —31 defeats in the last 41 games. Billy comments on the 11-game losing streak:

I think this is why so many teams get in slumps. Because everybody wants to lead the ball club. Everybody wants to win ballgames. And if you're not careful, you find yourself trying to hit the ball out of the park. We played well the first part of the year playing as a team. The answer then is to go back and start playing the kind of baseball you were earlier. A team effort. You get a guy on with a single, a walk or some way, you bunt him over, and another guy drives him in. It just won't work with one guy going up there trying to hit a homer.

August 17: Billy dumps Dodgers! Drives in four runs with bases-loaded single and a two-run homer as Cubs whip Western Division leaders, 5 to 1, and snap losing streak.

August 18: Billy does it again, delights over 24,000 fans. Cubs trail, 1 to 0, till sixth. Williams racks Claude Osteen for homer and 2 to 1 lead that holds up as Hooton shuts out Dodgers. Still playing first, Billy's four hits (two homers) in seven trips to the plate drive in six of the Cubs' seven runs in two days.

August 19: Reuschel holds Dodgers to four hits, but one is two-run homer in ninth and Cubs drop 2 to 1 heartbreaker.

August 21: Billy doubles and drives in two runs to beat Reds, 6 to 4, and help Jenkins record his first win since July 31.

August 22: In opener of three-game series Reds walk Cardenal to pitch to Popovich. Popo shocks Cincinnati by walloping game-winning three-run homer, his first of only two all year.

Monday scribbles on blackboard in Cub clubhouse: "Ruth 714 . . . Aaron 705 . . . Popovich 13." The glue-fingered "supersub," whose last homer came in August '72, cracks, "August is my big month!"

August 23–30: Cubs sweep series from Reds, winning 8 of 11 games after their losing streak. They're now in third, but trail by only three games.

During the month, Billy's average is .327, with 34 hits, including four doubles and four homers; he has 17 RBIs, and scores 11 runs.

August 31: In doubleheader with Pirates, Lockman rides with his two top winning pitchers. The chronic Cub-killers rack Reuschel for six runs, three of them unearned, to take the first game, then shell Jenkins to grab the nightcap.

September 1: Hooton and Pittsburgh's Bruce Kison tangle in brilliant scoreless duel for 8⅓ innings, but Pirates push over one run in ninth for their third straight win.

September 2: Billy bangs out a double, a single, and a two-run homer to break tie and salvage final game of Pirate series.

September 3, 4, 6: At Montreal, Expos dump Cubs three straight, despite Billy's flaming bat. As team limps home, he's hit safely in 11 of 12 games on the road for .388. Cubs return in fifth place, six games behind the division-leading Cards who open vital three-game set the next day at Wrigley Field.

September 7: Billy's bat still blazes. He leads Cubs in 8 to 2 romp over the leaders, tying National League high for season with five hits in five at-bats, including a double and three RBIs off Cardinal starter Rick Wise, who no doubt regrets ever throwing dusters at number "26." The onslaught sends his average, which had dropped during his slump, to .301, but Billy shakes his head.

That's just a figure. I'm not after the batting title this year. We still have a good chance. Not as good as a couple of weeks ago, but still good. And we've got enough time to get the job done.

September 8: Billy proves the word "quit" is another four-letter word he never uses. He raps out his sixth straight hit and scores the first run as Cubs slice another game off St. Louis lead. Relief ace Al Hrabosky strikes him out to snap hitting string.

September 9: "Mr. Ice in the Clutch" comes through again, with Monday the other half of an explosive one-two punch. Rick hits solo homers in the first and third, but Cards bounce back to take 3 to 2 lead in top of the fifth. Monday singles in tying run in Cubs' fifth, and Billy triples to drive him home with the go-ahead run. Cards tie it up again. In the eighth, Williams again faces Hrabosky. The lefty's the only one to get Billy out so far in the series and in over 30 relief appearances hadn't given up a homer. His luck runs out. Billy slashes a four-bagger for the winning run and a series sweep.

During the three-game series, with eight hits in nine at-bats, Billy drove in five runs, scored three, had a double, a triple, and a home run, and extended his batting streak to nine straight games. He had hit safely in 14 of the last 15 games.

Race has really tightened up. Cubs have a red-hot chance to move up—only three games separate first five teams. The Pirates, just one game behind the leading Cards, are at the "friendly confines" for four games starting September 10.

September 10: Ugly history repeating? Bucs batter Cubs, 11 to 3, with 21-hit barrage. Billy goes hitless in three trips for first time in ten games.

September 11: Hooton holds Pirates to only four hits, Blass gives Cubs only three. But Hundley homers and Billy drives in a run with a sacrifice fly to win, 2 to 0.

September 12, 13: Pirates pound Cubs, 4 to 2 and 6 to 1, Billy driving in only Chicago run of second game.

More bad news. Beckert no longer able to start. Available for pinch-hitting only. Will require postseason operation.

September 15, 16: Mets, creeping up, take two out of three from Cubs, move into fourth place, ahead of Cubs and only 2½ back of pace-setting Pirates. Expos are just half a game behind Pittsburgh.

When we got to New York, Maury Wills interviewed me. Now that I was beginning to hit pretty well again, did I think one player could carry a ball club? I said yes, if the pitchers will pitch to you. But when only one or two on the club are hitting well, it's easy for them to pitch around you. It comes up in their meetings the same as ours. They say, "Whatever you do, don't let Williams hurt you. Don't let him beat you. If you get into a spot where he can hurt you, throw him bad pitches, don't give him anything good to hit." Or, "If somebody's in scoring position, put him on first base."

I guess this shows I'm not a machine after all. Over the years, you develop a habit of going up to the plate to hit the baseball, not going up there to get a base on balls. I'm in a spot in the batting order where I've got the job of driving in runs. I want to knock 'em in, I want to swing the bat. So you get anxious up there sometimes, y'know, because you want to hit the ball, especially when the club's having trouble scoring many runs. But sometimes you just hurt yourself. You start by swinging at a ball one or two inches outside and all of a sudden, you find yourself going after 'em four and five inches outside. Whitey and I had a talk about it earlier in the season up in his office, and he told me it's better to be on first base than swinging at bad pitches. You know these things, but wanting and trying so hard to produce, it can get away from you, and then it's time to get back to basics. For me, that's to remember what Hornsby kept drumming into me—to be a good hitter, you've got to get a good ball to hit. Make sure it's in the strike zone.

September 17: "ONLY SOLUTION FOR THE CUBS: FIRE THE CUBS," writes Robert Markus, in the *Chicago Tribune*. Among his biting comments: "The Cubs have been dead for half the season now, and it's about time somebody notified the mortuary. This is nothing new for Cub fans who for time eternal have been warbling the mournful losers' song: 'Wait Till Next Year'.

"The Cubs have already tried one of the two accepted remedies for shaking up a bad ball club. They've fired the manager. I now suggest they take the alternative course and fire the team.

"Break 'em up. Splinter 'em. Back up the truck and ship 'em out. Sound cruel? Not at all. There isn't a key member of the team who wouldn't be better off for a change of scenery." He concludes: "If something isn't done—right now, before another season starts—the Cubs could well be on the brink of another 20-year voyage to the bottom of the earth."

September 19: After splitting twin-bill at Philadelphia, Cubs return to Chicago five games off the pace—and greet Gene Mauch's scrappy Expos who are challenging Pirates for division lead.

With only enough fans on hand to keep the Andy Frain ushers company, Expos bomb Reuschel for five runs in first, but he stays in the game. Cubs battle back and trail by just a run in fifth following homer by Monday. With two out and two strikes on him, Billy works starter Mike Torrez for a walk. Mauch waves for Mike Marshall, who set a new major league record with 92 relief appearances and led the NL in saves (31) in '73. Santo shocks the fabulous fireman with a shot into the seats, and Cubs lead, 6 to 5.

Marshall's still on the mound in the seventh, with Monday on first and Billy batting. The Sweet Swinger blasts the 376th homer of his career. Since the Expos scored in the ninth, it's the game-winning blow.

The homer puts him past Ralph Kiner (369), Gil Hodges (370), and Rocky Colavito (374) on baseball's all-time list. And at the end of the 1973 season, he's third among all active National Leaguers, behind Aaron (713) and Willie McCovey (413).

September 20, 21, 22, 23: Cubs virtually scrub Expos out of contention with two more wins. Billy's great throw cutting down runner trying to stretch a single is big factor in win on 21st. Another Williams' bulls-eye to the plate nips Philly trying to score as Cubs bounce Philadelphia twice to run winning streak to five games. Phils take final game.

September 25: "Corpse" shows signs of life. Bruins rally with three runs in ninth to down Cardinals, 4 to 3, and move ahead of slumping St. Louis in standings, 3½ games behind Mets, now entrenched in lead.

September 26, 27: Brock haunts his former team twice in two of the year's most gripping games. He scores a run in the first frame on the 26th, then Bonham and Wise both pitch scoreless baseball the rest of the way. Wise is the winner, 1 to 0, on a five-hitter, and Bonham the hapless loser, giving up only seven hits.

The next night, Reggie Cleveland picks up where Wise left off, and Hooton starts for Cubs. The first 16 Cub batters go hitless, and Hooton scatters hits but no runs score. Ken Rudolph singles to ruin the no-hitter but is rubbed out when Hooton's attempted sacrifice turns into a double-play. Brock snaps the scoreless tie with a two-run homer in the sixth. Cleveland sets down the next ten Cubs in order for the first one-hitter of his career.

Disheartened Cubs head home for the last four games of the season—against the Mets—who were in last place July 30, nine games back, and still in last place, 6½ games back, August 27.

The standings on September 28: the Pirates, 1 game behind Mets; the Cards 2½ behind; the Expos 3½ behind; the Cubs, in fifth place, 4 behind.

Even a five-way tie is a remote possibility at this stage. The only thing 100 percent sure is that the Cubs must win all four games from the Mets to stand any chance of picking up the marbles.

September 28: Rain washes out scheduled game. Cubs grouse. The odds aren't tough enough. Now they face two doubleheaders on two days.

September 29: Relentless rain still pelts Wrigley Field. Inside their clubhouse, the Cubs are edgy, irritated, frustrated. Over in Mets' quarters, Tom Seaver is savoring the extra day of rest he's getting thanks to the downpour. He tells reporters "the ball feels heavy," reminds them he's already pitched over 280 innings. The games are called off—so it's to be two games tomorrow (Sunday) and probably two more on Monday.

September 30: The field's sloppy and rain-puddled in the outfield but the umpires give okay to start. Surprisingly, a crowd of 21,432 turns out for the showdown. Reuschel rewards the fans with seven innings of shutout baseball. Jon Matlack, on the hill for the Mets, also hangs goose eggs on the board, and gives up only three hits, one by Billy. But after pitching to one man in the eighth, a blister on his pitching hand forces Reuschel to leave the game. Locker takes over in relief.

Rookie Dave Rosello singles to lead off in the bottom of the inning. Then, with two strikes on him, Kessinger surprises the Mets' infield by bunting, Rosello making it safely to second. Santo, up next, cracks a single and Rosello streaks in to make it 1 to 0. It's all the Cubs need. Locker mops up in the ninth. The Bruins are still alive.

The sounds of "Joy" reverberate throughout the park as Wrigley Field organist Frank Pellico happily runs his fingers over the huge console in the upper-deck booth overlooking the leftfield area. It's the song saluting every Cub victory in '73. Pellico also has a special song for each Cub player, either one that the player would like played or something appropriate. For example, with Rick Monday digging into the batter's box, it's "Never on Sunday"—naturally. He used to play "Billy Boy" for the veteran leftfielder, but he now introduces Williams with "Mr. Bojangles," one of Billy's favorites.

Unable to play in the final game due to an injury, Hundley doesn't know he's heard "Dixie" for his last time—unless they play it for the "Rebel" at Minnesota.

There are mixed reactions when Jenkins runs out to the mound for the second game. Some fans cheer, a few boo, but most are silent. The rangy righthander's quotes and misquotes have cost him popularity. One remark in particular came back to burn him. He'd said, in jest, how nice it would be playing in Detroit since it's so close to his home in Ontario. It was interpreted as a desire to be traded. Fergie's had a tough year—the four bats he threw cost him $100 each in fines, he's failed to win at least 20 games for the first time in seven years, and has given up the most homers (34) of any pitcher in the league.

The year doesn't get any better for Jenkins fast. A pair of errors lead to three unearned runs in the first inning. Again, it's the all-too-familiar story of the Cubs having to play catch-up baseball—not an easy job with Jerry Koosman serving them up for the Mets. The Cubs get a pair of runs back, but that's all, as Koosman scatters six hits. Jenkins racks up his 16th loss of the year, 9 to 2, Cleon Jones clipping him for homer number 35. Fergie has heard "Alouette" for the last time at Wrigley Field. Shortly after the season ends, he'll find out he'll be chucking his baseballs for Billy Martin of the Texas Rangers.

The strains of "For the Good Times" follow those who stayed to the bitter end of the game. Denoting a Cub defeat, it's been played all too often. The disappointed fans shuffle toward the exits, still finding it hard to believe that this year wasn't "next year" either. The Met win has eliminated the Cubs from any chance for a playoff and assures New York at least a tie. Only the Cards and Pirates remain in contention—and the Cubs hold the key. If the Cubs take two from the Mets, it could become a three-way playoff situation.

October 1: Another doubleheader on tap. But only 1,913 bother to show up. It's Seaver against Hooton, who gets through the first inning with no difficulties. Then a boot by Santo allows a gift run in the second. Seaver is happy to get it. He's not at his sharpest and allows 11 hits and four runs—an RBI by Billy and Kessinger and a two-run homer by Monday. Fortunately for the Met ace, New York bats are busy collecting five more runs off Hooton and Aker.

Tug McGraw comes in to relieve Seaver in the seventh and throttles the Cubs until the ninth when Rudolph gets an infield hit with one out. Number "18" is in the on-deck circle, and Pellico breaks out with Beckert's last salute—"The Pennsylvania Polka."

Glenn hits a soft liner that doubles up Rudolph and ends the game. The Mets are the Eastern Division champions. Pellico plays "For the Good Times"... one more time... as the Cubs trudge slowly off the field.

The word's waiting for them in the clubhouse—the second game's off. There's no purpose now. The Cards and Pirates are dead along with the Cubs. Milt Pappas is one especially disappointed Cub. He would probably have started the second game. Now he must "wait till next year" for his chance to become the third pitcher in history to win 100 or more games in both major leagues.

The Cubs don't say much. They have other things on their minds, especially the veterans, the members of the "old guard," who have been together for five straight, often frantic but always fruitless, campaigns—beginning with the "Hey, Hey! Holy Mackerel!" glory days of 1969.

It has to be running through their minds. Billy. Santo. Jenkins. Hundley. Beckert. Kessinger. Popovich. Hickman. How many would be dressing in the same clubhouse in 1974—if any? Billy, Santo, and Hickman must okay a trade under the new Players' Association ruling for ten-year veterans who have been with the same club for five years. But not the others. They can be sent anywhere.

A couple of Cub fans are polishing off their last brew before leaving the park.

"Ain't that somethin'? What happened? The way the Cubbies started out and those bleepin' Mets win. Now '69 don't look so bad.... The Mets couldn't do anything wrong at the end there. But *this* year... what went wrong?"

"Don't know. But I'll tell you *one* thing. No matter what they do with the Cubs over the winter... all I gotta say is... next time that guy shows up with the *goat*... they'd better let 'em in."

1973—A Postmortem

"I've been unhappy over the team's performances in other years, but there's only one word to describe my feelings about this season and that word is—disgust." So said Philip K. Wrigley, quoted by Harvey Duck in the October 3 *Chicago Daily News*.

"I feel Whitey did a good job. He can return as manager if he desires. I can't say that any of the others earned their money this season," the Cub owner went on.

In talking with *Chicago Sun-Times* columnist Edgar Munzel, Wrigley singled out only one player for praise, the same as he had done in his startling newspaper ad in '71, which kept Durocher on as manager, commended only Banks, and "fired" the rest of the team.

"We just didn't have anybody who could drive in any big runs except Jose Cardenal. I just hope the rest of them haven't killed his spirit.... They made a lot of mistakes and we must have set a record for leaving men on base."

Perhaps Wrigley didn't have the final statistics when interviewed. Indeed, Cardenal *was* valuable, leading the Cubs in batting, with .303, 33 doubles, and 19 stolen bases. However, Billy led in game-winning hits, 14. Monday belted a career high of 26 homers to lead the club, and Billy was club leader in hits (166), RBIs (86), and sacrifice flies (6); he hit .288 and tied Santo for second in homers, with 20.

Not a real bad season I guess, but for me, personally, it was a bad season, because I'm capable of doing better.

And as for leaving men on base, Wrigley apparently wasn't aware that only three other National League clubs left as *few* on base as the Cubs; in the East Division, only the Pirates left fewer on base than the Cubs.

Unfortunately, however, the Cubs also had the fewest at-bats and hits in the league and were tied for tenth for fewest total bases. And there's no denying that the "power shortage" hit Chicago earlier and harder than other National League teams. From fifth in batting in '72, the Cubs sank to tenth in '73. Only the Mets and Padres were punier at the plate. The Cubs' homer output also sagged from 133 in '72 to 117 in '73. Though the "friendly confines" are supposedly ideal for the North-Siders, the wind blows out for the other teams too. The invaders hit the long ball 72 times to only 66 by the Wrigleys in their home park.

The effect of a team slump on the productivity of an individual player becomes strikingly clear in view of the fact that Billy scored the fewest runs in his entire 13 full seasons, only 72. With 731 plate appearances, he reached base 223 times, including 76 walks, 14 of which were intentional. Homers aren't figured in the on-base figure. So the sad truth is that by hitting 20 homers Billy thus drove *himself* in 20 times, while his mates pushed him around only 52 of the 223 times he reached base.

"I think there's been some undue criticism going around, the fact that we haven't played as well as we should have this year, and putting the blame on the big guys... Jenkins, Santo, and Billy Williams." The speaker was Glenn Beckert, the day before the Mets clinched the 1973 East Division title.

"It's got to affect the player. The player who says it doesn't affect him is crazy. It affects him. Maybe this caused Billy to put a little more burden on his back, and he shouldn't. You don't win with three players on a club, although the press makes out that you do. But that's wrong. It's going to be the average players who surround the superstars having a good year that determines whether you win. Look at Pittsburgh. Stargell's having a good year, a great one, and he's their big guy. But the little guys haven't provided the punch.

"I know that some of the years I've hit second ahead of Billy were some of his best years. He's a better hitter with men on base. For one thing, it opens up more holes. With the first baseman holding a runner on first, it's easier for a lefthanded hitter like Billy to get a base hit. He pulls a lot of ground balls in the hole between first and second. He didn't get a lot of those this year. There were a lot of switches of the lead-off man and second hitter, and, for that matter, the guys batting behind Billy. Things like these all add up, but the average fan doesn't realize it."

Beck's right, said Billy. *There's been a lot of talk about how we would have won if Billy and Fergie and Ronnie had good years. But these are guys who've had good years the last five years, and we still haven't won. Speakin' about Fergie, this is the one year he didn't wind up winning 20 ballgames. It's the first year I haven't hit .300 or more in the last four years. Ron drove in 123 runs in '69 and 114 in '70. My best years were '70 and '72, but we still didn't win. The sports magazines that come out in February or March have felt that with the players we had and their past records, we were capable of winning from '69 on. The writers, they look at it this way: if this player and that one has his standard type year, the Cubs should win. But that's on paper. The thing that's forgotten is . . . we've got to play the games to win. And perform. I'd say it's a matter of five or six guys on a ball club all having a good year in order to win the pennant.*

Several important factors contributing to the Cubs' failure in '73 were overlooked. One of these was the surprising and sudden trade of "Mr. Unpredictable," Joe Pepitone, on May 19.

The flighty first sacker who used to roam about town in a chauffeured Rolls Royce—and once taunted Durocher with a "Leo Must Go" button in his mouth, with the "Lip" standing next to him—was hitting well when the deal was made.

With Pepi gone, first base, a problem ever since Banks hung 'em up, became more acute than ever. Billy said of Joe:

It could have been a big mistake. This was the year he really was going to play ball. And I'll tell you why I think so. Down in spring training, he and I had a $5,000 bet. If Pepi left the ball club during the season, as he'd done before, he was to pay me $5,000. And I said, "If you stay with the ball club all year, at the end of the season, I'll give you five grand." I did it just to let him show the talent I knew this guy had that could really help our ball club.

I know he was heart-broken about it when he found out he was traded. He called me that morning. I think it surprised the majority of the players. They'd heard how he talked in the clubhouse and could tell he was all enthused about playing this particular year.

He could have helped, because when he left, he'd been playing first, and the ball club was depending on him. It made a big difference when the others tried to come in and take over, coming in cold, since they hadn't been playing. Unfortunately, bringing up Pat

Bourque didn't work out either. He started out real well, but then his hitting fell down.

I'm not sure of the real reason they let Pepi go. But Joe could get himself pretty involved in all kinds of troubles, and that probably had a lot to do with it.

I do know there were some hard feelings the time Pepi resigned from baseball [in early May of 1972], *then changed his mind later on and came back with the club* [in mid-June 1972]. *Leo said he'd have to fight for his job, but within a few days, he was back playing first base.*

It gave me a shot at first base too. [Billy played 19 games at first, had 167 put-outs, 20 assists, took part in 14 double-plays, with only 2 errors.] *I enjoyed it and seemed to feel stronger. My hitting picked up. I played first some in the minors, but know I still have plenty to learn about the position. It extended Ernie's career. Maybe it can do the same for me.*

The loss of Glenn Beckert for full-time duty after July 19 was also a serious blow to the Cubs' hitting attack. Beckert jumped off to a flaming start with 81 hits in 82 games, running up the longest consecutive-game hitting streak in the league (26) and hit .358 during that stretch.

Another Cub problem was the giant slip by Santo due to a jammed thumb suffered in spring training. It never healed completely. Ron was off to one of the most blistering starts in his career and as late as July 5 was still hitting like a demon—.325, 93 hits, 47 RBIs. When the Cubs took their West Coast trip with their families, Santo needed a sponge to protect the thumb at bat and was in pain whenever he made contact. Unfortunately, when Billy's bat came to life, not only Santo but the other hitters went into their colossal slump.

The pitching was also dismal, a big drop from the previous year. After July 20, Reuschel was 4–9, Jenkins 5–8, Pappas 2–4, and Hooton 5–9.

The press has advanced many theories on the possible causes for the marathon of miseries which befell the Cubs in 1973, and with the help of Billy, let's see how much water they hold.

For one thing, the "boys" have never let the Cubs forget '69.

Jack Griffin, *Chicago Sun-Times,* June 6, 1973: Griffin told how the "Bleacher Bums" still gathered at Ray's Bleachers and still played their "varsity song," "Hey, Hey! Holy Mackerel!" but that there were a lot of new faces, and their celebrating was quite subdued.

"But there was a specter that hung over them, both the new and the old, and that was 1969, the Year of the Great Debacle, when glory ended and turned to dust in the air of late September.

" 'It's not like 1969, is it?' said one of the group.

"It was not a question really. But rather a plea for reassurance that what had happened four years ago would not befall the Cubs, and that the taste of victory would not go to their heads, as it had done in those dark weeks at the end of the season."

Edgar Munzel, *The Sporting News*, September 1, 1973: Comparing the '69 and '73 skids, Munzel added, "That haunts the veteran Cubs like a nightmare because the current tailspin of the Cubs is so similar."

Billy's comments: *I think a ballplayer plays from year to year, and that we go out and try to win the ballgames over a 162-game season, not just three-quarters of a season. A lot of people said that we lost it in '69. But the Mets played over .700 baseball the last quarter. And any time a ball club plays this kind of ball, they're bound to win. I always feel, and I think most of our players feel, it wasn't a case of our ball club losing it, it was a case of the Mets playing a tremendous percentage of baseball to win it. Really, it didn't have the effect on us that some people make out it did, at least that's how I feel about it.*

The question of Cub salaries too has always intrigued the press, especially when the investments don't pay off in a pennant.

James Enright, *Chicago Today*, September 14, 1973: "In the Cubs' country-club atmosphere, it's a never-ending I-me-my story at salaries ranging from $65,000 to $150,000."

Billy's comments: *When you get right down to it, only a few fellas on the ball club are making real good money. And it's only because these are players who've gone out and proved themselves, played good baseball not just a few seasons or two but over a period of 8, 10, 12, or so years. In many cases, they're also rewarded for their leadership. We all try to help the young ballplayers, get them to develop a winning attitude. Lots of times, they'd rather get the dope straight from a player who's had some good years in the big leagues, and success.*

You hear that "giving 100 percent" a lot from ballplayers, I know, but there's no other way to say it. Because we play in so many games, especially the big salary guys who can't be replaced or spared that easily, sometimes it might look as if we're not giving 100 percent. But you can be sure we're all giving 100 percent of what we've got at the time—and not because of the salary. It's because we have personal pride in playing our best and trying to win. There's no other way to play the game, and I know I'm not the only one who goes out every day with that idea.

Another thing people have a tendency to forget. I was fortunate enough to get the highest salary ever paid to a Cub ballplayer. But what kind of money do you think I made those five years I spent in the minors before making it up to the big club? And how much my first few years in the majors? It took ten full seasons of good, consistent baseball to get that figure—and I almost didn't get it then because of a policy against paying that much. And I haven't been getting it that long. So averaging it all out over what amounts to about 18 years of my life in baseball, maybe it comes to about $25,000 or $30,000 a year, if that. Men in other work can do just as well or better in that much time and get a lot of tax deductions we don't get as ballplayers.

I honestly think our salaries.... I'm talking now about the "big guys"—Santo, Fergie, and myself—are not out of line with what others with the same kind of records earn with other ball clubs. I really can't say, of course, how the other Cub ballplayers compare. But, and no sour grapes, take Reggie Jackson. An outstanding ballplayer, no question. He's been in the majors six full seasons. Up until last year, he never hit .300, had over 100 RBIs just once, never had over 157 hits. [Both in '70 and '72 when he finished second in the NL's MVP voting, Billy had better overall years than Reggie.] *All of a sudden, in '73, he has a big year and is chosen MVP. I see where he signed for $135,000. That's just one example I can think of right off.*

For years, there's been a suspicion that the Bruins live in a Shangri-la of the baseball world, spoiled, pampered "fat cats," overpaid for underproducing.

James Enright, *Chicago Today*, September 6, 1973: "After listening to all the off-field conversation, it's easy to understand why the Cubs are 15–35 since July 10 when they were 50–37 and owned a 4½-game lead in the East Division. Everything, especially personal pleasure, comes ahead of baseball where most of the troops are concerned. The Cubs' country-club label never was easier to understand."

Reporting from spring training March 1, 1974, Rick Talley informed his readers: "There aren't many smiling faces in the Cubs' camp this year. That doesn't mean anything is wrong. It means the country-club atmosphere is gone. It means there are young people here with their careers ahead of them . . . young men with serious intent and apprehension. Win the pennant? Hell, man, I just want to make the team first."

Billy's comments: *When things like this come out in the paper, the fans get the wrong impression. But the more you think about it, it's really kind of amusing. First, I'm not sure what Jim and Rick mean by "country-club atmosphere" . . . . it must mean something to them. Fans might get the idea we're a bunch of playboys who don't care about winning. But I wonder how many fans actually believe that good, veteran ballplayers don't have the pride and desire to play their tails off to get into a World Series. Especially those who've put in as many years as guys like Santo, Fergie, Beckert, Kessinger, Hundley, Hickman, Pappas, Popo, Cardenal, and me. A lot of us have had plenty of honors, but not one has been in a World Series.*

What it all boils down to is this . . . whether you win or not seems to make the difference. 1969 was a good example of what I mean. One day Ronnie clicked his heels after we won a game. I don't think it was because he had a big head. Ron's emotional, he was happy, and that was his way of showing it. The fans got a kick out of it. People made a big fuss about it. Of course, the teams who were behind us in the standings might have taken it the wrong way. They called it "bush." We played "Hey, Hey! Holy Mackerel!" a lot. The team did some singing and made some remarks on a record album called "Cub Power," and, I'll admit, some of the fellas might have gone a little overboard, talking like we'd already won the pennant. And because the fans were so excited, they wanted all sorts of things—Cub T-shirts, mugs, autographed baseballs, pictures, personal appearances—and somebody made up a pool so all the players, and Leo too, would share in the proceeds. Dick Selma led the "Bleacher Bums" in cheers, from the bullpen. Those were exciting days. Mr. Wrigley even paid to send a bunch of the "Bleacher Bums" to Atlanta. People were lined up at six in the morning or earlier to get seats for that afternoon's game at Wrigley Field.

Now, here's what I'm getting at. All the while we were winning, I don't recall anybody criticizing these things. Most people thought it was colorful . . . and made it a lot more fun to come out and see the Cubs.

But now, all of a sudden, we start losing games. Nobody can believe it. The Mets finally go past us, and we wind up second. People start saying things like we were over-confident, we spent too much time in things off the field, weren't keeping our minds on baseball, we faded under pressure, the "Bleacher Bums" made other teams mad at us and more eager to beat us, this was a jinx, that was a jinx, etc. etc.

Then, go back a few years, to the Cardinals in '67. That's when Orlando Cepeda was the leader, playing cha-cha records everywhere they went and in the clubhouse. They called themselves "El Birdos," bragged about their great spirit, and even had a specially painted ball for infield practice. People went crazy over Cardinal souvenirs, the same as our fans did. But the Cards won. Cepeda was named MVP. He was said to be the guy who kept the Cardinals loose and relaxed to play better baseball. Suppose the Cards had gone into a slump and blew the pennant? All the talk would have sounded silly then, wouldn't it? The same as it's embarrassing for us to listen to that "Cub Power" album now.

And how about Oakland in '73? With all their troubles, fights, complaints about the owner and manager and all that . . . if they'd lost, they'd probably be blamed for their country-club atmosphere too. Same thing in our division. Tug McGraw came out with "Ya Gotta Believe!" and that got played up big. But what if they didn't win? When you win, it seems most anything goes. When you lose, most anything the players, manager, owners, or anybody connected with the club does is wrong.

After these past few years, in a way, ballplayers aren't sure how to act. Say we lose a couple of games and somebody comes into the clubhouse right after the game. He sees us sitting around, staring at our lockers, slamming things around, or some guys arguing. They might write we're "down," our morale's bad, the pressure's getting to us, can't play as a team. You know the kind of stuff that gets said. Suppose we win, and we're all happy, laughing, and joking. They might say we're cocky, heading for a fall, taking things too lightly. If we lose and somebody cracks a joke, they come up with the idea that we don't care about losing.

Over the years, I've found what works best for me. After a game, win or lose, I sit at my locker for a while and go back over the game in my mind to think about what I might have done different or better. A lot of the other Cubs do too. Maybe they don't sit at their lockers, but they're thinking about it. When I finally leave the club-

house, I try to leave the game right there. It's not always possible, especially if you're not hitting the way you should or something, of course. But I try to adopt the attitude that even if I went 0-for-4 today, doesn't mean I'll do it again tomorrow. In fact, I go up there next time with the idea that the odds are better for me to get a hit. I figure getting down on yourself isn't going to help you or your ball club. It's best for me to get my mind off baseball, whether I go fishing, take in a movie, listen to my stereo, go out in the boat with the family, or talk to friends on the phone. Some guys play golf. I don't care for it too much, only because it's too much like baseball— too much concentration—and I do enough of that at the ballpark before and during and right after the game.

The world's oldest martini joke claims that if you're ever lost... anywhere, just start making a martini. Somebody will show up and tell you how. It's the same with a baseball club, only more so with the Cubs. What some told the Cubs they could do with their ball club was.... not too subtle.

Here's a letter, typical of those that flooded the *Chicago Tribune* "Sound Off" column, from Richard W. Sexton: "To the Cub players. Congratulations on your stretch drive to the bottom. Once again you have rewarded your many and long-suffering fans with a patented collapse. Never have I seen such good individual talent jell together to form such a collective failure. Do your fans a favor next spring: when you go to Arizona for spring training... stay there."

Said Bill Gleason of the *Chicago Sun-Times* amid the gloom of the Wrigley Field press box: "If Billy Williams had had one of his greatest years instead of just a typically very good Williams' year, the Cubs might have won the division and might have advanced to the World Series. Now, it isn't likely he'll ever be in a World Series with the Cubs....

"There's no question what Billy Williams means to baseball and *is* in baseball. He'll go into the Hall of Fame surely not long after his retirement." Gleason went on: "The fans need new people here, new heroes—and also new 'bums'... people to cheer and people to boo... people who haven't been here before."

Pat Sheridan, host of WMAQ Radio's "Sound Off On Sports" program, complained that the Cubs have too many one-dimensional ballplayers. "When they start swinging from the heels, they're beaten. They're just a beaten ball club. When they go back to their old ways—the way they played in '69, '70, '71, and '72, they're going to lose those ballgames."

Sheridan was all for adding more youth and speed, more base-stealers, more good bunters to go along with the lusty hitting that's characterized Cub teams through the years.

Billy agrees: *Now they're thinking about a change. They feel you've got to have speed to win ballgames, and I kind of go along with that, especially close ballgames.*

I stole a few bases in the minor leagues. But when I came up with this club, I was hitting in front of Ernie, batting third. They told me when I get on first base, I'm supposed to stay there, and let Ernie hit home runs. So this is how the team has been built over the years. I know with Santo, Banks, and myself, the guys batting ahead of us were also told to stay on first until we hit the ball out of the ballpark. The clubs that have won over the last few years have had guys who steal over 60 bases or four or five who steal 15 or 20 bases apiece.

Leave it to *Chicago Today* columnist Rick Talley to come up with the most drastic suggestion of them all: "When you talk about housecleaning . . . it should start at the very top. The Cubs need more than . . . youth and team speed . . . and a revamped front office (John Holland should retire) . . . and a revitalized farm system . . . and all of those other things which become necessary when an organization goes stale.

"They need new ownership.

"Like many people, I've always been intrigued by Wrigley's eccentricities and wealth. I've always been delighted, too, by his stand against night baseball, even tho he may be doing his teams more harm than good if you buy that theory about the Cubs 'burning out' under the July and August sun. But, I can't get too enthused about an owner who doesn't care enough for baseball to attend games . . . or an owner who treats his franchise like a toy and allows his generosity, which Wrigley certainly has, to affect front office and on-the-field performances.

"I wish Wrigley would sell the club," Talley concluded. "So do a lot of other people who are waiting with their checkbooks."

Bill Berg, WGN talk-show host, gave his reaction to that one. "Suppose tomorrow a new owner took over the Cubs. Let's say Bill Veeck. Think there'd be any changes?" he was asked.

After thinking a moment, Berg replied... "We'd have exploding vines!"

More to the point, however, the question is... *why* have the Chicago Cubs been the one major league team without lights, without artificial turf, and *without a pennant* since 1945? Some purists won't even count *that* one—like Bill Gleason, who stoutly maintains, "1945 should really be thrown out because it was a war year. Therefore, the Cubs haven't had a genuine championship team since 1938..... *that's 35 years ago!*" Either way, it's the longest pennant famine in baseball. Brushing up on their own history, the Cub hierarchy would probably find their biggest long-standing problem ... pitching.

Sure, when the Cubs were the scourge of the National League with pennants in 1929, 1932, 1935, 1938, and 1945, the talk was about "Cub Power." But all those teams had superb pitching along *with* that power, as well as gaudy base-stealers, top-notch catching, and all-round team balance. In two of those pennant years, the Wrigley's *bought* pitchers to help turn the tide—Dizzy Dean in '38 and Hank Borowy in '45. Also, in their last Golden Era, the Cubs acquired star players who were in or near their prime.

Sadly, though, from 1946 through 1962, the North-Siders went 17 straight years without a single 20-game winner. Case in point: in 1958, five Cubs walloped 20 or more homers to lead the league with 182—and Banks was a one-man gang, winning the MVP hands down, with 47 homers, 129 RBIs, 379 total bases, 119 runs, and slugging .614. But where did the Bruins finish? Tied for fifth. The top winner on the pitching staff was Glen Hobbie, with ten victories. Only the seventh- and eighth-place teams had higher ERAs. In other years of the "Dark Ages" since '45, the best Cub pitchers had as few as 11, 12, or 13 wins. Not only that, aging and almost "over the hill" veterans dotted the line-ups.

Across town, however, Al Lopez kept the White Sox in contention for years primarily with pitching, speed, and defense—and even unseated the Yankees for a flag in 1959, with barely enough power to blow out candles on a birthday cake.

Few teams belted the ball much better than the Cubs of 1969 through 1972, but the Bruins had no pitchers to beat Pittsburgh. The Bucs clobbered Chicago 11–7, 10–8, 12–6, 12–3, and 12–6 the last five seasons. And despite his six 20 or more victory seasons, Jenkins was only 9–22 against Pittsburgh.

You'd think that since the Cubs supposedly have the fattest, fastest checks in the game, plus good tradeable talent, they could have found *someone* who needed *something* in return for a hurler or two to give Chicago *some* respectability against the Pirates.

Then, too, in the years between Hartnett and Hundley, catching was at best mediocre, centerfield and first base often trouble spots, and outstanding lead-off men and base-stealing threats few and far between. What's more, Cub trades have seldom left the other teams in tears.

Wrigley Field has lost some of its magic due to the new type of ball clubs coming in from heavy schedules of night baseball. They often find it their hitting paradise. The Cubs, on the other hand, traditionally hit for lower averages than many other teams on the road, especially their first couple of night games.

Few true Cub fans really want lights. But wouldn't it be interesting to see how the baseball commissioner would handle the problem of televising night World Series games in lightless Wrigley Field? Let's see what the Cub owner is doing to burden Bowie Kuhn with this dilemma.

A New Broom, A New Season

*"When they said 'Back up the Truck',
I mean . . . . they really put it in reverse!"*

Billy Williams, Spring 1974

"I know somebody will say there's . . . no substitute for experience. But . . . I'm convinced baseball is a young man's game. We've been knocking at the door for about five years now and haven't made it. It's time to start over. We definitely have to rebuild." So said P.K. Wrigley to Edgar Munzel of the *Chicago Sun-Times*, at the close of the '73 season. The season had barely ended when Wrigley's promised rebuilding program got under way.

"If there'd been a team in Outer Mongolia, the Cubs would have sent me there." That was the comment made by Ferguson Jenkins on October 26, 1973. Fergie had asked to be traded. But where he went and who the Cubs received for him in return raised some eyebrows. The Texas Rangers exchanged promising rookie infielder-outfielders Bill Madlock and Vic Harris for the disillusioned righthander. So went the Cubs' lone Cy Young Award winner. Billy comments:

I was sorry to see Fergie wind up with a noncontending ball club. He deserved a chance at getting into a World Series or two, and I don't blame him for being hurt and disappointed. Of course, he's still got some good years ahead of him yet, he just turned 30 in December, and might be just the one to help the Rangers become a contender.

As I told the ball club, I'd prefer to stay in Chicago but, if they make a deal, to make it with a contending ball club, one that's expected to win in the next couple of years. Under the new ruling, I can accept or refuse a trade, but I haven't caused trouble before and don't plan to now. But with my record and loyalty all these years, I feel I've got that coming—a chance to be with a winner. (Which still could be the Chicago Cubs, and I'd like nothing better.)

By the way, that remark Fergie made about Outer Mongolia, he said it on the phone to George Vass [of the Chicago Daily News], and the way I know him, he probably said it with a smile. Things look a lot different in print than they sound when somebody says it. He has a way of saying things that people who don't know him misunderstand. He could be kidding, and they think he's serious.

One example of how remarks are misunderstood.... Remember when somebody told Durocher he was the "dumbest bleeping manager he ever played for"? First it came out that Santo said it. It wasn't Santo, it was Joe Pepitone. And stories said it happened during our big clubhouse incident with Leo in '71. But as I recall it, I'm pretty sure Pepi said it later in Cincinnati when things had settled down and everybody was in a good frame of mind. We were carrying on in the clubhouse, and Joe was clowning around as usual. He was always telling Leo "You wanta win?—put me in the line-up." And Durocher would come back with some funny remark. This time he might have said something like... "You? Why you're the dumbest bleeping ballplayer who ever played for me!" And Pepi came back with... "And you're the dumbest bleeping manager I ever played for." It was said jokingly anyway. See how things can get mixed up?

Fergie's trade was not the first move by the Cubs' front office. Changes in the coaching setup had been announced earlier. Al Spangler was named first-base coach, replacing Banks, who was given a new assignment of infield instructor for the major and minor league clubs in the Cub system. Jim Marshall, who won two division titles managing Cub farm clubs, replaced Pete Reiser as third-base coach. Hank Aguirre would be pitching coach, the '73 coach, Larry Jansen, having retired. Former catcher J.C. Martin would head bullpen coaching chores.

When trade talk started, the question naturally came up—"Is anybody untouchable?" And, of course, it opened a fall and winter guessing game for the other "survivors" of the last five frustrating campaigns—Billy on top of the list. Here's what Kessinger had to say: "I don't think there's such a thing as an untouchable—when Willie Mays was traded, I think that wiped out all thoughts of anybody being untouchable. Nobody likes to be traded, especially when you've been in a city as long as Billy or I have. I'd be surprised to see a Billy Williams traded, but you never know in this game. About his playing first base? I know Billy's the kind of guy who'd be perfectly willing to do whatever he felt would help the ball club win. He'd go at that just as he's done everything else—with 100 percent effort. He'd give it everything he's got."

The first veteran to feel the cold edge of the ax was Santo. Told the Cubs had arranged a deal with the Angels for him, Santo refused to give his approval. (And thus came the term, the "Santo-Clause.") Ron announced he wanted to stay in Chicago, period. Suggestions that he might take a healthy pay cut and/or sit on the bench kept him in a stew for a few days. But suddenly, the White Sox indicated an interest in him. Though they already had a pretty fair third baseman in Bill Melton, the American League's top home-run hitter in 1971, a deal was made. Billy's comment:

The way it worked out, it played right into his hands. When Ron made the statement that he wouldn't accept the trade, he got himself in a bind. And after he got himself there, he had to keep goin'. He probably would have gone to another ball club, but then he said he didn't want to play for anybody but the White Sox, and they played that up big. I was telling Shirley the other day—Ron's not used to sitting on the bench, and he's not going to be contented over there. Of course, going to that league, they have the designated hitter, and maybe it can work out.

I do know one thing. Somebody asked me about Ron on Pat Sheridan's show one night, asked if he could compare Santo to Brooks Robinson of Baltimore, and could he make the plays. All I said was, I'd played right behind Ron for a long time in leftfield and I don't think I'd seen anybody any better.

Two of the Cubs' "walking wounded" the past couple of seasons, Beckert and Hundley, were the next to be sent packing—Glenn to the Padres and Randy to the Minnesota Twins. Billy's comment:

If Glenn's heel operation is a success, he could have a real good year with San Diego. There's another great competitor. He said walking was like stepping on an ice pick near the end of the '73 season, but whenever we'd need a pinch-hitter, he'd go on up there. He was a real good player to hit behind and helped me have some of my best years. As much as I like Beck, I hope he doesn't come back to "haunt" us the way Brock has. I'll just say I hope he has one of his best seasons ever—against everybody but us.

By the way, he's some driver. Guys like Glenn and Ron, they don't get enough excitement playin' ball—they go in for snowmobiling and all that type of thing. There was one time that Glenn gave me an experience I'm not sure I'll ever forget. We were driving back home from a baseball clinic, me at the wheel. I'm doing things by the law, maybe just a little over the speed limit. All of a sudden, I see the cherry behind me. The policeman pulls me over, gives me a speeding ticket, and takes my license. I suppose I could have taken a chance and driven the rest of the way, but I wasn't in a very good mood to drive. So Beckert gets under the wheel.

We were about 20 miles out of Davenport, and from there till we get to the Outer Drive on Route 55, Beckert's doing an average of about 110 miles per hour. He doesn't get stopped. I don't think anybody paid any attention!

I suppose this is why a person doesn't do a lot of things. It keeps running through your mind. The other person can go ahead and do something and get away with it. But if you do it, it seems you get caught every time. It sure makes you wonder sometimes.

Beck also tells one on Billy. "I really got a laugh one time when we were playing I think at Cincinnati. I'd been on a hot streak and for the only time I ever had it happen, they walk me to pitch to Billy. And it worked, they got him out. I couldn't resist giving him the needle. He just looked at me, trying not to smile, trying to look real mean, shaking his head, and saying: 'They'd–better–not–do–that–again'."

In a more serious vein, Beckert remarked: "I think we're living in the era where the guy who's the pop-off artist, the guy who has the ability to be eccentric and do crazy things, is the one that gets all the glory and prestige.... There's one thing you can't keep down and that's ability. And Billy definitely has that. Billy's attitude is great. Super. I can sense times when I think Billy would just like to explode when things aren't going well, but he keeps things inside probably better than any other individual on the club."

The Padres gave up outfielder Jerry Morales for Beckert. The Twins, meanwhile, traded a younger catcher, George Mitterwald, for slow-talking, fast-thinking "Rebel" Hundley. Billy's comment:

Everybody had respect for Randy ... and his great desire to come back after those two knee operations. Nobody knows whether he can come back to the way he was when he first came to the big leagues. You have to feel for a guy like this who gets hurt but still puts out with everything he's got. Shoot, there were times last year when Randy would drop down a surprise bunt to try to get on base. And even with those knees, he's still pretty fast out there. Randy's a real fine bunter.

The pitchers respected him because he always called a good game.

If there was a problem out on the mound, he knew just how to handle the pitchers. I'm quite sure our old teammate, Bill Hands, who's also with Minnesota, will have a better year with his favorite catcher back with him. (That is, if "Froggy" doesn't get traded. There's been a few stories saying the White Sox would like to get Hands.) Bill and Randy had a thing going, and Hands pitched some outstanding baseball for us. This move could benefit both of them.

By January 1, 1974, the Cubs' front office indicated that, barring an overwhelming development, the major trading was over. They had Harris and Madlock in the infield to work with Kessinger; Billy the top candidate for first; Cardenal, Monday, and Morales in the outfield; and Mitterwald behind the plate. From the White Sox, they'd picked up lefty Ken Frailing, a rookie with an 11–3 record at Iowa; one-time National League pitcher Steve Stone, who had a 6–11 mark and 4.29 ERA with the Sox in '73; and catcher Steve Swisher, from Ohio University, a top draft choice of the Sox.

Still, Billy's mind was far from at ease.

I remember a time earlier in my career. During the off-season, I was selling cars. Well one morning I pick up the paper and read where they're talking about a possible trade that could send me to Baltimore. So right away I get on the phone and call John Holland about it. He assured me at the time that nothing would come of it. So I pretty much forgot about it. Then, we're out in spring training, and Frank Lane, who was with the Baltimore organization, comes up to me. And he says, "Billy, we missed you by just that much!" And he held his fingers up about half an inch apart. I guess the deal fell through because Baltimore didn't want to give up Curt Blefary [outfielder-first baseman and 1965 American League Rookie of the year].

Although the Cubs had shipped out "name" players, they had yet to obtain an established, front-line player in return. As a result this naturally pointed to the Sweet Swinger as probably the most valuable prize to dangle in front of another club. The possibility of his being traded was still very much alive. It was hardly a blissful winter for Billy.

This was the first time they started out by offering me a salary with a cut in pay. I guess you know my reaction to that. I can see their thinking—a young ball club and being worried about less fans coming out, and wanting to keep expenses down. But I think it's going to make it a more exciting season and fans will want to see the new kind of club we can put on the field. Besides, I feel I'm the same type ballplayer I was last year, and next year I'll be better.

My feelings are the same . . . I'd prefer to stay in Chicago, but if they come up with a deal with a contender, I'd have to give it a lot of thought.

That's how matters stood when spring training started in Scottsdale, Arizona. Billy was there, and, as usual, he had Shirley and the girls with him for a few weeks' vacation. But one thing was different. Daddy still hadn't signed his contract.

The quiet man was quiet, even for the quiet man. Although he was in camp, Billy wasn't in uniform. After more than two months of contract talks, he wasn't signed, he wasn't happy, and he wasn't talking about it. At a meeting with John Holland on February 28, Billy made one last try to reach a two-year agreement, then he gave in and signed a one-year pact.

After he got into his uniform, he looked at the two gloves in his locker, picked up the first baseman's mitt, and stepped out into the bright Arizona sunshine.

"Billy! How about a TV interview?"

"Okay . . . sure," said Billy, "as long as we don't talk about my contract."

"Oh? How come?"

"I'm afraid I'll say something wrong . . . something I may regret saying later on."

"Yes, Billy was down for a few days," said Shirley. "And there were still those rumors that he was going to be traded, right up until the day he signed. He really wasn't concerned about the money, he just wanted the security of a two-year contract. When he couldn't get it, that really hurt him." Billy's comment:

I signed practically against my will. I know John was only doing his job. He and the Cubs have been real good to me all this time. But still, it was a slap in the face. You keep reading about all this loyalty, y'know. And well, after a player's been with one ball club over 14 years and asks for a two-year contract, he feels they'll give it to him. But we're dickering right down to the wire. I'm the kind that when things start to get to me, and I can feel it, I stop fightin' it. That's the thing. After you go in and get all riled up, you have to try and forget about it. You're more hurt than anything else when something like this happens. Am I happy? No. Maybe I counted on too much, mainly because they kept me on the ball club, and I hoped they might have something to offer me later on with this organization.

But I guess they want to see how all these changes are going to work out and don't want to be involved with a longer contract. Could be they want me to hang around only this year. I really don't know, but it seems like the only reason they wouldn't give me the two years. So I'll just stay prepared. Whitey said on a TV interview that he would play me at first about three fourths of the season, and in the outfield other times I imagine.

Everything will work out in the end. As you know, I've always felt everything that's done is done for a reason. That's how I have to look at it.

Not too long after Billy signed, the new broom swept out two more Cubs, Rudolph and Hickman. Rudolph went to the Giants, and Hickman suited up with the Cardinals. In April, Pappas was released, and Popovich went to the Pirates. As Billy said, they didn't just "back up the truck . . . they *really* put it in reverse!"

Now, only two players remained from the 1969 team that had been mashed by the Miracle Mets—Kessinger and the Classic Hitter. Some reports out of Scottsdale gave the impression that Billy was accepting the move to first base grudgingly. Actually, he was all fired up on making the switch as far back as early August 1973.

Confided Brickhouse, "First of all he *wants* to be. This may be the first time in his life he's really *wanted* to be the first baseman for the Chicago Cubs. We talked about it on a bus trip in New York. He was interested, too, in a remark Phil Cavarretta made to me one time. Cavarretta said he hit better when he played first base than when he played the outfield because he felt he was more in the ballgame.

"The way he said it, a certain glint in his eye, a certain determination in his voice indicates to me that Mr. Billy Williams is going to be a very good first baseman for the Cubs one of these days." Billy's comment:

What Jack says is true. I do like playing first and want to make good at it for two or three years. I really think I can be more of a leader on the field because when I played first in some games last season, I found myself getting a lot more involved in the game. Like

I'd go out to the pitcher when they had a power hitter coming up and we had a base open. He probably had it in his mind, but I wanted to make sure he knew what he wanted to do. And it seemed to help my hitting... I felt stronger.

A charged-up, jovial Billy was gushing on the phone when he talked to us from Scottsdale.

Hey! When I first came out here, I thought it was a young bunch of guys and it'd take a little while to get together—but they proved me wrong. They're playin' good baseball! Real good baseball! The two guys they got in the trade for Jenkins—Madlock and Harris—they're doin' a tremendous job. First? Oh yeah, I like it... I'm making the change and getting adjusted to it. Yeah, I'm getting there! Now I'm happy. You have a tendency to try and forget about things ... I experienced that in 1972 after the Most Valuable Player thing, y'know, when I lost out. You can't go through a season with a chip on your shoulder.

"What's this about you tripping over the pitcher's mound?" Billy laughed:

Oh yeah! I was trying to catch a pop fly. Somebody put a mound there. It's been there 150 years but it got in my way this time!

"Feeling any stronger now that you're playing first?"

Uh huh! That's what I've got to do now ... get adjusted to my strength. I might be too strong!

Although he had signed reluctantly, he was already showing his tremendous resiliency—to weather disappointments and shrug off obstacles. He had new goals to attain.

It might be well to remember the hardy breed of these boys from Alabama. Aaron's still clouting at 40, Willie Mays made his final World Series appearance in 1973 at 42. Too, it's only fair to warn opposing pitchers that even including 1973—when he batted .288 with 20 homers, a fine season for almost anyone but him—the Sweet Swinger *averaged* .311, 107 RBIs, 98 runs, 185 hits, 31 homers, and 29 doubles a season for the last four years. And with the start of the 1974 season, except for Aaron with 20 full years, Billy in his 13 has the *most hits, the most runs, the most total bases, the most doubles, and the most RBIs of any active National Leaguer.*

Trivia nuts might take delight in this as well. Although Hammerin' Hank is baseball's all-time leader in total bases and led the

200

league eight seasons, he surpassed Billy's 373 of 1970 *only once.* The 348 in 1972 by Billy also topped Hank in four other years.

Back in '61, the kid with the fastest wrists in the West, a tiger in his bat—and a reputation for shaky glovework—was trying to make the club as an outfielder. The Cubs were in a rebuilding and youth program that year too.

Santo was already there, coming up in June of 1960, and 30-year-old Banks was slowing up at shortstop. To extend his glorious career, he moved to first, giving Billy a chance to clinch a regular job. Now, it's *Billy* "trying to make the team" at first base.

He's the only one left of the old gang... the only one with a chance to realize the dream they all chased and missed—a pennant and a World Series in Wrigley Field. Could it be, as Billy always says, that "What's supposed to happen will happen... what's done is done for a reason... and everything's for the best"?

As the Classic Hitter starts the 1974 campaign, here's how he sees the "new" ball club:

As we get closer to the season starting, I kind of like this ball club better than the last two or three years. It's exciting... it is. This team's beginning to look real *good. I thought it would take two or three years to rebuild, but it seems like these guys are ready to play now.*

We're really changing the attack. Y'know, last year, we were always looking for the big hit from somebody like Ron, Rick, Jose, or me. But this year, most of the guys have speed, so we're stealing bases, hit-and-running, getting a single, getting a guy over, and scoring the runs. We're trying everybody on the hit-and-run. Like today [the Cubs beat the Brewers]. *Jerry Morales, who's got my old spot in leftfield, is doing a real fine job. He's batting third right now, and I'm in the cleanup spot. It looks like I might stay there. And it's going to be a real solid, sound batting order. Vic Harris has been leading off—he's a switch-hitter. Monday's batting second, then Morales, Williams, Jose, then Bill Madlock, Kessinger, and the catcher, Mitterwald or Lundstedt, and, of course, the pitcher.*

I really enjoy playing first base. Every play a first baseman has to make during the season has come up during spring training, and that's what I need, eperience. My big troubles were in cutoff plays, positioning and stuff like that. Movies have helped me a lot, watching Cub defensive plays. If I don't learn, it's my own fault, I've sure got a lot of help. Ernie, Whitey, Jim Marshall... they all played first. And Andy Thornton has been a tremendous help. I try to help him with his hitting, and he gives me a hand with my fielding.

Of course, it's pretty hard to tell at this point about our pitching. Bill Bonham's been most effective so far I'd say, and last time out, Hooton looked good. And this Ken Frailing, the lefty we got from the White Sox in the deal for Santo ... he knows how to pitch. One thing's sure, we're going to shake things up a bit this year. The young guys all have a lot of spirit and desire, and it keeps us "Senior Citizens" on our toes.

Another thing. Whitey's been good for the club because he believes in giving 25 guys a chance to play—and this is what a manager has to do. The nine guys who are playing every day, they're happy. But the biggest thing is keeping those on the bench satisfied by letting 'em get in there and play now and then. That way, you can't help but have guys who are rooting and pulling for each other. It makes for good teammanship, and sometimes that can make up for a lot of things. Now, I think we can play the kind of game some of the other teams have been playing against us. Besides, and it's not an alibi, I think I mentioned it before, when I first came up to the big leagues, the wind seemed to blow out a lot more at Wrigley Field. A big lead didn't mean too much, but in those one- and two-run ballgames, the kind of kids and speed we've got now can change things around. We don't need that long ball as much, even though we've got quite a few who can hit 'em out. That never hurts.

Something else that I think's important. We're having fun playing the game. Myself, I like to play the game to have fun. There are plenty of things you can do in the infield to keep the fellas loose. Sometimes we're passing the ball around, I slip 'em a curve. You don't want to go into too deep a concentration. It's like hitting. You get concentrating too much up there and you blank out.

A guy'd be kind of foolish to make any wild claims as to how we're gonna wind up this year ... I guess they've picked us anywhere from last in the division to second or third. It'll be an exciting season.... I'm getting excited about it. I think the fans'll like this kind of a ball club too.

Billy Wraps It Up
—A Postscript

When a ballplayer gets to be around 35, people have a tendency to think he's about finished. If I want to feel old, all I have to do is look at the rest of our Cub ball club this year. The average age is about 26 or 27, I guess. But then I see my good friend Aaron tying Babe Ruth's record in the first inning on opening day off one of the finest pitchers in the league, Jack Billingham, and Hank's 40, so I think I have some good years left too.

For one thing, God's been very good to me . . . I haven't received any serious injuries, my weight's pretty close to what it was when I came up in 1961, I feel strong, and I'm going to give everything I've got to try and become a dependable first baseman. I can still swing the bat, and playing with all these young guys has me just as enthused about playing baseball as I ever was, maybe even more.

Besides, I have a few goals I'd like to reach before I'm done. I'd still like a chance to complain about *my* World Series ring. And it'd be great if I could come up with a year good enough to win an MVP or the Triple Crown. Maybe my biggest goal is to reach 3,000 hits. Right now, only 11 have done it, though Al Kaline will probably make it in 1974 (he needs only 139 more), and Frank Robinson needs only 217. I like to kid Ernie that I'm out to catch up with him. I've got a good chance to pass him in a lot of batting departments. Ernie leads all Cubs since 1900 in nearly every batting category . . . and if I'm able to play two or three more years, I could become the team leader in all but one (providing I'm still with the Cubs, of course). I doubt if the wind will *ever* blow out enough for me to tie or beat his 512 homers.

Of course, too, I'd like to finish with a lifetime batting average of .300 or more. Not that there's so much difference between my .297 and .300, but the magic number has always been .300, so it's just one of those things a guy'd like to do.

Right here, maybe I should answer some of the questions people ask me most. I understand Fergie made a statement a few weeks ago that "Ernie always said the *right* thing," and I "never said *anything*" when it came to our relations with the Chicago Cubs. I laughed when I heard it—that sounds like Fergie. So, the question comes up: Would I still be a "good guy" if I had the chance to start my career all over again? In one way "no"... in another way "yes."

Baseball's become such a big business since I first came up to the major leagues, and after certain things that have happened, I think they have a tendency to take advantage of those who don't speak up. I see cases where guys demand to be traded or get into some kind of controversy—and usually seem to end up with a contender, maybe play in a couple of World Series. You see some players who have a real good year or two demand a salary that's almost twice what they made. They go to arbitration and get it. Then other guys do the same thing—guys who are valuable too—but they have to take less than they're really worth.

So you start getting the idea that loyalty doesn't mean much anymore, on either side. I think that's wrong. Loyalty should mean a lot. But as long as the squeaking wheel gets the most grease, I think I'd be a lot more outspoken than I have been—about the business part of it. It's good business for the ball club to get the best players they can for the least amount of money they can. And I'd have to take the attitude that it's strictly business with me too. Baseball careers are short compared to other lines of work, and I'd want to get the most I could for as long as I could, and still be fair, not trying to hold up anybody.

About popping off, stirring up controversy, or things like that—no, I don't think I'd change. If I can't get my name in the papers by driving in runs, hitting homers, and having good years, it's no use being in there playing. I can't be phony, I've got to be myself. Nobody would believe me if all of a sudden I was a different kind of guy. People can see right through me when I try to be anything but Billy. The time I did spout off, I don't think anybody took me seriously—they knew it wasn't the real me talking.

Sure, I get upset, hurt, and disappointed, especially when another player refuses to be traded, goes to another ball club, a contender, gets a longer contract and a raise in pay besides, and I'm not even able to get the longer contract. But I can't stay bitter. I've found it does me more harm than good. It gets under my skin when people keep telling me that after I've given everything I can all these years, I'm still the "invisible" superstar or "the superstar hardly anybody knows."

On the other hand, there's not much I can do about it now except hope they don't forget me when it comes to voting for the Hall of Fame and that Billy's still around to shake hands and sign autographs when and if they put me in. There's no question that losing out on the MVP and Triple Crown and World Series cost me a lot in recognition and money. But I've got some things a lot of other players haven't got. I've been proud and happy of the recognition by my fellow players and being chosen by the fans for the 1973 All-Star Game for the first time, and I've played in a great city for great fans and a fine organization.

That's why, even though I'm grateful for all the nice things people said about me in this book, something Joe Torre said stands out—when he said I'm the same whether I go 0-for-4 or 4-for-4, and that "anybody can take a 4-for-4 day." What it all boils down to is this: I'd rather be known as that type of ballplayer, especially by the young kids who come out to see us play.

I'm often asked if I have any advice for kids. Y'know, like, What does it take to become a star? That's pretty hard to answer in so many words, but I do know what most of the stars I've met in baseball and other sports have. Most of them have six outstanding qualities, and they all start with "D." DESIRE. DIRECTION. DETERMINATION. DEDICATION. DISCIPLINE. DEVOTION TO GOD.

It's hard to do anything well unless you really want to—in baseball, your job, or your life—and you have to direct your efforts at some goals to get anyplace. Determination is one of the most important of all—I've seen case after case where a player with less ability than another player gets the job and does the job and where the player with all kinds of ability but without determination never reaches his potential. You must dedicate yourself to things that will help you achieve your goals and avoid those that won't—and that takes discipline. It's pretty hard to have your cake and eat it too, so you should recognize that you'll have to make sacrifices in order to stay on the right track. And then, since nobody does anything by himself, I think it pays to ask God for help, for strength and courage when things get tough—and don't forget to thank him for what he's given you.

About the black and white situation? I'll say straight out, I don't think I'll forget some of the treatment given other black ballplayers and myself years ago. Forgive, yes, but forget, no. I'm sure I'll always ask myself the same question. Am I being treated as well as I am in Chicago because I'm Billy Williams the major league ballplayer? How would I be treated, how would Shirley and the family be treated if I were just another guy named Billy Williams?

Not too long ago at a nice Chicago restaurant, we were seated way back by the kitchen even though there were a lot of other tables, better ones, available. Then we sat and waited and waited for service. Finally, I got the waiter's eye and asked if we could have a nicer table. He disappeared for a while. When he came back, he had another man with him, probably the manager. Anyway, he recognized me and right away hustled us to the best table in the place, and the table was set up and everything like we were the king and queen. The sad thing is, things like that happen enough to make you wonder—How many of our race aren't fortunate enough to be well known and get treated badly only bebecause they're black?

Before we moved into our new home, the man who sold it to us suggested sending letters out, telling people in the area about our moving in. All I said was, "How many people who get that letter do you think will be surprised? They *know*." We've had one heartbreaking experience since we moved in—I'd rather not go into details. There's no ignoring the fact that this kind of thing is still going on, but, it's getting better and I think it'll all work itself out. Programs like "All in the Family" have done a lot of good because we find it's possible to laugh about things that used to be insults—and that's what this old world needs.

I hope we're getting to the day where it's like my grandfather told me so many years ago back in Whistler. "It's the outside of a man they care about. But, the *inside* is what's important." I think that's all any of us, white or black, really wants—to be judged on the way you are as a person, not on your color. It might sound corny, but I'd like to see the time—and soon—when the only race problem we have to worry about is the pennant race.

If it works out, I'd like to end my playing career with the Chicago Cubs ... I'm really looking forward to this 1974 season. After that? I'm going to try to take the next years as they come. With luck, maybe some day Aaron will be in *his* rocking chair watching TV and say to his wife, Billye .... "Hey, look at that *old* Billy Williams ... he still can swing that bat!"

Billy Williams

BILLY WILLIAMS' LIFETIME RECORD (Through 1973 Season)

Year	Club	G	AB	R	H	2B	3B	HR	RBI	TB	RP	SO	BB	IBB	E	FA	BA	SA
1956	Ponca City	13	17	4	4	0	0	0	4						1	.835	.235	
1957	Ponca City	126*	451	87	140	40**	3	17	95						25**	.903	.310	
1958	Pueblo	21	80	9	20	2	1	2	11						2	.939	.250	
1958	Burlington	61	214	38	65	7	0	10	38						4	.960	.304	
1959	San Antonio	94	371	57	118	22	7	10	79						21	.968	.318	
1959	Fort Worth	5	21	7	10	4	1	1	5						1	.923	.476	
1959	CUBS	18	33	0	5	0	1	0	2	7	2	7	1		0	1.000	.152	.212
1960	Houston	126	473	74	153	28	3	26	80						7	.968	.323	
1960	CUBS	12	47	4	13	0	2	2	7	23	9	12	5		1	.962	.277	.489
1961	CUBS	146	529	75	147	20	7	25	86	256	136	70	45	11	11**	.954	.278	.484
1962	CUBS	159	618	94	184	22	8	22	92	288	164	72	70	3	10	.967	.298	.466
1963	CUBS	161	612	87	175	36	9	25	95	304	157	78	68	9	4	.987	.286	.497
1964	CUBS	162	645	100	201	39	2	33	98	343	165	84	59	8	13	.950	.312	.532
1965	CUBS	164*	645	115	203	39	6	34	108	356	189	76	65	7	10	.968	.315	.552
1966	CUBS	162*	648	100	179	23	5	29	91	299	162	61	69	16	8	.976	.276	.461
1967	CUBS	162	634	92	176	21	12	28	84	305	148	67	68	8	3	.989	.278	.481
1968	CUBS	163**	642	91	185	30	8	30	98	321**	159	53	48	10	9	.967	.288	.500
1969	CUBS	163*	642	103	188	33	10	21	95	304	177	70	59	15	12	.957	.293	.474
1970	CUBS	161*	636	137†	205††	34	4	42	129	373†	224†	65	72	9	3	.989	.322	.586
1971	CUBS	157	594	86	179	27	5	28	93	300	151	44	77	18	7	.977	.301	.505
1972	CUBS	150	574	95	191	34	6	37	122	348†	180	59	62	20	4	.986	.333†	.606†
1973	CUBS	156	576	72	166	22	2	20	86	252	138	72	76	14	6	.985	.288	.438
Major League Totals		2,096	8,075	1,251	2,397	380	87	376	1,286	4,079	2,161	890	844	148	100		.297	.505

* Tied for lead in league ** Tops in league † Tops in majors †† Tied for lead in majors